So Who The Heck Was Oscar Mayer?

▼

The Real People Behind Those Brand Names

So Who The Heck Was Oscar Mayer?

The Real People Behind Those Brand Names

DOUG GELBERT

BARRICADE BOOKS, INC. NEW YORK

Published by Barricade Books Inc.
150 Fifth Avenue
New York, NY10011
Copyright © 1996 by Doug Gelbert

Library of Congress Cataloging-in-Publication Data
Book design and page layout by CompuDesign

Gelbert, Doug.
So who the heck was Oscar Mayer? : the real people behind
those brand names / by Doug Gelbert.
p. cm.
ISBN 1-56980-082-0
1. Businessmen—United States—Biography.
2. Entrepreneurship—United States—Case studies.
I. Title.
HC102.5.A2G45   1996
338' . 0092'273
[B]—dc20   96-21037
                                                CIP

First printing

34926765

Contents

4. In The Medicine Cabinet

5. On The Vanity

6. In The Yard

7. Around The House

8. In The Closet

9. At The Store

Preface

Household names. They are names we know so well we forget the people who bore those names: Pillsbury, Kraft, Maytag, Hertz, Kellogg, Gerber. Yet, open a copy of the *Information Please Almanac* and turn to the chapter on famous people. You won't find these names. Although over four thousand names are listed from every walk of life—most of whom no one knows—the one group conspicuous by its absence is American businessmen. Hundreds of business founders whose companies have made their names commonplace are omitted. How many names are more famous than Howard Johnson? Milton Bradley? Oscar Mayer? John Deere? But *who* were these men?

We can't blame the *Almanac.* While the names of America's best-known companies live on, the founders are forgotten. We all know *what* a Buick is, *what* a Schick is, *what* a Boeing is but no one remembers *who* David Buick was, *who* Jacob Schick was, *who* William Boeing was. Let's find out now.

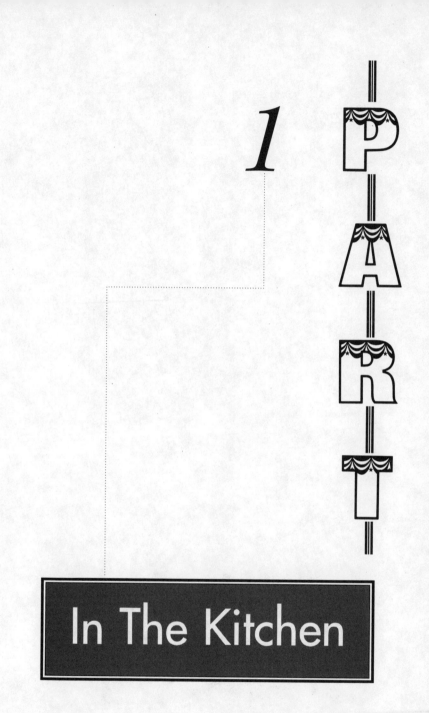

1

PART

In The Kitchen

Armour

Philip Danforth Armour, "Phil" until he died, grew up on a farm in Stockbridge, New York with, as one biographer dutifully noted, "no tradition of zeal for scholarship." In 1849, at the age of seventeen, he was discharged over a matter of discipline from the Cazenovia Academy and thrust into the working world.

Armour clerked in a store for two years until he could no longer resist the romantic tales coming east from the California Gold Rush. He set out for the West Coast on foot and by rail. When he arrived in California, Armour quickly noticed that most miners never struck it rich—and those that did lost their fortunes more often than not.

Rather than grab a pick and axe, Armour went to work building sluiceways so the miners could have water in which to pan their gold. In five years he saved eight thousand dollars, and then headed home to New York to buy a good farm. On the way home Armour stopped to visit his brother Herman in Milwaukee. He would stay for another nineteen years.

Armour was impressed by the thriving community he found in Milwaukee. He established a produce and commission business and, in 1863, Armour entered into a partnership with John Plankinton, a pioneer packer in the Midwest. In the winter of 1864-1865 Armour traveled to New York, then the center of the pork packing industry.

At the time pork was selling for forty dollars a barrel and spiraling upward. The consensus among veteran New York commodity traders was that the price was going nowhere but up. Armour saw things differently. He believed that with the end of the Civil War in sight, the price of pork would fall when the Confederacy did. The New York traders were eager to buy as much pork as the brash young man from Milwaukee could sell at forty dollars a barrel.

As Armour gambled it would, pork collapsed as Richmond fell. He filled all his eastern orders with pork he purchased for eighteen dollars a barrel. As many brokers tried to repudiate their contracts with Armour he stayed in New York for ninety days forcing his debtors to settle. Thereafter, Armour's business grew with unprecedented rapidity.

In 1867, Armour and Plankinton set up a packing plant in Chicago as Armour & Company. 1860's Chicago was a city renowned for its muddy, unpaved streets, but with a bustling railroad business it began looking like the midwestern city of the future.

In the first year, Armour's pork business outgrew the company's Bell House plant, and the partners acquired the Griffith House plant. Beef and lamb were quickly added to the line. Armour's four brothers joined the business as Armour's influence spread to Kansas City and New York.

At the time, meat processing was a seasonal business limited to cold weather months. There was no system other than salt curing to preserve perishable meat. In 1872, a method using natural ice in large coolers was devised, and Armour & Company built the world's first large chill room, with temperatures cooled by massive blocks of ice cut in the winter and stored under sawdust through the summer.

Armour had converted the meat business into a year-round industry. He not only now offered Americans fresh meat daily, but he also created an ice industry and stimulated the transport of live hogs for slaughter in Chicago rather than on the farms where they were raised. He built the massive Union Stock Yards in 1872. For the first time, more hogs than pork carcasses arrived in Chicago.

In 1878, the first crude refrigerator railroad cars and ships— known as reefers—began to appear, and Armour's markets spread across the globe. He created an oval-shaped label bearing the legend "Armour Star Ham" which became one of the best known trademarks in the history of the American food business. The star appeared in yellow on a dark blue background and told buyers they were getting the very best ham on the market. It was the first of nearly a thousand Armour trademarks.

In 1882 Plankinton left the business. In 1884, Armour finally retired from his business in Milwaukee, where he had lived until

1875, to devote himself to the bustling Chicago empire. By this time, Armour & Company was involved in every facet of the meat packing industry. The Armours controlled vast grain and feed interests, owned their own railroad cars, and had distribution plants across the country.

In the 1880s, Armour & Company became a leader in converting byproducts into useful products like buttons, combs, and glue. Armour added a department to sell pepsin—a digestive aid—which became the forerunner of the Armour Pharmaceutical Company. Other industries included oleomargarine (1880), ammonia (1891), fertilizer (1894), curled hair for cushions (1895), laundry soap (1896), glycerine (1896), brushes (1897), and sandpaper (1900).

The man who built one of the most splendid enterprises of the nineteenth century began to fade away with the end of the epoch. He became sick in 1899 and died early in 1901. He had enough time to carefully plan for the future of Armour & Company in the interim. "There's no such thing as luck," Armour said, "Brains always have and always will command the highest market value."

 aker's

It is known that the Aztec Indians of Central America used chocolate as many as three thousand years ago, mixing cultivated cacao beans into a frothy drink. Columbus was served the drink on a voyage in 1502, and other explorers started trading in the exotic flavor, which rapidly gained popularity in fashionable European chocolate houses.

The American chocolate business did not begin, however, until 1755, when Massachusetts sea captains sailed to the West Indies to trade cargoes of fish for the precious cocoa beans. The beans were sold to apothecaries who would grind the beans into a medicine. This is how James Baker, a Dorchester, Massachusetts physician, came to know chocolate.

In 1764, Baker provided the capital for John Hannon, an Irish immigrant, to mill the first chocolate in North America. The water-powered mill opened on the banks of the Neponset River in the center of Dorchester. It sold ground chocolate and also milled beans brought in by others. By the time of the American Revolution, Hannon's chocolate business was flourishing.

Meanwhile, Baker was experimenting with other recipes for chocolate. He leased space in a local paper mill and in 1772 sold his first chocolate. In 1779 Hannon sailed for the West Indies in search of greater supplies of cocoa beans. He was never heard from again. The original mill came under Baker's full control, and in 1780 he began producing chocolate under the brand name Baker's.

Although James Baker retired in 1804, the chocolate business remained in family hands for nearly another hundred years. Other chocolate factories ground beans throughout the United States, but none seemed as efficient as the Baker mills. Today, over two hundred years later, the Baker name remains synonymous with unsweetened and semi-sweet baking chocolate in America. It is the oldest American concern manufacturing the same product in the same location.

irdseye

Clarence Birdseye had been traveling to the Arctic north since vacation breaks from Amherst College. Later, he returned as a naturalist for the United States Biological Survey. In 1916, the thirty-year old Birdseye journeyed to Labrador as a fur trader and medical missionary.

The house which the scientist and his young family occupied was but a tiny cottage perched on storm-gnawed rock above the Labrador Sea. Outside, the great gray wall of an Arctic winter pressed upon them. Here, amid the towering snowdrifts and biting Arctic wind, was born "the most revolutionary idea in the history of food."

Birdseye hunted and fished to provide food for his wife and weeks-old child. The deer carcasses he hung outside the cottage quickly froze into blocks of meat which could be sliced only by axe. Fish drawn through a hole in the ice congealed in the middle of a flip.

Birdseye came to realize that his frozen meat and fish retained their fresh flavor. Cold storage meat, however, always lost much of its original flavor in the freezing process. What was it about the natural freezing process in Labrador that preserved the flavor of food?

Birdseye returned home to Gloucester, Massachusetts and began a series of experiments in the freezing of food. At the start he could afford to spend only seven dollars for equipment, including an electric fan, ice and salt. Eventually Birdseye came to realize it was the quick freezing that sealed in the flavor and freshness—and it remained sealed in until the food was thawed and cooked.

Perishable food was cleaned and prepared and then wrapped in moisture-proof cellophane. The packages, with the food at the peak of freshness, were plunged into a patented Birdseye Quick-Freezing Machine at minus fifty degrees. Since the food was frozen in the package no flavor-enhancing juices escaped. Birdseye frozen foods cooked and handled just like fresh foods. He had perfected a new freezing process.

And the business failed. The process was a success but the

manufacturing and distribution were not. Retailers were not ready to invest in the specialized refrigeration equipment necessary to merchandise the frozen food. Birdseye hocked his life insurance and tried again. This time he got it right. In 1924 Birdseye and three partners formed the General Seafoods Company, and a year later quick-frozen fish filets fresh off the Gloucester wharfs were available. Soon Birdseye Foods included more than a hundred varieties of meats, fish, poultry, fruits, and vegetables. Housewives quickly adjusted to the cooking directions on the new frozen food packages.

In 1929, Birdseye sold the business for $22,000,000, including 168 patents on quick-freezing. A $50,000 yearly stipend was thrown into the package. At the time it was the largest sum ever paid for a patent. The name of the company was immediately changed to General Foods Corporation, which made back their investment hundreds of times over.

Clarence "Bob" Birdseye later invented a reflector and infra-red heat lamp. One of his hobbies was whale tracking, leading to his perfection of a kickless harpoon gun. In 1949 he devised a method for dehydrating food. He continued working in the frozen food field and was singlehandedly responsible for every important development in the young industry. All told he received nearly three hundred patents before his death in 1956. "I like to go around asking a lot of damn fool questions," he always said.

Borden

Gail Borden drifted through early nineteenth-century America waiting for the times to catch up with his creative mind. Borden was born in New York state in 1801, and worked his way to Texas as a surveyor, school teacher, farmer and customs collector. In Texas he became one of the leaders along with Sam Houston and Stephen F.

Austin, in the movement that freed the region from Mexican rule. Working as a newspaper publisher, he penned the famous headline *"Remember The Alamo!"*

Borden was of intensely religious Puritan stock and turned to invention to better serve God by improving living conditions. He battled yellow fever with ether, invented a Lazy Susan-type device, and devised a "terraqueous machine"—a prairie schooner with sails to use in crossing rivers. It was the forerunner of amphibious vehicles used in World War II a hundred years later, but when he demonstrated his sail-powered wagon it overturned, dumping his select group of guests into the Gulf of Mexico fifty feet from shore.

He developed a meat biscuit that was all but inedible; he believed it would be the ideal food for the army, navy, and explorers. The tasteless biscuit was a commercial failure, and he lost between $60,000 and $100,000. But it was hailed as a scientific breakthrough and Borden sailed to England to accept an award. On the journey back he watched horrified as children died from drinking contaminated milk.

While futilely promoting his meat biscuit, Borden began experiments with condensing milk. In 1853, he developed a milk of good flavor with excellent keeping qualities. Borden thought it was the condensing that kept the milk fresh for long periods of time. In fact it was the high temperatures he employed that destroyed disease-carrying bacteria, as the world would later learn from Dr. Louis Pasteur. Borden had produced not only the first condensed milk but the first "pasteurized" milk as well.

He applied for a patent which was finally granted three years later. Gail Borden was fifty-five years old. He had a patent but he had no market, no money, no credit. He persuaded one man, on the strength of a handshake and Borden's earnestness, to give him use of equipment in his Wolcottville, Connecticut factory. The company failed. So did another.

On a train trip home to New York, the gregarious Borden struck up a conversation with the stranger sitting opposite him. By the time the two men stepped off the train, Borden had a backer for the New York Condensed Milk Company. His factory was a small mill in the town of Burrville, Connecticut.

The nation was finally fed up with dangerous, unclean milk. Condensed milk caught on quickly. Borden's company, the oldest national dairy business, solidified during the Civil War with orders from the government to feed the Union Army. After the war his milk fueled a migration west, just as he himself had made fifty years earlier.

Borden was involved in every facet of his operation. He visited dairy farms, lectured plant workers on sanitation, and worked alongside the mechanics on the machinery. He solicited orders. He could often be seen sweeping floors and cleaning windows.

Borden died in 1874 at the age of seventy-three. The next year his sons took the company into fluid milk. Eventually Borden would bring milk into more homes than any other firm in the world. Gail Borden had selected his burial site several years before his death, choosing a shady knoll in Woodlawn Cemetery which he marked with a huge granite milk can. The can was replaced with his epitaph: "I tried and failed, I tried again and again, and succeeded."

Breyers

Ice cream was known in colonial times; Dolly Madison introduced it to the White House in the early 1800s. But it was troublesome to make and rarely seen on American tables in that time. The first major improvement in the manufacture of ice cream was Nancy Johnson's hand-cranked freezer in 1846.

After the Civil War, in 1866, William Breyer took a hand-cranked freezer and made his first ice cream. Breyer used rich cream, cane sugar, fruits, and nuts to make his frozen treats. He loaded his wagon and hawked his ice cream to his neighbors on the streets of North Philadelphia. Breyer called his customers out of their homes with a dinner bell. That first year he sold a thousand gallons of homemade ice cream.

Philadelphia was America's ice cream capital. Philadelphians enjoyed more ice cream than anyone, in the city's famous public ice cream houses. A frozen concoction of vanilla-and-egg earned the moniker "Philadelphia" and was wildly popular. Amidst such competition, William Breyer could afford to make his ice cream from only the freshest natural ingredients.

In 1882, Breyer had sold enough ice cream to move his trade off the Philadelphia cobblestones and into his own retail ice cream store. A manufacturing area was built in the back of the shop and a soda fountain out front. The store was his last contribution to the firm; he died later that year.

William Breyer was able to survive in the carnivorous ice cream business only by using the purest, highest quality ingredients obtainable. Aware of the legacy entrusted in him, when Henry Breyer took over the business in 1882 he wrote a "pledge of purity" that continues to adorn every Breyers ice cream carton today. Breyers, now America's largest selling ice cream, still blends its ice cream with the same basic formula William Breyer used in his kitchen in 1866.

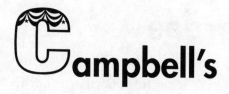

Campbell's

In 1860, Abraham Anderson opened a small canning factory in Camden, New Jersey. Across the river in Philadelphia, Joseph Campbell was a produce merchant who wanted to get into the processing end of the business. In 1869 Campbell and Anderson became partners, forming Anderson & Campbell. The two men canned vegetables, minced meat, jams, jellies, and a variety of soups.

In 1876 Campbell bought out the founder, and changed the company name to Joseph Campbell Preserve Company. A few years later Campbell invited his son-in-law and nephew into the canning business. His son-in-law brought along a friend named Arthur Dorrance, who provided the firm with a needed infusion of cash. The company name was changed to the Joseph Campbell Preserving Company.

By 1896 the cannery was prospering, and a large factory was built in Camden to expand the product line. Campbell's company now offered prepared meats, sauces, canned fruit, ketchup, and plum pudding. In 1899 John Dorrance, Arthur's nephew, developed a revolutionary way of canning condensed soup. The innovation enabled Campbell's to ship and sell soup at a third of the cost of its competitors, effectively eliminating them. As soup varieties increased, the firm canned less and less produce.

A year later Joseph Campbell died. In 1915, John Dorrance purchased total control of the company, ending any Campbell family involvement in the food processing giant.

hef Boyardee

Hector Boiardi came to the United States from northern Italy in 1914 at the age of seventeen. He already had six years of experience working in kitchens in his homeland. Despite his young age, he had no problem lining up a job as a chef at New York's Plaza Hotel, where his brother worked as a waiter, Word of Boiardi's skill spread rapidly, and he was soon called upon to cater President Woodrow Wilson's wedding reception at the Greenbrier Hotel in West Virginia.

In 1929 Boiardi migrated to Cleveland, Ohio where he opened a small restaurant of his own. Soon he was sending home bottles of his tomato sauces to customers who wanted to take that special Boiardi taste with them. When he heard that the flavor did not translate to kitchen tables he started including a package of his special blend of cheeses. Then he added a package of uncooked spaghetti. His home Italian spaghetti dinners were the talk of Cleveland.

Boiardi began marketing his spaghetti dinners and other specialty dishes to neighboring stores. Soon he was spending more and more time selling his new line of products. To maintain his restaurant, Boiardi formed a company with his brothers Richard and Mario. But while his foods were popular, his name was not. Even his sales representatives had difficulty pronouncing the name correctly. Reluctantly, Hector Boiardi changed the brand name to spell phonetically: Boy-ar-dee. The national launch was under way.

In 1938 Boiardi moved his operations to Milton, Pennsylvania, where the former Susquehanna Silk Mill was transformed into an Italian wonderland of canned pastas. Boiardi's canned foods were an important ration for Allied troops in World War II and his Americanized name became well-known enough to sell the company for six million dollars after the war. Hector Boiardi remained an advisor in the canned pasta business until his death in 1985, at the age of 87.

Dole

When he died at the age of eighty, *The New York Times* wrote, "Mr. Dole was personally responsible for the pineapple industry, the popularity of that fruit in the United States, and in large measure, for the prosperity of the Hawaiian Islands." James Drummond Dole certainly earned the calling card, "The Pineapple King."

The Dole family were New England traders and missionaries as far back as the eighteenth century. Daniel Dole, grand-uncle to James, was an early missionary to the Polynesians in Hawaii, establishing a branch of the family on the islands. In 1899, after graduating from Harvard, Dole sailed to Hawaii, where his cousin Sanford was governor of the territory, to seek his fortune. With him he packed a twelve hundred dollar nest egg.

At the turn of the century, the Hawaiian Islands were an isolated chain in the Pacific whose economy turned on the market fortunes of a single commodity—sugar. Efforts had been made to introduce rubber, coffee, sisal, rice, and other tropical crops on the lava islands. All had failed.

Dole was going to Hawaii to boldly stake his future on pineapples. The pineapple is a bromeliad believed to originate in Brazil. Columbus discovered the fruit in the West Indies on his second voyage. Fresh pineapple is a poor traveler and spoiled before Columbus could reach Europe with the golden fruit. Pineapple thus became a great delicacy and was raised in Royal European hothouses.

The fresh pineapple that did reach markets in 1900 was not enthusiastically received. Wrote one observer, "Pineapples resemble pine cones and have about the same flavor and texture." This was the fruit on which the twenty-four-year old James Dole chose to risk his life savings. He knew absolutely nothing about growing pineapples.

The pineapple came to Hawaii in 1813, where it thrived in the red Hawaiian soil. But sporadic attempts at growing the spiny fruit commercially were all abandoned. Natives scoffed at Dole's claim to "extend the market for Hawaiian pineapples into every grocery store in the United States." But Dole was not going to try and ship perishable fresh pineapples twenty-three hundred miles to the Pacific Coast. He was going to grow them and put them in cans.

In 1901 Dole organized the Hawaiian Pineapple Company, and planted 75,000 pineapple plants across twelve acres of homestead land at Wahiawa near Honolulu. A half century later there would be over one billion pineapple plants in the Islands.

With $20,000 invested by friends and a San Francisco food firm, Dole built a tiny frame cannery using hand-operated equipment. Broken slices of pineapple were inserted through a small hole in the top and the cans were soldered shut. From this would grow the world's largest fruit cannery. In its first year Dole's sixteen employees canned 1,893 cases of pineapple.

The product was a success. Others followed Dole into the pineapple business and the mainland markets absorbed all the canned pineapples Dole and his contemporaries could produce. Still, pineapple was a luxury food on American tables. In the Panic of 1907, demand evaporated. The year 1908 began with plantations harvesting 400,000 cases and holding orders for only 120,000. The infant industry faced ruin.

Under Dole's leadership the eight island packers fought back as a united industry, formulating a marketing plan unique to American business. They pooled their money and launched a $50,000 national advertising campaign. It was the first advertising done by an industry with no regard to individual brands. Housewives were told to "not ask for pineapple alone, insist on Hawaiian pineapple." The effect was startling. "Hawaiian" became the hallmark of the finest pineapple. Warehouses emptied and consumption quadrupled in eighteen months.

In 1914, the Hawaiian Pineapple Company produced a high-speed peeling and coring machine. With the new machine, Dole had the means to outproduce his rivals. But he believed that one pineapple company could not prosper at the expense of the others. He shared the technology with his competitors, charging only a modest royalty for its use.

Dole continued to search for ways to meet burgeoning pineapple demand. He bought the uninhabited island of Lanai and planted a fourteen thousand acre plantation, blasting an artificial harbor out of the lava to ship the pineapple. When the Depression again threatened the industry, Dole began popularizing pineapple juice as a beverage, which bore the Dole trademark for the first time.

Dole was fascinated by aviation. On the heels of Lindbergh's solo Atlantic crossing in 1927, Dole began envisioning the day when Hawaii would be connected to the Pacific Coast by air service. After the first nonstop flight from California to Hawaii by two Army Air Corps pilots, Dole offered a $25,000 first prize and a $10,000 second prize for the first civilian flight to Hawaii.

The Dole Race captured the imagination of the public and the name of James Dole, "the pineapple King of Hawaii", became known in households across the land. Five tiny planes set off on August 12, 1928. Two landed safely to claim the prizes, but the other three, carrying six men and one woman, vanished. Dole was criticized for promoting a dangerous stunt but his efforts led directly to the establishment of trans-Pacific air service.

Dole's success had irritated Hawaiian sugar planters for decades. Taking advantage of Depression prices they bought up more than half of the Hawaiian Pineapple Company stock. Dole was elected chairman but no longer wielded major control. The Hawaiian pineapple king retired in 1948. He died ten years later in 1958, the same year Hawaii was to become the fiftieth state.

Drake's

There was nothing in Newman Drake's background that indicated he would have a successful career as a baker. Drake left school in 1873 at age thirteen and gained employment as a ship's cabin boy and later a carpenter. He worked as a repairman on the

Lackawanna Railroad. And in 1896, after eight years of preparation in his chosen craft, his first-day sales of $3.24 did not bode well for his baking future.

In 1888 Drake was traveling in England selling biscuit machinery when he discovered a fast-selling, mass-produced pound cake called a "slab cake." Grocers would slice slabs of the ready-made cake for customers who didn't feel like baking at home. In America, wholesale baking of biscuits was common but cakes were still the exclusive province of daily bakeries and home kitchens.

Drake returned to the United States and set about developing a recipe for wholesale baking of pound cakes, as well as arranging financing. He invented the machinery necessary to mass produce cake. A friend helped construct a bakery in Harlem, and Drake's first cakes were ready for sale in 1896. He hired a salesman who reported back with the $3.24 and a disheartening message that delicatessens and groceries were not ready to accept mass-produced cakes.

Drake began extensive missionary work on behalf of his pound cake. He personally visited hundreds of retailers explaining how the slab cakes sold in England. His one consolation was that there was no competition. Slowly his slab cakes gained acceptance among retailers.

In 1899 the emerging colossus of the National Biscuit Company purchased the Drake Baking Company and appointed Newman Drake as manager. But Drake had just begun to taste the success of independent enterprise. He left in 1900 to form the Drake Brothers Company with his brother Charles, who had left the Drake Baking Company in its early days to sell jams and preserves.

The Drake brothers began with five thousand dollars and five horse-and-wagon delivery vehicles. Newman Drake had conquered the skepticism of retailers and now tackled the doubts of housewives. He reduced the portions of his recipes so housewives could replicate his "Pure Food" cakes and compare them with their own.

The strategy worked, and sales gradually grew—surpassing one million dollars annually by 1913. Wax paper was developed during World War I, which enabled Drake to individually package his cakes. Popular Drake coffee cakes were introduced in 1916, and sales surged further.

By the early 1920s, Drake's health began to fail and he sought more time for his avocations of travel and hunting. He sold the company in 1924 while remaining as chairman of the board in the new organization. Drake spent the remaining years of his life near his birthplace of Andover, New Jersey, devoting his resources to Sussex County. He donated a park and erected the town's first movie house. He often had anonymous deliveries made to fill coal bins of poor families throughout the area.

Newman Drake died in 1930 at the age of seventy. Drake's was ultimately acquired by Borden's in 1946, and the last family member left the original cake and pie company in 1954.

Folger's

The Folgers were an old Nantucket family who traced their roots to the founding of the island's colony in the early 1600s. Generation after generation of Folger men worked in or around the whaling business as Nantucket grew into the greatest whaling center in the world. All that ended one morning in 1846 when a great fire destroyed the entire business district and waterfront—thirty-three acres in all. The townspeople set about rebuilding immediately, but it was clear that a young man's prospects in Nantucket would never be the same again.

Accordingly three of the five Folger brothers—twenty-year old Edward, sixteen-year old Henry, and fourteen-year old James—set sail for the Gold Rush taking place in California in 1849. They arrived in San Francisco on May 5, 1850 to find a town whose population had burst from eight hundred to forty thousand in two years. Most were males between 20 and 40 seeking the same fortune as the Folgers.

It was decided the two older brothers would head for the gold country while James remained in town, working as a carpenter. James had helped rebuild Nantucket and recognized the same sort of building boom now embracing San Francisco. Work was plentiful, and wages were high enough to temper some of his disappointment at not joining his brothers in the gold fields.

Folger signed on with William Bovee, then age twenty-seven, to erect a spice and coffee mill. Bovee had tried his hand in the gold fields himself, but soon decided to return to the coffee trade he had learned in New York. There was no roast coffee then available in northern California, and ground coffee was unheard of in the mining camps.

Bovee called his new business the Pioneer Steam Coffee & Spice Mill, although there was no steam engine and the mill was often powered by Jim Folger's hands. From his time digging for gold, Bovee knew that ground coffee, ready to brew, was what busy miners would want. He roasted, ground, and packaged ready-to-brew coffee in labeled tins.

The business grew, and after a year Folger left to finally seek his fortune in the northern California hills. Just in case, he took along a trunk loaded with coffee samples and spices to call on provision stores. In between gathering orders, Folger actually made a strike. With a small bag of gold dust he made his way deeper into gold country to Auburn. He found plenty of miners but no store, so he opened his own in 1852.

His timing was perfect. A big strike hit near Auburn, and he was able to sell his business for a handsome profit and return to San Francisco. He dallied for awhile as a hardware merchant before returning to Bovee's and investing money in the coffee firm. In 1859 Bovee's own gold fever returned, and he sold all but a small interest in the coffee mill to Folger.

Now twenty-four, Folger took on a partner and aggressively expanded the business of the newly named Marden & Folger. When the economy collapsed following the Civil War, the partners found themselves badly overextended and went into bankruptcy. Folger's first response was to buy out his partner after convincing creditors their best hope of recovering outstanding debts was to allow the mill to stay open.

It took until 1874 for J. A. Folger & Company to return to solvency, but by then the business was thriving with the West. Folger bought into several mines and part of a newspaper. He moved across the bay to the oak-lined coast of Oakland, joining several prominent clubs. He was elected to the Oakland City Council and the Board of Education.

Folger died unexpectedly of a coronary occlusion in 1889, at the age of fifty-four. Flags were lowered to half-mast throughout Oakland. James Folger III followed his father as company president, just as Folgers had continued in the family business back in Nantucket for centuries.

French's

In 1880, Robert T. French was winding down a career as a New York wholesaler of coffee, tea, and spices. He had been born fifty-seven years earlier in Ithaca, New York, but rather than move back to the farm in retirement, French had other ideas. He was going into business for himself.

Together with his sons George and Francis, French began to deal in a wide assortment of products, from spices to birdseed. By 1883 the Frenchs had moved upstate to Rochester, and the little wholesale trade continued to expand. Robert French died in 1893 without ever considering the mustard that would propel the family name into everyday American life.

It was George and Francis who decided to counter the volcanic mustards of the day with a milder blend of seasonings. They blended a creamier mustard, colored bright yellow, and called it "French's Cream Salad Mustard." A nine-ounce jar sold for ten cents. For the first time, consumers could buy a prepared mustard in a jar. The novel yellow mustard was introduced with the hot dog at the St. Louis World's Fair in 1904. By 1912, a new plant was needed in Rochester to satisfy demand. Another plant opened ten years later and in 1926 the French family sold their business to a British food company for nearly four million dollars. By 1980, one hundred years after R. T. French set off on his own, 500,000 jars of French's famous yellow mustard were being sold every day.

Gerber

In 1928, seven out of every hundred babies born in America died. Seven-month old Sally Gerber, like many babies, suffered from a troubling illness, and a physician advised her worried parents that strained fruits and vegetables might serve as a nourishing treatment. Home preparation of strained fruits and vegetables was tedious and time-consuming, but little Sally was luckier than most American toddlers—her family owned a cannery.

The Gerbers had emigrated to central Michigan in 1875, settling in the small town of Fremont, two hundred miles from Detroit. Joseph Gerber organized the Fremont Canning Company, and his son Frank returned from school in Indiana in 1901 to join the family business. Frank worked his way through the plant and office, until in 1917 he became president.

In 1928 Gerber, joined by his son Dan, applied the process used to make tomato puree to produce strained fruit. The experiment was a success. Word about little Sally's food spread around Fremont and local mothers began requesting samples.

The Gerbers knew their baby food could be an important money-maker for them but several questions needed to be answered. Would the medical profession accept the new food? Would the grocery trade handle the product? And did the mothers in a small town of three thousand represent a workable sample?

Dan took samples to a Grand Rapids physician who was more enthusiastic about the strained food than even the Gerbers. So they tested market acceptance with a survey, rare for the times. They found that mothers would buy the strained food only if it was cheap and readily available at stores. The Gerbers decided to sell the new baby food for fifteen cents a can at a time when drugstores carried other baby foods for thirty-five cents.

In Autumn of 1928, the Gerbers spent $40,000 advertising an introductory assortment of six cans to mothers for one dollar and a coupon with their local grocer's name. Dollars poured in and the Gerbers took the coupons to grocers to demonstrate demand. Within six months Gerber strained peas, prunes, carrots, spinach, and vegetable soup were available across the country.

Within a few years, the cannery was devoted solely to making baby food. Frank Gerber changed the name of his company to Gerber Products Company as his name became known the world over. Baby foods expanded into infant nutrition; Gerber's was offering sixty-nine varieties after its first twenty-five years.

Aggressive competitiors entered the marketplace, which helped expand the entire baby foods industry. When Frank Gerber died in 1952, in the midst of the post World War II baby boom, the business he founded because his granddaughter was sick was selling $54,000,000 worth of baby food each year.

Harry and David

If one were to list the types of businesses best suited to withstand the Great Depression of the 1930s, selling fancy pears would not be on the first page—or likely any page. Harry and David Holmes, both Ivy League-educated, did not need to have their bleak prospects pointed out to them.

Harry, born in 1890, and David, born a year later, had returned to Oregon from Cornell in 1914 to take over the family pear orchard in Medford. The star of the orchard was a giant DuComice pear that was served at elegant tables in New York and Europe. The brothers built a steady and reliable income from their pear business, which was threatened when the Stock Market crashed in 1929.

Desperate for anything to save the orchard, the brothers decided to try and sell gift boxes of fruit by mail. At the suggestion of an advertising friend, G. Lynn Sumner, Harry and David prepared fifteen sample packages and sent them by special messenger to some of the most powerful corporate leaders in New York City. An hour later, the brothers had their first order; it was from Walter Chrysler. The fifteen sample fruit boxes pulled in a total of four hundred and sixty-seven orders.

Harry and David Holmes were in the mail order fruit business, battling the local produce stand. In their first year they sold six thousand gift boxes, and the next year another fifteen thousand. In 1937, Harry and David founded the Fruit-of-the-Month Club. Each of the millions of catalogs they mailed featured the brothers' images, clad in a friendly plaid shirt. By the time they died in the 1950s, Harry and David were more recognizable to most Americans than their local greengrocer.

Heinz

Henry Heinz looked around at his company exhibit at the 1893 World's Columbian Exposition in Chicago. The hand-carved antique oak glistened with polished oil. The small pagodas at each corner—graced by four international beauties—were stocked with a dizzying variety of free Heinz food samples. A trade paper had raved, "the Heinz exhibit is most comprehensive, showing every variety of sauce, relish, and preserve put up, many of them being original with the firm."

The pavilion had everything—except visitors. Heinz thought a bit and left for the nearest print shop. He designed a small white card promising the bearer a free Heinz souvenir when redeemed at the Heinz Company Exhibit at the fair. He directed his men to hand out the cards and hired boys to scatter the tokens by the thousands around the fair grounds.

The souvenir in question was a small charm one and one-quarter inches long shaped like a pickle, emblazoned with the name *Heinz*. And the people stampeded. The next day *The New York Times* reported, "It has just been discovered that the gallery floor of the Agricultural Building has sagged where the pickle display of H. J. Heinz Company stood, owing to the vast crowd which constantly thronged to procure a watch charm."

Fair officials had to call on Chicago police to regulate the crowds until the supports of the gallery could be strengthened. Other exhibitors filed an official complaint with fair authorities, charging unfair competitive methods. All told, Heinz gave away one million pickle charms at the fair. The *Saturday Evening Post* lauded the promotion as "one of the most famous giveaways in merchandising history."

By the time of the Chicago Exposition, Henry Heinz had been selling food for forty-one of his forty-nine years. At the age of eight, Heinz sold the surplus from his mother's garden in Sharpsburg, Pennsylvania, north of Pittsburgh. By the time he was twelve, Henry was cultivating his own three-and-one-half acre plot. At an early age Heinz showed an intuitive sense of seed and soil, drawing on his German heritage.

Heinz specialized in bottled horseradish, a delicacy of the area. The food was prized as an appetite sharpener and hailed as a medicinal marvel. But its allure was not obtained without tedious kitchen preparation and a legacy of scraped knuckles. Heinz's bottled, prepared horseradish—packaged in clear bottles for housewives to inspect for any trace of fillers—anticipated the desire for processed foods that was eventually to establish his company in twentieth century kitchens around the world.

Despite his success in the horseradish business, Heinz was primarily a brickmaker until he was twenty-five, first in his father's brickyard and then as owner of his own brick factory. In 1869, he married and decided to forego all non-food business interests. His Anchor Brands started with horseradish and gradually expanded to include sauerkraut, pickles, and vinegar.

By 1875, Heinz and his two partners had "built up the business with a rapidity seldom witnessed," reported a commentator of the day. But it was too much too fast. A bumper cucumber crop left Heinz strapped for cash and the firm went bust. His parents' house and furniture went to a sheriff's sale; Heinz had to beg for credit for groceries his family.

The stigma of bankruptcy did not settle long on Heinz. He was shortly back in the food business, managing a company started by his brother and cousin. His debts paid off, Heinz was solvent again by 1879, a year ahead of his self-imposed schedule. A small dervish of a man, the restless Heinz now set out to expand the business.

An inveterate traveler, the Pittsburgh food merchant sailed to England in 1886 with dozens of jars of pickles, chili sauce, and other condiments. Brazenly he marched into the leading London grocer of the day, Fortnum & Mason, and sold all his samples. Heinz products were quickly staples in every pantry in the British Empire.

While riding a New York elevated train in 1892, Heinz studied a car placard that advertised "21 styles" of shoes. He reckoned the phrase would work for his own products. Although there were more than sixty of them at the time, Heinz hit on the number fifty-seven. Within a week the sign of the green pickle with the "57 Varieties" was everywhere Heinz could "find a place to stick it."

He ordered New York's first electric sign, a six-story, twelve-hundred-light display that advertised "good things from the table" from Heinz. Enthralled New Yorkers gathered nightly to watch the mechanically orchestrated lines of flashing lights, each of which cost ninety dollars a night to burn.

His most successful promotion was the Heinz Ocean Pier at Atlantic City. Jutting nine hundred feet into the Atlantic Ocean, the pier was popularly known as "The Crystal Palace by the Sea." An estimated fifty million people visited the pier, most of whom left sporting their tiny Heinz pickle pin. In 1944, when the amusement pier seemed to be outliving its novelty, a September hurricane tore apart the pier, casting the "5" from the giant "57" into the sea.

By 1900 Heinz had dwarfed his competitors. "Any one of our present buildings in Pittsburgh—there were seventeen—is as large as the entire plant of any other concern in the same business in this country," boasted a company statement. Heinz invited the public to visit his plant, one of the first industrialists to open his doors to factory tours.

In an era of reviled sweatshops, Heinz proudly showed off his operation, where Heinz girls stuffed pickles and peppers into glass jars and in their off hours enjoyed a paneled wood locker room, a library, and a swimming pool. All food handlers enjoyed a free weekly manicure.

In an age when Americans began to turn away from home-grown foods, concern grew over the quality of prepackaged food products. Practically alone in the food industry, Henry Heinz stood in favor of the 1906 Pure Food and Drug Act and helped shepherd it into existence, generating priceless favorable publicity for his firm.

In his seventies, Heinz left much of the business details to his son and devoted himself to the national Sunday school movement. Still globetrotting, he had little time to enjoy his private museum collection and the ten greenhouses at his Pittsburgh mansion. He was busy making plans for their expansion when he was stricken by pneumonia and died in 1919, at the age of 74.

Fifty years later in 1969, on the 100th anniversary of the founding of the food processing firm by Henry Heinz, company officials quietly dropped the celebrated "57 Varieties" trademark. At the time the H. J. Heinz product list numbered more than 1,100.

Hellmann's

Richard Hellmann sold several varieties of his wife's mayonnaise in his little deli on Columbus Street in New York City in 1905. To simplify his wife's life, he polled several customers and discovered the "blue ribbon" formula was the most popular. And so it was that "Richard Hellmann's Blue Ribbon Mayonnaise" became the first mayonnaise that most Americans ever tasted.

Hellmann was born in Vetschau, Germany in 1876, and apprenticed in the wholesale food business as a boy. He then traveled the globe for Crosse & Blackwell, a British grocery concern. He landed in America in 1903 to work in a wholesale grocery business, before opening his deli two years later.

To flavor his sandwiches and salads, Hellmann offered mayonnaise, a French cream sauce known since the mid-1700s. He sold ten-cent portions, ladled into wooden bowls. In 1912 he began packing his salad dressing in jars with his name emblazoned on the label beneath a bright blue ribbon. Within a year, Hellman realized his small shop could not produce the amount of mayonnaise his customers demanded.

In 1915 a modern factory was up and running in Queens. By 1920, a second manufacturing facility was set up on Long Island. Hellmann merged his company with the newly formed General Foods Corporation in 1927, remaining on the board of directors of the parent company. He pursued other business interests, including banking, before his death in a Greenwich, Connecticut nursing home in 1971, at the age of ninety-four.

Hormel

Meat-packing was in George Hormel's blood. After several false starts, Hormel finally settled into his life's work, establishing a reputation for innovative meat products that continues today. In an eighteen-month period during the late 1980s, the Hormel Company introduced 134 new products.

George Hormel was born in Buffalo in 1860 before moving to Toledo, Ohio, where his father opened a tannery. His mother came from an immigrant meat-packing family and at age fifteen George left to work in his uncle's butcher business in Chicago. His health failed however, forcing Hormel back to Ohio.

The convalescing youth filled out his six foot two inch frame, and after stints in his father's tannery and a railroad yard, he set out for Kansas City to seek his fortune. Hormel found a job as a wool-buyer calling on accounts in dusty frontier towns in the upper midwest. He was especially fond of the northernmost town in his territory—Austin, Minnesota. Here, Hormel spent much of his leisure time joining several recreation clubs.

His Kansas City company failed, and Hormel landed in Chicago as a hide buyer. On a trip to visit friends in Austin in 1887 he learned of a butcher shop which had been damaged by fire. With five hundred dollars borrowed from his employer, Hormel joined a friend in refurbishing the building into a retail meat market and pork packing business.

After a disagreement over the direction of the business, the partnership dissolved in 1891 and George opened the Hormel Provision Market. The next year, in a small grove of oak trees along the Red Cedar River, Hormel converted an old creamery into a packing house. George handled the production of sausage, hams and bacon himself. The first year he slaughtered 610 hogs.

Hormel poured every dollar of profit back into his business. Output increased to 2,532 hogs in 1893, and soon he controlled most of the meat market in the region. That year, large Chicago packers introduced improved refrigerator cars which allowed them to sell and deliver product in faraway communities, virtually eliminating competition from small midwest packers. All but four of several hundred packers west of the Mississippi closed their shops.

Hormel decided he needed more and better products to survive. He concentrated on a superior sausage which became popular locally, and in 1895 he introduced the first of his company's new products—"Hormel's Sugar-Cured Pig Back Bacon", known today as Canadian bacon.

Before 1900, ice plants were nonexistent. Meat shops butchered fresh beef and pork mostly on demand. This constricting system was inadequate for Hormel's ambitious operation. He installed an ice storage plant with ice cut in eighteen-inch slabs from the frozen Red Cedar. The business expanded rapidly, and in 1899 Hormel sent for his father and three brothers to join him in the business. Their arrival allowed George Hormel to put down his cleaver forever.

Hormel's own son, Jay, returned from World War I to join the firm, and uncovered a scandal that rocked the Hormel Packing Company. An assistant controller had embezzled $1,187,000 leaving the company short of funds to pay three million dollars in bank notes. Hormel's integrity won him extensions that kept the business afloat.

He aggressively restructured the organization, and in 1926, the year George Hormel retired from active management of the company, he introduced "Hormel Flavor-Sealed Ham", America's first canned ham. Hormel added Dinty Moore beef stew in 1935 and canned chili in 1936.

In 1937 Hormel developed a spiced ham and ground pork product destined for pop culture immortality. Because the canned meat included shoulder meat it couldn't be called ham. Hormel sponsored a contest to name the new meat. The winner received eleven hundred dollars and Spam entered American lexicon. It became a World War II staple and—though roundly ridiculed—it sold one billion cans in its first twenty years.

Hormel withstood a bitter labor strike in 1933, when disgruntled employees armed with clubs physically removed Jay Hormel from his office and threatened to shut off the plant's refrigeration system—endangering millions of pounds of meat. A compromise was reached in three days, and Hormel subsequently became a leader in innovative labor relations policies. When George Hormel died in 1946, the company he founded in 1892 by dressing 610 hogs was processing five thousand hogs a day.

Jeno's

Ettore Paulucci came to Aurora, Minnesota from Italy to work in the iron mines. Work was sporadic and his son Jeno began hustling for money at the age of twelve. It was 1930, and the Depression was just getting underway. Jeno collected cardboard boxes to sell for a penny apiece, and gathered lumps of coal that fell off the passing trains. He unloaded boxcars for a dollar a car, sold ore samples to tourists, and conducted tours of the mines.

When he was fourteen, Jeno got a job as a barker on Duluth's produce row. The five foot five Paulucci paraded around his stand hawking fruit so loudly that the city passed an ordinance outlawing fruit stand barking. Meanwhile the Great Depression continued to beat down on his father, who deserted the family in 1933. He would not return until Jeno was successful.

There were never enough hours in a day for Jeno Francisco Paulucci. He worked in the city markets of Hibbing, Minnesota after school and from five A. M. to midnight on Saturdays. At sixteen he became a sales rep for a food wholesaler, a business he worked in until 1945.

During World War II, fresh vegetables became scarce, and Paulucci noticed that Oriental families were growing bean sprouts in hydroponic gardens. Paulucci decided to form a partnership in the Bean Sprouts Growers Association. "I don't think I'll ever forget the look on the banker's face when I told him I wanted to borrow twenty-five hundred dollars to grow sprouts from mung beans," he said. But he got the money.

The bean sprout business struggled, but as he talked to retailers, Paulucci realized that they never had any canned Chinese food on the shelves. He would make chow mein. Paulucci named his food line Chun King, the first Chinese-sounding name that came to mind. But how was an Italian from Minnesota going to sell Chinese food?

He added flavor to the typically bland Chinese fare. He worked constantly to improve his profit margins. When the Minnesota growing season was too short to grow celery, Paulucci had to buy his celery in Florida like everyone else. But when he noticed that farmers cut the stalks in even bunches to facilitate shipping, he negotiated to buy the cut-off celery, typically discarded for cattle feed. He paid one-quarter the going rate.

Every dollar saved in production became a dollar spent on advertising. The food processor who began in a Quonset hut in Grand Rapids, Minnesota was the leading Chinese food maker by the early 1960s. But there were growing pains—especially in quality control. Food Fair, a major grocery chain and Paulucci's largest customer, threatened to discontinue handling Chun King over a rash of customer complaints.

Paulucci flew to Philadelphia to meet Food Fair's head buyer. Opening a can to demonstrate Chun King's quality, Paulucci looked in and met the bulging eyes of a huge grasshopper. He reached in, snatched the grasshopper, and ate it before the buyer noticed. The account was safe.

Paulucci sold Chun King for $63,000,000 in 1966 to R. J. Reynolds Foods. He came along as chairman of the board. The arrangement did not last long. Paulucci was used to arriving for work at 6:00 A.M. On his first day of work at R. J. Reynolds, the guard wouldn't let him in the building at that hour. Paulucci took his sixty-three million dollars and tackled the frozen pizza business.

At the time, only local and regional brands of frozen pizza were available. Using the same formula of low-cost production and an aggressive national advertising campaign Jeno's became America's number one frozen pizza by 1972. The big food processors now entered the field. To compete, Paulucci needed more central distribution, so he moved to Ohio.

He was vilified in Duluth for taking away thirteen hundred jobs from a depressed area, and he vowed to replace every one of the lost jobs. The effort consumed him. It crushed Paulucci's ego to take jobs from his hometown. He offered his terminals rent-free for two years but was only able to attract five companies and two hundred jobs to town. Paulucci helped build a new arena, recreation center, and a downtown retail center. Still, the battle with Duluth raged.

In 1986 Paulucci sold Jeno's to hated Pillsbury for $150,000,000 and made one last attempt to revive Duluth. Nothing worked. And now the failures of Duluth haunted his business ventures as well. An Italian-American magazine failed. He opened and closed pizza delivery and Chinese food delivery businesses in Florida. A billion-dollar real estate project in Orlando floundered. But throughout his ordeals, Jeno Paulucci remained a man of boundless energy still pursuing his dreams.

Keebler

Godfrey Keebler opened a small bake shop in Philadelphia in 1853. Around the neighborhood, word got out that Keebler was baking the best cookies and crackers in the area. At the time there was no way to expand a bakery business, no matter how good; the available transportation just didn't allow it. All around the country, fine local bakeries like Keebler's proliferated.

As horses and buggies gave way to automobiles and trucks, fresh baked goods could be delivered in a wider area than the neighborhood; distribution expanded to a regional level. Owners of local bakeries realized that certain advantages, such as purchasing economies and pooled transportation, could be derived by banding together into a business federation.

In 1927, the Keebler family bakery, now passed down from Godfrey, joined a consortium of bakeries to form the United Biscuit Company. The network eventually marketed cookies and crackers in every state east of California under a wide variety of brand names. In 1966, the company decided to operate under a single name. Of all the existing names, "Keebler" was judged to be the most sound and memorable. The Keebler elves, created by a Chicago advertising firm in 1968, have made Keebler one of the most recognizable names in America.

Today, Keebler is America's second largest producer of cookies and crackers in bakeries across the country. None, however, operates in Godfrey Keebler's hometown of Philadelphia.

Kellogg's

William Keith Kellogg once estimated that forty-two cereal companies launched in the breakfast cereal boom during the early years of the twentieth century. His, the Battle Creek Toasted Corn Flake Company, started when he was forty-six years old, was among the last. How did his company become the most famous?

Today Battle Creek, Michigan is widely known as the cereal food capital of the world. But in the middle of the nineteenth century it was a small town of a thousand people, where the seeds of the Seventh Day Adventists were sown. The Kellogg family made the pilgrimage to Battle Creek to be nearer the center of Adventist teachings. Kellogg's father manufactured brooms in addition to his church activities.

In 1878, at the age of eighteen, Will went to Texas to help start

a broom factory for an Adventist family in Dallas. When he returned
to Battle Creek, he began a stretch of twenty-five years living and
working in the shadow of his brother Dr. John Harvey Kellogg, a
celebrated physician and director of the Adventist Battle Creek
Sanitarium. Dr. Kellogg invented and marketed various health
foods based on Adventist beliefs in health reform.

While searching for a more digestible form of bread, the
brothers ran boiled wheat through rollers in the sanitarium basement. The day was long, and one failed experiment followed
another. They retired for the night. The next day they discovered
the wheat dough had dried out. When broken up by the rollers
thin flakes fell out. Flaked cereal was born.

The original flakes would be unrecognizable today. They were
tough and rather tasteless, but popular with patients at the sanitarium. Soon mail-orders came in from ex-patients. The Kellogg
brothers called their cereal "Granose," and marketed it through
the Sanitas Food Company. The factory on the sanitarium grounds
turned out 100,000 pounds of flakes in the first year.

The Kelloggs sold a ten-ounce box of wheat flakes for fifteen
cents—a return of twelve dollars for a sixty cents bushel of wheat.
This sort of profit did not go unnoticed. The secret of the flakes
leaked out and triggered a cereal boom in Battle Creek. Soon there
were thirty cereal companies in a town of thirty thousand people.

Will Kellogg broke with his brother in 1905, after building a
new factory for $50,000. Dr. Kellogg said he had not authorized
such an expenditure, and Will would have to pay for the plant himself. Will started his new company in 1906. He was forty-six. The
thin, brown-haired boy had given way to a stocky man with thinning
hair. Kellogg was a shy, deeply religious man with strong convic-
tions. So it was no surprise that despite the enormous popularity of
wheat flakes and the sneers of the cereal community Kellogg never
wavered from his plan to make corn flakes his main product. To
that point, only one company had manufactured corn flakes, and
that company had gone bankrupt. Only Will Kellogg saw the
future of this breakfast table staple.

His first flakes were ground from whole corn and their taste
was indistinguishable from the box. Kellogg switched to corn grits
and the boom was underway. He built his company on advertising
in a market glutted with look-alike products. He spent one-third of

his initial capital on an advertisement in *Ladies Home Journal.* It is not clear why the famous "W. K. Kellogg" signature began gracing company cereal boxes, but it probably was an attempt to ward off imitations. Orders outpaced production from the beginning.

In 1907, a fire destroyed his main factory building. Kellogg made plans for a new plant with a capacity of forty-two hundred cases a day. "That's all the business I ever want," he told his son John. By 1920 capacity had reached twenty-four thousand cases a day.

Kellogg advertised relentlessly. He made cases oversized so he could pack samples for grocers to distribute free. His ads hinted, "Wink at your grocer and see what you'll get." You got a free sample of corn flakes. He pioneered test-marketing his products with trial runs in Dayton. Later, during the Depression when sales drooped, he doubled the advertising budget.

The Toasted Corn Flake Company became the Kellogg Corn Flake Company in 1909, but his brother had renamed Sanitas the Kellogg Food Company in 1908. A decade of litigation began between the brothers in 1910, before Will won the use of the name in 1919. Afterwards the two men saw each other only briefly two or three times a year.

Will's son John was instrumental in the company from its early years, helping to invent All-Bran cereal and waxed paper inserts. In 1925 Will forced his son, who served briefly as president, out of the business, after John Kellogg bought an oat-milling plant and divorced his wife to marry an office girl. Will Kellogg objected both to his son's moral lapse and to his preference for oats.

The two men remained close, and there were hopes John Jr. would carry on the Kellogg dynasty. The young Kellogg resigned, however, after trying to sell his grandfather a process he developed on company time for puffing corn. Shortly afterward the twenty-six-year old Kellogg committed suicide.

After 1930, although he received weekly reports and a daily statement of the cash status of the company, Will devoted most of his energies to the Kellogg Foundation, endowed with a million shares of company stock. The Foundation was dedicated to the promotion of the "health, happiness, and welfare of mankind, principally of the children and youth." Mr. Kellogg gave over forty-seven million dollars of his fifty million dollar fortune to the foundation.

Kellogg lived to the age of ninety-one, spending time at several fabulous houses. Despite blindness caused from glaucoma, he indulged a passion for German shepherd dogs—one descended from Rin-Tin-Tin—and Arabian horses. He had lived long enough to see his name become synonymous with breakfast in America.

Kraft

For the consumer in the early 1900s, buying a wheel of cheese was as risky as a spin of the roulette wheel. Quality and flavor varied from cheese to cheese. Big wheels dried rapidly and shrank noticeably. Shelf life was measured in hours, not weeks. There were no brand names nor advertising to guide the buyer. All in all, the average American bought less than a pound of cheese a year.

One of eleven children born into a Mennonite family, J. L. Kraft developed a lifelong love of cheese while working behind the counter at Ferguson's store in Fort Erie, Ontario. In the summer of 1903 the twenty-nine-year old Kraft set out for Chicago with sixty-five dollars and an unshakable desire to start a cheese business. The sixty-five dollars paid for one month's lodging and breakfast rolls, rental of a horse named Paddy, a wagon for Paddy to pull, and a small stock of cheese to be sold to Chicago grocers. Paddy and his wagon would grow to be a Kraft company trademark.

A popular early Kraft item was a variety of club cheese, and his profits soon moved him into larger quarters. He asked his four brothers to join the business and the young company became J. L. Kraft & Brothers in 1907. Kraft expanded his business into the vibrant cheese markets of New York and began importing popular European cheeses.

All the while he toiled over his double boiler and old copper kettle, searching for the elusive process that would enable him to package the highly perishable commodity. After years of failure he finally perfected a method of blending and pasteurizing natural cheese that could be packaged in tins and stamped with the Kraft name. For the first time, the consumer could expect high quality and uniformity when buying cheese in convenient packages.

In 1921 Kraft introduced his famous five-pound loaf of pasteurized, blended cheese—cheese without rind or waste and carrying the name and guarantee of its maker. National per capita consumption of cheese soon increased by half. To meet demand, Kraft persuaded farmers in regions outside the traditional milk-producing regions of Wisconsin and New York to expand their herds for his cheese factories.

Kraft & Brothers became the Kraft Cheese Company in 1924, and expanded the line to include Velveeta, a cheese food with milk sugar and minerals incorporated to form a nourishing "family" cheese food. Kraft merged with the Phenix Cheese Company and began marketing Philadelphia Brand Cream Cheese, a spread first made in New York in 1882 but named Philadelphia because it was considered the home of quality foods at the time. Destined to become the largest selling package cheese in the world, Philadelphia Brand Cream Cheese was never manufactured there.

J. L. Kraft purchased several salad dressing companies as its diversification continued. Finally in 1930, Kraft and his company were acquired by the National Dairy Products Corporation. Kraft, now in his fifties, was absorbed with other pursuits. Prior to his death in 1953, *Popular Mechanics* called him "America's #1 rockhound." Among other achievements James Kraft was credited with discovering American jade.

Lance

P. L. Lance always tried to look out for his customers while operating his food brokerage business in Charlotte, North Carolina.
Although he dealt primarily in coffee, from time to time Lance was
asked to obtain peanuts for his customers.

On one such occasion he obtained an order for five hundred
pounds of peanuts, only to have the customer turn down the order
at time of delivery. Rather than back down on his bargain with the
farmer from whom he obtained the peanuts, he decided to roast
the goobers in his own kitchen and sell them in small bags on
downtown streets.

It was 1913 and, after much deliberation, Lance decided to roast
peanuts, make peanut butter and deliver it to Charlotte merchants
to promote the use of this nourishing food. With sixty dollars to
start, he installed a peanut roaster and peanut butter mill on the
second floor of a downtown building. He called his new venture
the Lance Packing Company, because the partners actually packed
the peanut butter into containers.

The product line expanded in unconventional ways. It was
Mrs. Lance who came up with the idea for the company's famous
peanut butter cracker sandwich, believed to be the first such combination sandwich ever offered for sale. A soldier at nearby Camp
Greene offered the Lances a recipe for peanut brittle and it
became a big seller.

Lance products were offered by mail, and soon Lance was the
largest parcel post business in North Carolina. P. L. Lance died in
an automobile accident in 1926 when the company was still mainly
a candy manufacturer and peanut processor. The big shift in product
line took place during World War II, when Lance decided its sugar
allotment would go farther in crackers than candies. Production
shifted to the five cent peanut butter sandwich, the staple of the
Lance line today.

Lay's

Herman Lay's business career started in 1919, when he was ten years old. He opened a soft drink stand in his front yard in Greenville, South Carolina. Location is everything, and the Lay home was opposite the town ballpark. Business was so good Herman opened a bank account, bought a bicycle, and hired assistants to tend the stand.

His business career was interrupted by schooling. Herman attended Furman University on an athletic scholarship, but dropped out after two years, anxious to resume selling. Lay worked at a succession of jobs before setting up as an independent snack food distributor in Nashville in 1932.

By the end of the decade, Lay was able to buy a financially ailing snack food manufacturer in Atlanta. He renamed the company H. W. Lay & Company and made Lay's Potato Chips the star of his line. Over the next two decades, Lay's potato chips became the most asked-for brand in the South. There were no national brands of potato chips at the time but Lay was about to change that.

He merged his company with the Frito Company of Dallas in 1961 to form Frito-Lay. As board chairman of the new company he advertised extensively, and Lay's Potato Chips were soon on grocery shelves across America next to regional brands. In 1965, he negotiated another merger with the Pepsi-Cola Company to form the massive conglomerate Pepsi-Co. In his role as chairman, Lay pushed the company into many new product lines.

Although sitting at the pinnacle of corporate America, Lay was an active advocate of entrepreneurship. He spoke frequently promoting entrepreneurship and endowed chairs at several colleges to encourage young people to go into business for themselves. When he retired from Pepsi-co in 1980, he heeded his own advice.

As soon as he departed the corporate world, Lay began starting new businesses. He set up several family corporations engaged in real estate and oil and gas exploration. When cancer caught up with him in 1982, Lay was still starting businesses; echoing his early

career he had just returned to the food business with the launching
of State Fair Foods, a manufacturer of frozen foods.

Lea & Perrins

In 1835 Sir Marcus Sandys returned to England from a stint as governor of Bengal in India. A renowned gourmand, Lord Sandys
carried with him a secret recipe for a flavorful sauce. He settled
back into his country estate in Worcester and sought the assistance
of two chemists in town to conjure up some of the exotic sauce for
his personal use.

He selected John Lea and William Perrins, who had been in
business since 1823, building a catalog of more than three hundred
items in their apothecary. Company lore maintains that the original brew from Lord Sandy's recipe was so foul it was dispatched to
a dark corner in the cellar and forgotten for two years. When it was
rediscovered, with great trepidation, the partners tasted the sauce
and were greatly surprised.

Lord Sandys began serving the sauce at his extravagant parties
and delighted guests soon carried word of his exotic sauce beyond
the shire. Lea and Perrins obtained permission to sell some sauce
to other customers, and by 1839 bottles of Worcestershire Sauce (it
was only "Worcester" in England) were finding their way to New
York City packaged amid boxes of Lea & Perrins surgical supplies.

Lea & Perrins supplied luxury liners with cases of sauce, helping spread Worcestershire Sauce around the world. The sauce was
amazingly versatile; it held its flavor in the hottest jungles and in
the coldest tundra. It would eventually be marketed in more than
a hundred countries—each batch made exactly as it was when it

was brought back from India in 1835. Lea and Perrins would go on to become the first Englishmen to open a chain of drugstores, but they are remembered today for the sauce "from the recipe of a nobleman in the county."

Libby's

Arthur Libby was born in 1831; his brother Charles seven years later. Like many others in mid-America in the middle nineteenth century, the Libbys gravitated towards the slaughterhouses of Chicago. In 1868 Arthur, Charles, and a third partner, Archibald McNeill, pooled three thousand dollars to start producing corned beef in barrels to ship to eastern markets.

Arthur got up at 3:00 each morning to scour the stockyards on the South Side of Chicago for the very best beef. But others were hustling the yards as well. The Libbys separated themselves from the competition in 1875 when they became the first firm to market meat in tin cans. By 1879, the Libbys were processing 200,000 cattle a year.

Charles Libby—the youngest—died first, in 1895. Arthur Libby died four years later at the age of sixty-eight. Their tinned meats insured their name would carry into the new century.

Lipton

Many of the fortunes made in the nineteenth century were by European immigrants who applied Old World skills in their adopted land of America. Thomas Lipton was different. He came to America, looked around for a while, and took what he learned in the New World back to Scotland to make one of the greatest fortunes of all.

Lipton began work at the age of ten in 1860 to help his family. He toiled as a stationer's apprentice, a hosier's helper, and a cabin boy before scraping together eighteen dollars for steerage to New York City in the spring of 1865. He arrived with a mere eight dollars in his pocket, but struck a deal at dockside to round up a dozen lodgers in exchange for free room for himself.

The post-Civil War South needed labor to rebuild, and Lipton headed there for the next forty months. He showed up in the South Carolina rice fields, on the New Orleans streets as a carman, in Charleston fighting fires and keeping books on a plantation. He finally returned to New York as a grocery clerk, where he became entranced by the American way of merchandising—attractive displays, salesman interested in customers, and especially flamboyant promotions.

At a time when ambitious young men were exploiting the unlimited potential of America, Lipton took the five hundred dollars he had saved and returned to Scotland. He opened his first shop in Glasgow on May 10, 1871. He bought directly from farmers and crofters, paid cash, never borrowed, and lived for his work. But so did many others. What set Lipton apart was his flair for advertising and showmanship—techniques he had learned in the United States.

Lipton hired one of Scotland's leading cartoonists to produce a fresh poster for his shop window each week. He employed an Irishman in knee breeches, cutaway coat, and a cocked hat to promote his Irish bacon by driving two scrubbed and polished pigs named "Lipton's Orphans" through the Glasgow streets to his shop—always by a different route.

He erected a pair of mirrors on the walk in front of the shop. One was concave, producing an elongated body with a haggard face. That was "Going to Lipton's." The other was convex, which caused a paunchy look and an inevitable smile. That was "Coming from Lipton's." He provided entertainment for children to free mothers to shop.

In six months he set up another shop—the forerunner of the food chains of today. By 1880 Lipton operated twenty shops, with the goal of a new one every week. Each opening was preceded by an elaborate street parade and a blitz of posters and newspaper ads. Lipton would be on hand, dressed in white apron and overalls, offering a prize to the first purchaser.

For Christmas 1881, Lipton determined to bring Glasgow the largest cheese ever made. For six days eight hundred cows and two hundred dairymaids gave all for the behemoth cheese—to the delight of townsfolk who were kept informed of every detail by Lipton. When the steamer carrying the cheese chugged into port crowds were waiting. They lined the streets to cheer the progress of the cheese on its trip to the store.

When it arrived Lipton ostentatiously inserted gold sovereigns into the cheese. It was on display all December in the shop window and when it was finally sliced up on Christmas Eve police had to be called in to control the crowds. Lipton sold every ounce of cheese in two hours.

Monster cheeses became a Lipton Christmas trademark. When police advised that the public might choke themselves by innocently swallowing coins Lipton gleefully advertised the "Police Warning" that anybody buying a portion of Lipton's giant cheese was in danger of being choked by one of the many gold sovereigns concealed in it. Lipton couldn't sell the cheese fast enough.

Thomas Lipton was forty years old before he sold an ounce of tea. In 1890 he sailed to Australia, ostensibly for rest, but he stopped in Ceylon to investigate some supplies of tea. The British had been drinking tea for two hundred years, but it was expensive, sold from ornate chests and carefully weighed out. Lipton reasoned that he could attract business by packaging tea in tiny packets and creating one brand, rather than a commodity. He sent some tea home with the slogan "Direct from the tea gardens to teapot." By the time he returned to Scotland, his three hundred shops couldn't handle the demand.

He bought a tea plantation in Ceylon to supply his stores directly. As his teas became known around the world, he bought more and more tea and coffee plantations. The man who once opened every one of his stores personally never saw all of his world-wide properties.

His first recognition from the British royal family came in 1898, when he was knighted for contributing $125,000 to supply the tea consumed by 300,000 poverty-stricken Londoners in the week of Queen Victoria's Jubilee. That same year, Lipton sent his various businesses public; his fortune was estimated at $50,000,000.

For the final thirty-three years of his life Sir Thomas Lipton pursued yachting's America's Cup, which at that time had never left America. He made five challenges in all, building all con-tenders himself at a personal expense in excess of $5,000,000. Sir Thomas was never successful, but gained an international reputa-tion for sportsmanship.

He so endeared himself to Americans that on the occasion of the defeat of *Shamrock V*, his final challenger, money was raised to present Lipton with a golden loving cup, the symbol of his election by Americans as "the gamest loser in the world of sport." Before he died the next year at the age of 81, Sir Thomas stated, "My great-est regret is that I have never lifted the America's Cup."

McCormick

"Make the best—some will buy it." That is the credo by which Willoughby M. McCormick ran his business of flavor extracts, exotic spices, and teas. McCormick was born in rural Virginia in the midst of the Civil War in 1864. After hostilities ceased, his family emigrated to Texas, where he found work as a clerk in a general store at the age of fourteen.

As a young man, he returned east to begin a career in food merchandising. He chose Baltimore, then one of America's largest distributing centers. His first plant in 1889 on Hanover Street was one room and a cellar. The small back yard was used to store the flavoring extracts, spices, and teas. McCormick never revealed where he happened upon the financing for the venture. "I saved a little and borrowed a little," he always said.

At the time, food distribution was controlled by wholesale grocery houses. Quality was not a consideration to these profiteers, who sought only the best margins in their dealings. McCormick was convinced that if a manufacturer supplied consistently high quality brand name products, he could create consumer demand.

McCormick produced such goods under private names and trademarks for wholesalers. His business prospered until the Great Baltimore Fire of 1904. The entire business district was consumed, including the McCormick building. As he rebuilt, McCormick began to realize that the goodwill generated by his products was reaped by his customers and not his company. He decided to market his own brands.

McCormick teas, introduced in 1905, became his leading seller. For his line of insecticides McCormick chose the Bee Brand because, " The study of bee culture has always been fascinating to me. One of the cleanest and most valuable of insects, the bee is discriminating. He selects the best for his production."

McCormick, who died in 1932, pioneered several marketing techniques. He always believed in sales conferences to train his field personnel. McCormick distributed a book of recipes using his exotic food products, and published books on teas and spices. He opened the plant to tours of how spices, extracts, and salad dressings were prepared. As one Baltimore paper paid tribute to the McCormick legacy: "Within the brick walls are all the odors of the Orient."

McIlhenny

Edmund McIlhenny's world was being torn apart., Approaching Union troops forced the self-made banker of Scotch-Irish descent to flee New Orleans in 1862 for the safety of his wife's ancestral home on Avery Island in the Louisiana bayou country.

The McIlhenny's refuge was short-lived. The family island yielded minable rock salt - the nation's first salt mine is there—and salt was needed to preserve meat for feeding troops. The Union invaded Avery Island in 1863. The Averys and McIlhennys fled to south Texas for the duration of the War.

When they returned, their house was plundered, their plantation in tatters. About the only thing that seemed to survive the Yankee occupation was a patch of hearty Capsicum peppers that thrived in a kitchen garden. No one knew exactly how the peppers got there, but Edmund McIlhenny knew what he wanted to do with them.

He chopped the peppers and blended them with vinegar and Avery Island salt. The fiery potion was left to age in wooden barrels. When ready, McIlhenny portioned off the resulting sauce into discarded cologne bottles. Local opinion was unanimous: the former banker's pepper sauce was extraordinary.

In what must be one of the most eclectic of all product christenings, McIlhenny called his sauce "Tabasco" after the name of a river in southern Mexico. He had heard the name and liked it. Tabasco sauce was an immediate hit. His initial shipment of 350 bottles in 1868 sold swiftly, and the next year he sold many thousands of bottles for one dollar apiece. Within three years McIlhenny opened an office in London to service European tastes for his spicy sauce.

For the next twenty years until his death in 1890, Edmund McIlhenny sold as much pepper sauce as he could make. Today, the company started by a former banker whose life was turned inside out sells fifty million tiny bottles of Tabasco sauce in America alone.

Oscar Mayer

Sausage was a popular table food in America in the late 1800s, served up by thousands of German wurstmachers cooking up old family recipes in corner butcher shops. But Oscar F. Mayer, who was to become the most famous of the sausage-makers, descended from a family of ministers and foresters.

Mayer came to America in 1873, at the age of fourteen. He joined family members in Detroit, where he immediately went to work in a meat shop. The family moved on to Chicago, and Mayer found work in Kohlhammer's Meat Market. In 1883, the twenty-four-year old Mayer opened his own small butcher shop on Chicago's North Side.

Pork was selling for eight to twelve cents a pound, and first-day sales were fifty-nine dollars. From the beginning Mayer placed an emphasis on quality above all else, and soon his salesmen could be seen carrying large orders in wicker baskets out of the neighborhood. The business grew rapidly to meet the lively demand for quality Oscar Mayer meats. The business was so successful that the former owner of the shop refused to renew Mayer's lease after five years, saying he wanted to make some money himself.

Mayer bought property and moved the business into a new two-story building. At the turn of the century, Oscar Mayer & Company ledgers listed forty-three employees, included among them "five wagon salesmen, one pig-head and feet cleaner and cooker, and two stablemen to take care of the delivery horses."

In 1929, Oscar Mayer became the first to break the traditional anonymity of meat producers by branding its weiners with a yellow paper ring. It guaranteed that Oscar Mayer wieners could be distinguished from others in the grocer's case. This brand identification paved the way for consumer advertising—an unheard of concept for meat products. The "Oscar Mayer Wiener Song" eventually became so famous it was performed by the Vienna Symphony Orchestra.

Mayer remained active until his death at age ninety-five. His obsession for quality had steered his company away from the herd of local butchers in the nineteenth century to the forefront of national processing in the twentieth.

Perdue

Arthur Perdue was a Railway Express agent in the years after World War I who loved living on Maryland's Eastern Shore. Rather than accept a transfer away from Salisbury to another station, Perdue quit his job. He built a small chicken coop and began raising fifty Leghorn chickens. Soon Perdue's eggs were showing up in produce markets in New York City and other eastern towns.

During the Depression, Perdue's always slim profit margins tightened even further. He mixed his own feed and salvaged leather from his shoes to make hinges for the coops. Perdue stayed out of debt through the hard times and even made a little money. He took great pride in his eggs, never missing a chance to boast about their quality.

The Depression forged the Perdue business values, which would foster further growth. He scrutinized costs and never borrowed money or took on partners, fearing an inability to pay and a loss of independence. By 1940 his flock had grown to two thousand Leghorns—until the chickens were decimated by leukosis, a fast-spreading avian disease.

Perdue couldn't take the chance of another devastation in his barnyard. He switched from eggs to chickens, and bought eight hundred hardy New Hampshire Reds. With his broilers, he needed new distribution outlets, but World War II generated great demands for all farm products and soon Perdue was realizing his greatest profits to date.

Perdue hatched chicks by the thousands, and raised them on a special blend of feed superior to any on the market. He trucked his broilers to market in Selbyville, Delaware, where they were snapped up by large meat packers like Armour and Swift.

In 1953 Perdue was selling eight million dollars worth of chickens each year and raising 2.6 million broilers when he turned the daily operations of the farm over to his thirty-three-year old son Frank. The poultry business was changing completely in the 1950s. Chicken raising evolved from a labor intensive business into an automated one, with a chick going from egg to store in eight weeks virtually untouched by human hands. Frank Perdue convinced his father to keep up with the radical changes and build a huge chicken processing complex in Salisbury.

The new plant opened in 1958. Company growth continued modestly until 1967, when Frank convinced his father to do the unthinkable—borrow $500,000 to expand into the New York retail chicken market. In a short time Perdue Farms was selling 800,000 broilers a week and advertising the new Perdue Farms chickens in a small way. Then Frank Perdue decided to expand again.

Account executives from his advertising agency came to visit the Perdue operation in Salisbury for ideas. They focused on the unique yellow color of Perdue chickens, which was achieved with marigold petals in the feed, as a way to distinguish Perdue chickens as meat of the highest quality.

One other thing caught their eye. As one adman would recall, "Frank was very, very involved in everything to do with his company. So we realized that what really set Perdue chickens apart from other chickens was Frank Perdue. He looked a little like a chicken himself and sounded a little like one. He squawked a lot."

They decided to use Frank Perdue as his own spokesman, one of the first executives to do his own commercials. Revenues jumped from $58,000,000 to $500,000,000 over the next decade. Other established packers leaped into the brand chicken market, launching the "Great American Chicken War" in the mid-1980s, but Perdue continued to take command, exceeding one billion dollars in annual sales.

illsbury

John Sargent Pillsbury was the first of the New England Pillsburys to leave the East. He settled in St. Anthony Falls, Minnesota in 1853 and became a hardware merchant. Shortly after he arrived, fire destroyed his entire inventory—$40,000 worth.

Slowly John Pillsbury paid off his creditors. He and his wife had no new clothes for six years. When he finished settling his debts, Pillsbury was so well-respected that the new Farmers & Mechanics Bank loaned him a thousand dollars when they had only eight thousand dollars in deposits.

Within a few years, Pillsbury became prosperous and was offered the presidency of the bank. He diversified his business interests to include land, railroads, and timber. Sawmilling was the number one industry in Minnesota in 1865, but Pillsbury believed the new reaper invented by Cyrus McCormick would make flour milling the new big business.

Pillsbury persuaded his nephew Charles Alfred Pillsbury to bring his new bride to join him in milling flour. Their first venture was a broken-down 250-barrel Minneapolis flour mill. The Minneapolis business community regarded it as a very foolish investment. In the heart of "America's Bread Basket," Minnesota was actually importing flour. Minnesota wheat was hard, brittle, and produced inferior flour. It cost more to make and sold for less than other flours from the region.

The Dartmouth-educated Charles Pillsbury, however, saw potential in the unpopular grain. He believed he could make *superior* flour from the gluten-rich kernels. He installed a new purifier that blew the bran out of the wheat kernel and made a six thousand dollar profit in his first year.

Charles took the profits and started a new firm, C. A. Pillsbury & Co., in 1872. By now John Pillsbury had become more involved in community affairs. He was an early benefactor of the University of Minnesota, establishing the faculty and even recruiting the first student, an unwilling Easterner. John Pillsbury eventually became a popular governor of Minnesota.

Charles Pillsbury was always quick to adopt new milling technologies that were bursting on the scene, and the fine, strong flour he produced—which made more and better bread per barrel than soft winter wheat—soon commanded a premium as the best flour on the world market. In 1880, he set out to build the world's largest flour mill.

Minnesota was in the throes of four years of crop failures, including the Grasshopper Plague of 1877. Grasshoppers flew so thickly that Governor Pillsbury called for a day of prayer to end it. A sudden temperature drop the next night froze every grasshopper in the state stiff. Despite the grain shortages, Pillsbury began turning out ten thousand barrels of flour a day.

In 1889, Pillsbury's vast milling interests were sold to an English syndicate which also operated The Washburn Mills, England's leading flour producer. Despite the considerable clout of the Pillsbury-Washburn Flour Mills, Pillsbury, who headed the organization, opposed the establishment of a monopolistic trust and the attempt ended.

Through the last decade of the nineteenth century, Charles Pillsbury's influence over the company waned. He was still spending two hours a day in the office, however, when he died suddenly of heart disease in 1899.

Post

At the age of ten Charles William Post watched solemnly as his father walked through the streets of Springfield, Illinois as a member of the honor guard laying Abraham Lincoln to rest. The patriotic fires burned inside young Post, and he left the Illinois Industrial College at Urbana, the forerunner of the University of Illinois, at

the age of fifteen to join the Springfield Governor Guards. He
served in Chicago in 1871, after the Great Fire left the city under
martial law.

This exciting event led Post to abandon the course set for him
by his businessman father and his mother, a writer of verse. He left
to explore the West with a friend. They borrowed a thousand
dollars from Post's mother and opened a hardware store in
Independence, Kansas. After a year, the young partners had doubled their money. Post sold his half-interest and returned home to
pay back his mother and marry a neighborhood girl.

Post left his bride with his family and went to work as a traveling salesman with the Climax Corn Planter Company to study the
frontier and earn money. Commercial travel in the mid-1800s was
fraught with hardships: bad water, worse food, and uncertain
accommodations. Post suffered from digestive disturbances, the
first of many years spent in broken health.

In 1880 Post came home to manufacture his own improved
seed planter and in 1881, at the age of twenty-seven, he formed the
Illinois Agricultural Works. He patented cultivators, a haystacker,
and a harrow. Post prospered to such an extent that the banker
who made his loans tried to take over his business. In 1885 Post
collapsed from nervous exhaustion brought on by his work and
bank problems.

In 1887, Post moved to Fort Worth to recuperate more fully.
While in Texas, Post became involved in papermaking and in a
woolen mill. Always a fastidious dresser, Post began marketing a
"Scientific Suspender" he developed. But the strain of his new
business ventures and lingering difficulties from his past entangle-
ments led to a more serious nervous collapse in 1890.

Early in 1891 the family moved to Battle Creek, Michigan to
entrust Post's care to Dr. Kellogg's nationally famous health sanitarium. Post was a patient for nine months, confined to a wheelchair. Nothing seemed to work. Dr. Kellogg called Mrs. Post to say
her husband had little time left, that he was not getting well.

She wheeled the frail Post across town to Elizabeth Gregory, a
practitioner of Christian Science. Post listened to Gregory's theories and decided to stay under her care, even though she had no
facilities. She remodeled her home to accommodate Post. She
admonished him over his fear of impure food and convinced him
that he had to *act* well to *get* well. And Post recovered.

He liquidated all his holdings to establish *La Vita Inn* in Battle

Creek to teach patients about dietary and mental influence in health care. Word spread around town of a patient rejected by Dr. Kellogg who got well on his own. Post devoured medical books on spiritual healing and medicine. He conducted experiments with food and dietetics. He wrote a book on "mind over matter," *I Am Well*, which sold well. In the meantime he revived his suspender business, which also did well.

Post developed a cereal drink as a coffee substitute in 1895. He called the food drink "Postum," and it reached the market when the American health and fad foods craze was at its zenith. Post was the first to introduce foods to the public through advertising. A two hundred dollar ad produced five thousand dollars in sales. Post eventually became the largest advertiser in the world.

He wrote most of the advertising copy himself, using "plain words for plain people." He developed Grape-Nuts in 1898 as a "scientific food" that made red blood. In 1908, Post introduced Post Toasties, and in 1911 came Instant Postum. Along with Postum these were Post's only foods—and they generated one of the country's greatest fortunes.

Aside from his food business, Post created the Post Check Currency to end the problem of mailing money through the mail. In 1907 he developed his own community in Texas, but Post City, the most ambitious of projects, couldn't sustain its original momentum and Post sold most of his holdings. Charles William Post died in 1914, leaving the business in the capable hands of his daughter.

Reynolds

Richard Reynolds began working for his uncle R. J. Reynolds as a law student in the summer of 1902. His uncle told him flat out he was too good a businessman to stay in law. "We can hire all the lawyers we want," he said. Now it had been ten years, he was in his mid-thirties, and it was time to leave R. J. Reynolds Tobacco and do something on his own. R. J. offered him $100,000 to stay, but Richard had made up his mind.

Reynolds went out to Bristol, Tennessee and bought himself a mountain of pure silica crystal. He was going to grind it up into soap powder. Reynolds put his "Spotless Cleanser" in a can with a sifter top, and his cleaning products quickly became popular around the mid-south. As Reynolds prepared to expand to national production his plant burned down.

Just as he got going again, World War I broke out. When the government declared "Spotless Cleanser" a nonessential product Reynolds was out of business with no money. He reasoned that there must be products deemed "essential" by the War Department that nobody was producing. He went to Washington but the only product no one seemed to be making was waterproof barrels constructed of paper and not crucial steel.

Reynolds had no idea what this business was about, but while walking around Washington, by chance he saw some workmen applying paper material to a roof. If that paper kept roofs from leaking it must, he reasoned, be waterproof . He bought a roll of the asphalt felt and fashioned a barrel with steel on the top and bottom. Reynolds quickly entered into frenzied production of waterproof barrels for the war effort.

After the excitement of wartime production Reynolds had no desire to make cleanser again. He had a natural interest in metal foil for cigarette packaging and, with financial assistance from R. J. Reynolds he formed the U.S. Foil Company. He changed the way a factory produced tin foil and saved six and a half cents a pound, which enabled him to survive a price war by more established firms. Soon the Reynolds Metal Company was the country's biggest producer of tin foil.

From the time Richard Reynolds saw his first piece of aluminum foil, he knew the tinfoil business was doomed. He found himself the creator of a business that would soon be obsolete. He would not wait around. Reynolds immediately set up an aluminum fabricating plant in Louisville, Kentucky.

In 1937, while in Europe seeking sources of aluminum,

Reynolds discovered that Adolph Hitler was producing eight hundred million pounds of aluminum a year—twice the combined production of the United States, England, and France. Clearly he was planning to fight with light metal in the air. Reynolds appealed to the United States government to expand their production of aluminum, but he was ignored.

Reynolds expanded on his own without orders. His production capacity expanded seven times, and he bought all the bauxite he could find. As a result of expansion, Reynolds had to make Americans aluminum-conscious and he did this by heavily promoting Reynolds Wrap. Soon aluminum was used everywhere—including by the United States government—because of the foil's strength, lightness and corrosion resistance.

Consumption exploded, growing 1500 percent in the last fifteen years of Reynolds's life. Time and again before his death in 1955 he had turned crisis into opportunity since leaving the safe harbor of R. J. Reynolds Tobacco.

mucker's

Johnny "Appleseed" Chapman planted the apples, but it was left to Jerome Smucker to sell them. Chapman devoted his life to sowing the fertile Midwestern soil with domestic apple trees. In 1897 Smucker set out to process some of the bounty from the apple orchards around his Orrville, Ohio home.

Smucker started out in a wooden cider mill, with a steam-operated press to convert his neighbors' apples into cider. He charged a penny a gallon. It wasn't long before he discovered that cider in wooden tanks could be concentrated quickly by heating it with steam piped through copper coils. The concentrate formed the basis for apple butter.

Smucker used an old family recipe for his butter. He was proud enough of his product to hand-sign the paper lid on every stoneware crock of apple butter he made. He peddled the crocks to neighboring housewives from the tailboard of a drummer's wagon.

Smucker's Apple Butter was indeed well received, and local sales climbed steadily over the next two decades. Sales in 1915 topped $59,000. With the adoption of automatic machinery and glass jars, Smuckers was able to expand distribution past Orrville.

In 1923 the "Apple Butter King" branched out into the jam and jelly business, and soon the Smucker line included a full complement of preserves and jellies. In 1935, the company began fruit processing operations in Washington state, their first plant outside Orrville. National distribution of Smucker's products began in 1942, when the first shipment of preserves and jellies was sent from Orrville to Los Angeles.

When Jerome Smucker died in 1948 at the age of eighty-nine, he was the largest single apple-butter producer in the world; his fruit products were available in every state. Each year Smucker's was processing nearly a million bushels of apples—enough to cover half a billion slices of bread.

Stouffer's

As they reached their middle years, Abraham and Mahala Stouffer decided to leave their creamery business in Medina, Ohio and move north to the big city—Cleveland. It was the beginning of a long and fortuitous bonding between city and family.

The Stouffers opened a small stand-up dairy counter in 1922, in an arcade in the downtown area. The counter featured wholesome buttermilk, fresh-brewed coffee, and three types of sandwiches. The star of the menu was Mahala Stouffer's deep-dish Dutch apple pies. The little stand was an immediate hit.

Two years later, the Stouffers' son Vernon, a graduate of the Wharton School of Finance at the University of Pennsylvania, returned to Cleveland and helped the Stouffers open their first full-service restaurant. The Stouffer Lunch, housed in the Citizen's Building, used the same formula of clean, fresh-tasting ingredients that made the dairy stand a success.

The restaurant's popularity spawned new eateries in Detroit and Pittsburgh. Growth continued even during the Depression; by 1937 the family had opened their first restaurant in New York City. Big city dwellers could always count on a respite from the impersonal urban life at the restaurants where they came to recognize the family motto: "Everybody is somebody at Stouffer's."

After World War II, the Stouffer formula of locating in major cities changed rapidly with the times. Stouffer restaurants and inns followed families relocating in the suburbs. Again the Stouffers used Cleveland as their base, opening their first suburban restaurant in the Shaker Square area of Cleveland.

It was here that manager Wally Blankinship began filling customer requests by freezing popular menu items, like Macaroni & Cheese and Spinach Souffle, for them to take home. At the time, the typical frozen dinner consisted of peas, potatoes and a few small pieces of meat. Blankinship realized the potential of a higher quality frozen food, and sold items at a retail outlet called the 227 Club located adjacent to the restaurant. Suddenly, the Stouffer family was in the frozen food business.

In 1954, Stouffer Foods Corporation began—again in downtown Cleveland—to turn out distinctive frozen dishes. The food was always at the core of Stouffer businesses. Near the end of his career Vernon, who became president of the family firm, conceded that he was often more comfortable in the kitchen than the office. His Cleveland suburban home featured two kitchens, marked "His" and "Hers."

NASA selected Stouffer's products to feed quarantined Apollo 11, 12, and 14 astronauts following their landmark trips to the moon. Stouffer's advertising proudly claimed, "Everybody who's been to the moon is eating Stouffer's." It was a long way from Medina, Ohio.

Swanson

Until World War II, turkey was a treat reserved for holiday meals. The man who brought turkeys to American tables was a large, rough-hewn Swedish immigrant who arrived in the United States with a tag around his neck: "Carl Swanson, Swedish. Send me to Omaha. I speak no English." The year was 1896. He was seventeen years old.

Swanson joined his sisters in Omaha, working on a farm as he learned a second language. He studied at the local YMCA, where he paid thirty-five dollars for a lifetime membership. In 1899 he invested $125 as part owner of a consignment store. Swanson started with one horse, one wagon, and a little cash.

He soon moved into commodities trading. Swanson quickly became noted for his iron nerves in the risk-pervasive business, becoming one of the leading "butter and egg" men in the Midwest. In his spare time, Swanson also enjoyed non-business wagers on roulette, horses, and cards.

Dealing in fresh food opened the company to the vagaries of nature and producers. In the early poultry business, the birds were transported live to the retailer. Many chicks died or were appropriated during the trip. Others were pecked to death by aggressive cellmates, and still others succumbed to "roup," a fatal disease.

By the 1930s, shippers began using the "New York Style" dressing of birds—killed, bled, plucked, eviscerated, and refrigerated. But by 1943, only ten percent of all chickens shipped were eviscerated.

Dressing a bird was still considered the province of the man in the retail store. Many food processors were slow to adopt expensive plant changes to allow evisceration and delivery to supermarkets.

Carl Swanson was not one of them. He converted his business to quick freezing in 1934, and in 1936 moved into turkeys. Turkeys are difficult to raise, and in the 1930s most growers felt fortunate to keep their turkey casualty rate at fifteen percent. 1936 was a particularly bad year for turkey growers, but Swanson guaranteed raisers a price of eighteen cents a pound to convince them to continue production.

Swanson invested heavily in poults (chicks), production, processing, and promotion. In 1937, he developed a bronze-colored, full-breasted bird with more meat. It looked better, sold better, and became known as the "Mae West Turkey." He changed American's eating habits. From 1934 to 1942, Swanson's production increased by a factor of two hundred. In 1943 *Fortune Magazine* tagged Swanson "the turkey king of the country."

Swanson applied his technology to eggs, and developed powdered eggs. Demand soared in World War II, much to the distaste of enlisted men. One soldier wrote to Swanson, "I wish you would take some of your dried eggs, compare them to dirty water from the Missouri River, and tell me which is which." Demand continued strongly until the 1950s, however.

Swanson changed the company name to C. A. Swanson & Sons in 1944. To heighten the visibility and corporate image of the company, he plunged into a new butter substitute, oleo, despite being in the heart of butter country. Sales were tepid at first, until color was added to make the oleo look like butter. The product flew off grocers' shelves.

Carl Swanson remained president until he died in 1949. He had witnessed a revolution in the kitchen as women worked during World War II. There was a growing need for convenient prepared dinners for these working women. Swanson was soon to be a leader in the new frozen dinner market, introducing its "TV Dinner" for America's freezers in 1952.

wift

In 1855, when Gustavus Swift was fourteen, his father gave him twenty-five dollars to go into the meat business. He purchased a heifer for nineteen dollars, and when the young cow was ready, the man who would eventually sell more beef than anyone killed her himself in a shed. Swift turned a ten dollar profit on his twenty-five dollars.

Swift went to work for his brother, a Cape Cod butcher, that year and drove around New England buying and selling cattle. In 1869, he opened Swift's Market in Clinton, Massachusetts, incorporating all the ideas he had discovered in his sales trips. Above all else, Swift valued cleanliness in what was a traditionally messy business. He deplored waste, and always searched for new markets that could use his byproducts.

In a day when a good meat meal could be had for fifteen cents, Swift did $40,000 of business in a small New England town. But Swift was always restless to expand. In 1875 he traveled to Buffalo to buy cattle closer to their source and eliminate middlemen. He saved money, but realized how much more could be saved if he didn't have to ship live animals, feeding and caring for them, back East.

He knew he had to deal in dressed beef from the Midwest. He borrowed every penny he could to expand; Swift was never one to turn down a loan offer. Daily he staked his business on faulty refrigerator cars, which often failed to keep his perishable goods cold. No one took his efforts seriously; others had tried and failed. Technical problems with the cars hounded him, sending him perilously close to ruin.

Railroads didn't want dressed beef, and refused to build reefer cars. Swift convinced the Michigan Car Company to build him cars which blended the best features of their previous failed efforts. Swift built ice stations on the route in the event of failures, and finally Swift had a hundred train cars a year coming east with Chicago dressed beef.

The battle was hardly over. Some Eastern towns boycotted the refrigerated beef they couldn't accept as fresh. When this happened, Swift refused to allow his agents to move elsewhere. They sold beef directly out of the train cars until local agents accepted the shipments. Swift simply pounded on prejudice against Western beef until he won over his customers.

Swift borrowed all the money anyone would lend him. Sprawling plants went up in Kansas City in 1888, Omaha in 1890, East St. Louis in 1892. Across the Midwest, Swift established slaughterhouses and shipped refrigerated beef to now eager Eastern markets.

The great speed and growth of his business caught Swift unaware. When the Panic of 1893 hit, over ten million dollars of Swift's notes were called in. Swift employees lent him money to help pay the debts, and nearly all the company assets were converted to cash. Throughout the crisis Swift remained tranquil and composed in both his business and personal life as rumors of collapse swirled around his company.

The huge meat-packing firm survived. It was Swift's last major battle. Western beef was now accepted everywhere, and the only things he spent his time on—his company and his family—were stable and prospering. The years until his death in 1903 were unsettlingly peaceful.

Thomas'

The story of Samuel Bath Thomas was the story of tens of thousands of American immigrants in the nineteenth century. Born in Plymouth, England in 1855, Thomas came to New York at the age of twenty-one. He worked a succession of menial jobs until he had saved enough to set up a business of his own. In 1880 Thomas opened a bakery.

He didn't even have enough money to hang a sign over his door. For the most part he relied on the aroma of his breads and muffins to bring customers into the shop on Ninth Avenue. Thomas baked the English specialties he knew so well. And they caught the fancy of New Yorkers, so much so that Thomas began supplying restaurants with his creations.

Thomas was making a living, but so were millions of others whose names are unknown to us. But for one thing no one would remember Samuel Thomas either. He delivered his baked goods, especially his popular English muffins, to New York restaurants in glass-domed cases with "S. B. Thomas" stenciled on them. People began asking for Thomas's English muffins in their corner stores as well.

With Thomas's retail trade established, it was not long before Samuel Thomas was selling throughout New York. He died in 1919, having created a taste for the English muffin. Thousands of bakers plied their trade in tiny shops throughout the 1800s; Samuel Thomas is one of the few whose name survived.

Tyson

During the Depression, John Tyson sold his first chickens to pull his family through the tough times. In 1935, Tyson purchased fifty "springer" chickens and hauled them from his farm in Arkansas to Chicago to sell at profit. Two years later, he christened his business Tyson Feed & Hatchery.

The company prospered by buying and selling chickens, but

Tyson constantly needed to monitor the quality of the chickens he bartered. Gradually he became involved in raising his own chickens. In 1947, the company was incorporated.

In 1952, Tyson's son Don joined the company as head of operations. The younger Tyson pushed his conservative father into expanding production. Don convince his father to raise Rock Cornish game hens, a market Tyson would come to dominate.

Tyson took pains to achieve complete vertical integration, opening a processing plant in Springdale, Arkansas in 1958. By the 1960s chicken was becoming a regular visitor to America's dinner tables; consumption increased fourfold from 1950. A drop in feed-grain prices lured many amateur chicken producers into the industry, and the resulting glut caused big price cuts which drove several small companies out of business.

Tyson's step into increased automation saved the company. In 1963 Tyson took his company public and changed its name to Tyson's Foods, Incorporated. In 1966, John Tyson and his wife died in an automobile accident, and Don Tyson took over the business as president. The next year he began promoting the corporate name by labeling chicken wrappers with "Tyson Country Fresh Chicken" instead of the supermarket name. Tyson was on its way to being a giant in the poultry industry.

Underwood

In 1819, at the age of thirty-two, William Underwood walked from New Orleans to Boston. He had landed in Louisiana two years earlier, hoping to parlay his experience as a tinsmith in England into a career as a canner in America. After New Orleans did not work out, he set off for Boston. On foot. This sort of determination would serve him well in his attempts to establish the new industry of canning in America.

Food preservation began during the Napoleonic Wars, when French foodmakers discovered heated food could be sealed in jars and safely eaten later on the battlefield. Commercial applications quickly sprang up in France, England, and eventually, the United States.

Once in Boston, Underwood joined up with his brother James. Here they started preserving local delicacies such as cranberries and broiled lobsters in a shop on Russia Wharf. Underwood sold tomatoes, an exotic food in 1820s America, that he grew from English seeds in his yard. The early Underwood products were processed totally in glass bottles. By all accounts, the Underwood cannery was America's first successful canning operation.

William Underwood discovered a prejudice against American canned goods in his new country and was forced to ship most of his food to South American and Far East markets. He overcame this resistence by stamping "England" on his containers, and gradually he built his American market. Canning was expensive and time-consuming, but as developments in machine cutting and soldering advanced, cans became the main vehicle for Underwood's processed foods. Underwood canned meats went to sea, rolled west with the wagon trains, and eventually traveled to battle in the Civil War.

The canning business was run by Underwoods for almost a hundred years after William Underwood's death during the Civil War. In 1868, three years after the founder's death, Henry Oliver Underwood introduced the "red devil" trademark for the company's line of deviled meat spreads. The devil, a heavily-muscled, horned demon, was assigned trademark number eighty-two (the list went past one million in 1974). It is the oldest food trademark in the United States.

Welch's

As a minister with deep theological beliefs and an ardent prohibitionist, it always seemed to Dr. Thomas Welch that the use of wine as a sacrament was a heretical contradiction. One Sunday in 1869, a visiting minister to the Welch family home in Vineland, New Jersey was "led astray" by the communion wine. Welch vowed to develop a nonalcoholic fruit juice that could be used as a communion wine.

Welch began cooking grapes and straining them through cloth bags. He quickly immersed the remaining liquid into boiling water. It worked. Dr. Welch's Unfermented Wine would surely end the great contradiction of the ecumenical world. Proudly Welch began taking his nonalcoholic wine to local pastors. But he found that churchmen demanded only wine. By 1873, after four years of increasing futility, he abandoned plans to sell his grape juice.

Welch had an earnest desire to solve an important problem for his church. And no one cared. A graduate of Syracuse Medical College, he returned full-time to the practice of dentistry. In his autobiography, Thomas Welch never even mentioned the achievement.

In 1872 his twenty-year old son Charles left home to begin a dental career in Washington D.C. but grape juice flowed through his veins. In 1875 he returned to Vineland to revitalize the idea of commercial grape juice. His disillusioned father favored dentistry over juice, so young Charles compromised and split his time with his dental practice in Washington and his fledgling grape juice business in Vineland.

In 1881, Thomas and Charles operated Welch's Dental Supply Company in Philadelphia, while Charles sold an occasional gallon of grape juice. After returning to Vineland in 1886, the balance of Charles' activities began to tilt toward his fruit juice over dentistry. A new brick factory was constructed.

It was not an age of advertising, and bold newspaper ads were a novelty. But Charles Welch had no choice; he had to educate the public about the uses for his new grape juice. FOR THE SACRAMENT AND FOR MEDICINAL USE Welch's headlines screamed.

Finally in 1893, twenty-four years after the first grape juice dripped through his father's cotton cloths, Charles Welch left dentistry and plunged into the grape juice business full time. He traveled to Chicago and gave away samples of "Welch's Grape Juice" from his booth at the Columbian Exposition.

His success at the Exposition convinced Welch to seek areas that attracted crowds. The Welch's stand became a staple of the Atlantic City boardwalk, America's premier seaside resort at the time. He exhibited at medical and drug conventions. The Welch Palace dispensing pavilion at the San Francisco Exposition in 1912 was a big hit.

Welch was tireless in his promotion of his new drink. Like many beverages of the day, Welch touted the medicinal benefits of his grape juice. "Juice makes rich red blood," claimed his ads. Welch always retained the family Prohibitionist zeal for the nonalcoholic wine and he found several converts.

William Jennings Bryan, four-time loser for the Presidency and long-time teetotaler, served as secretary of state under Woodrow Wilson. He disliked the tradition of serving alcohol to his guests, and used Welch's juice instead. It became known as Grape Juice Diplomacy. At the same time, Secretary of the Navy Josephus Daniels banned alcohol on ships, and cartoonists dubbed his charges the "Grape Juice Navy."

By this time, Welch had relocated his business to the winegrowing regions of New York. Black Rot disease decimated the Vineland grape vines in 1895, forcing the migration to Westfield, New York. His first year in Westfield, Welch pressed 288 tons of Concord grapes to bottle 50,000 gallons of juice. In 1909, production reached one million gallons a year. Welch tried new products in 1912, and found success with jams and jellies. Others, like tomato juice and ketchup, failed.

Welch, still an ardent Prohibitionist, campaigned for governor of New York on the Dry ticket in 1916. He died in 1926, in the midst of Prohibition, still in full control of the company he founded on his father's nonalcoholic beverage.

2

PART

At The Candy Counter

adbury's

Eating chocolate was unknown when John Cadbury, the first tradesman to introduce the plate glass window to the streets of Birmingham, England, opened a grocery in 1924. Window shoppers who gathered to gawk at 93 Bull Street could go inside and find a real Chinaman, ornately clad in Oriental garb, dispensing tea.

Chocolate was popular in an often-bitter drink and widely used in cooking, and Cadbury sold a bit on the side. In 1831, John and his brother Benjamin began making some of their own chocolate in a small warehouse near the store.

The first eating chocolate was still nearly twenty years away, and the Cadburys were among the first to mill "French eating chocolate" in England. Cadbury became the dominant confectioner in 1853 when the brothers received a Royal Warrant to provide an assortment of chocolates for Queen Victoria. The English monarchy counted on Cadbury for chocolate until the 1990s; in 1986 a Cadbury Milk Tray tin was created to celebrate the union of Prince Andrew and Sarah Ferguson.

In 1860, John Cadbury bought out his brother Benjamin, but he retired a year later. Under his sons Richard, then twenty-six, and George, twenty-two, Cadbury improved the quality of its eating chocolate from cocoa butter. After dominating the chocolate-crazed English market Cadbury, then under the direction of John Cadbury's great-grandson, entered the United States market in 1978, seven years after the creation of its famous Cadbury Creme Eggs

Clark

David Lytle Clark, the "Pittsburgh Candy King," came to western Pennsylvania from County Derry, Ireland at the age of eight in 1872. He earned his first money toting market baskets along the city streets for pennies.

At age nineteen, he opened a one-room candy business. While his one employee, a cook, concocted the candy, Clark drove from store to store in a wagon selling it. In 1886, Clark chewed his first gum. He asked a druggist how the new novelty was made and learned about chicle. Clark went to New York and returned with a bale of chicle.

Clark colored his new gum pink because he thought it was pretty. He flavored his new gum with mountain leaves because as a boy he liked to chew them. Clark's personal tastes appealed to the market. His gum sold so fast he had to open a new factory to meet the demand. The D. L. Clark Company was big business.

Over the next thirty years, Clark made candies, including a big-selling candy-coated popcorn. In 1917, as a treat for soldiers, Clark made his first five cent bar, a honeycombed ground roasted peanut bar covered with milk chocolate called the "Clark bar." The wrapper encouraged buyers to "Try eating a Clark bar every day between 2 & 4 P.M. Drink a glass of water and see how much pep you have when the day is done."

It must have been an energetic America at day's end because Clark was soon selling one million of his chocolate bars a day. In 1981 the largest candy bar in the world was created—a monster thirty-one hundred-pound Clark bar fifteen feet long and twenty inches thick. It was the equivalent of 19,000 Clark bars.

Clark did his best to ensure the continuance of his family candy business. He sired thirteen children with his first wife and when she died, he married her sister. But one thing could not survive. The Clark bar went out of production in 1994.

anny Farmer

Fannie Farmer hated to cook with "a pinch of salt." It wasn't the salt she found distasteful; it was the pinch she could never abide. She set out to eliminate guesswork in cooking by codifying measurements in teaspoons, tablespoons, and cups.

The "Mother of Level Measurement" was seventeen years old in 1874 when she suffered a debilitating paralytic stroke which ended her dreams of a college career. She turned to cooking during her convalescence, and eventually entered Boston Cooking School—where she taught and, in later years, became director.

In 1896 Farmer wrote *The Boston Cooking School Cookbook*. When she took it to venerable Boston publisher Little, Brown & Company they were not interested. The cookbooks of the nineteenth century could contain anything from recipes for face cream to potions to kill vermin. The manuals were written for servants, and Farmer was out to train housewives.

Undaunted, she persuaded Little, Brown to publish three thousand copies of her book, which she would pay for herself. They were the first of more than four million that were sold—and are still selling. Farmer went on to start her own cooking school, Miss Farmer's School of Cookery, with five assistants and five maids.

Blessed with unbridled energy, Fannie Farmer maintained an impossible schedule of lectures. Too impatient to cook an entire meal, she lectured while an assistant cooked. When she suffered another stroke, she continued to deliver her lessons from a wheelchair. Her final lecture was only ten days before her death in 1915, at the age of 58.

Frank O'Connor admired Fannie Farmer's career, and when he started his first candy shop in Rochester, New York in 1919 he wanted to name his emporium in honor of her. He was granted permission, provided he spell the first name "F-A-N-N-Y" and not as Miss Farmer had spelled it. The Fanny Farmer Candy Company never sold any candy using a recipe by Fannie Farmer.

Heath

Lawrence Heath was different from most of America's candy pioneers. He came to candy bars late in life, after a career as a schoolteacher and principal. In 1914, at the age of forty-five, Heath opened a small confectionery on the west side of the public square in Robinson, Illinois. With his sons, Heath sold fountain drinks, ice cream, and a distinctive English toffee he cooked in his kitchen in the back room of the shop.

In 1932, at the height of the Depression, Heath decided to package his toffee in individual candy bars. At the time, most five cent candy bars were four ounces, a full quarter pound. Heath's toffee molded in milk chocolate also sold for a nickel but was only a one-ounce bar. The Heath Bar was popularly known as the "H and H" bar. Heath had selected a logo with bookend capital "Hs" and a small "e-a-t." People assumed the "e-a-t" was an admonishment to try the "H and H bar."

However the candy was known, it soon became apparent Americans had a taste for the English toffee. The demand for the Heath Bar soon exceeded the capacity of the tiny shop. Lawrence Heath clearly spent more time making his candy than eating it; he lived to be eighty-seven and seldom weighed more than 105 pounds.

Hershey

The Hershey Chocolate Bar was once the most famous product in the world, maybe still is. Yet Hershey never advertised. "The best advertising," said Milton Hershey, "is the right kind of goods. People will learn about them and buy all you can make." And Milton Hershey had simply developed the most popular goods in the history of commerce.

Milton Snavely Hershey was born into a Mennonite family in central Pennsylvania in 1857. His mother estimated the family moved thirty-seven times over the years, and Milton attended seven different schools in eight years, never advancing past a fourth grade level. He got his first job as a printer's assistant, but lost it when he dropped his hat into a press. It was the beginning of a long series of setbacks.

Hershey next found work as a confectioner's apprentice in Lancaster, Pennsylvania and at age nineteen he established his own shop in Philadelphia to take advantage of the bustling 1876 Centennial Exhibition trade. Making candy by night and selling it by day, without capital and battling strong competition, his health broke down and the enterprise failed.

He followed his father to Denver to join in a silver boom. Hershey arrived after most of the silver had been mined out, but he did discover his fortune—while working in a candy shop he learned that fresh milk, if used properly, made the best candy he ever tasted.

Father and son tried selling fresh milk caramels in Chicago and failed. They tried selling caramels in New Orleans and failed. Why not try the biggest market of all? They decided to set up shop and sell caramels in New York City. They failed. Hershey's father remained in New York to try and peddle his paintings, while Milton returned to Lancaster.

Milton's trail of failures had labeled him as financially irresponsible within his family. He found himself a pariah among his relatives when he got home. But Hershey believed that opportunity knocks at least once on every man's door, and he was darn sure he wanted to be making candy when it did. He borrowed some money from one of his still-civil aunts—just enough for a bag of sugar and a room on the wrong side of town. He made candy by night and peddled it by day from a basket.

His business picked up and he bought a pushcart. Pushcart rivalries were ferocious in Lancaster in 1887, and Hershey was actually stoned out of rival territory. But opportunity was looking up his address.

An English importer tasted Hershey's fresh milk caramels and placed a substantial order. His meager equipment could not possibly fill the order. He persuaded a local banker to visit his humble operation. The tiny room sandwiched between a carriage factory and a carpet beating establishment did not impress his prospective loan officer. But Hershey did. The banker personally endorsed a note to finance equipment and hire candymakers. Hershey caramels became so popular that by 1900 the forty-three-year old candymaker was able to sell his business for $1,000,000.

With his money, Hershey and his wife began a trip around the world. They made it as far as Mexico City when Hershey leaped out of his chair on the hotel porch and announced: "I can't stand this; I've got to get back to work."

Hershey had been dabbling with chocolate since 1893 when the confection started to gain some favor and he thought it might flavor his caramels. He now planned to stake his future on chocolate, specifically the mass production of a new milk chocolate bar.

Hershey decided to erect a great chocolate factory, not near the centers of industry, as was common at the time, but out in the country. He chose Derry Church, Pennsylvania—near the site of his birth. It was not sentiment but calculated logic which brought Hershey home. The good dairy country provided the best environment for manufacturing milk chocolate. The streams were clear, and the Pennsylvania Dutch people supplied an intelligent, hardworking labor pool.

The chocolate factory opened in 1904 and the first five cent milk chocolate bar was ready in 1905, as well as an almond bar. The world fell for milk chocolate like nothing else ever. The business succeeded beyond Hershey's dreams, beyond anyone's dreams.

A model town of four thousand, named Hershey, sprung up around the factory. When the Depression hit many years later, Milton Hershey made certain no one in his town was unemployed and instituted a vast building program. When labor unions tried to organize Hershey workers in 1937 with a sit-down strike, they were routed by local farmers and citizens. The CIO union was rejected by a vote of 2–1.

Hershey used little of his wealth personally. He would never have a telephone in his home or office. He never even owned his home, having given it away to his employees for a country club. His wife died in 1915 and Hershey had no heirs. Thus he endowed the Milton Hershey Industrial School with a trust fund of $60,000,000 for "the orphan boys of America." The rest of his money went to the Milton S. Hershey Foundation.

Hershey continued as chairman of the board of the Hershey Chocolate Corporation until he was eighty-seven, one year before his death. Just prior to his resignation, Hershey received the Army-Navy "E" production award for creating ration "D," familiar to all service men as the "iron ration." The Hershey bar was now a world currency.

Mars

Frank Mars was a Pennsylvania native who worked his way across America as a candy salesman in Minnesota and Washington state in the early 1900s. It was a meager existence, and in 1910 his wife Ethel divorced him on grounds of nonsupport. She was awarded custody of six-year old Forrest Edward Mars. After that, Frank Mars rarely saw his family and only occasionally sent twenty dollars a month in support payments.

Frank Mars married another Ethel after his divorce. He failed in a Seattle candy business and creditors even took his personal belongings. He started again in Tacoma and again declared bankruptcy in 1914. During the World War I years, Mars endured one business disaster after another. Finally, he and his wife returned to Minnesota in 1920 with four hundred dollars in cash.

Settling in Minneapolis-St. Paul, the couple set up yet another candy business. They lived in a one-room apartment over the factory and worked long hours making candy and distributing it in local stores. At the same time Mars was experimenting with candy bars.

In 1923, approaching forty years of age, Mars developed a recipe for a malted milk bar with a chocolate coating. He called his new confection Milky Way, and his sales skyrocketed from $72,800 to $792,000. Mars seized upon his first success and built Milky Way into a nationally distributed candy sensation. By 1929 Mars Inc. had sales of $24,000,000 and profits of more than two million dollars. Mars moved his factory to Oak Park, Illinois to expand production.

By this time his son Forrest had graduated from Yale University and joined his father's candymaking business. Immediately the headstrong young Mars began criticizing the way his father ran the business and made no secret about his beliefs that he could do better. By 1932 Frank Mars had had it with his son. He gave Forrest $50,000, the recipe for Milky Way, and the foreign rights to Mars products and sent him on his way. Frank Mars could not be accused of nonsupport this time.

Although the Depression cut his sales by almost two thirds, Frank Mars continued to operate a successful business until his death in 1934. Control of the candy company passed to his second wife, but she preferred spending time handling the family racing stable on the 2,700-acre Milky Way Farms in Tennessee. At her death in 1945, Forrest Mars, who had settled in England and built a pet food and candy colossus on the Milky Way bar, returned to gain control of his father's firm.

Forrest Mars grew into one of the world's richest and most secretive men. He has granted only one interview in his life to date. He established company headquarters in McLean, Virginia, home of the clandestine CIA. As one competitor observed, "Mars may *be* the CIA for all I know."

Nestle

The man who gave his name to the largest food company in the world spent the first fifty-four years of his life plying his trade as a merchant, peddling mustard and seeds and artificial fertilizer. In 1857, at the age of forty-six, Henri Nestle set up a small company for the manufacture of liquid gas. For the next six years he supplied gas to the twelve street lamps of his hometown of Vevey, Switzerland.

Nestle, a luxuriously bearded man, was a born inventor. In 1867 he turned his attentions to the alarming infant mortality rate in Switzerland—one out of every five children was dying in the first year of life. Nestle set about to create a "good cow's milk," and he shortly had a prototype. "The basis of my milk food is good Swiss milk," he said, "concentrated by an air pump at low temperature which keeps it as fresh as milk straight from the cow. The meal is baked by a new process of my invention."

But who would risk their child's health on an untested food? By chance, a friend brought to Nestle's attention a young mother named Wanner who was seriously ill after giving birth one month prematurely. The convulsing child refused mother's milk and everything else. The doctor suggested that Nestle's milk food be tried. The little boy took the milk and nothing else for months and was never ill again.

Nestle was now convinced that he had the ideal food for infants who could not be breast fed. He was a tireless proselytyzer of the wonders of his new product. He first sold mainly through doctors, and received many medical endorsements for his baby food. By 1868 the milk food was on sale in Vevey and Frankfurt on Main, Germany, the town of his birth.

He soon pitched his baby food directly to mothers, and demand for Farine Lactee Nestle soared to over one thousand tins a day. Nestle's energy in promoting his milk food was endless; however his financial resources were not. During his early years he did everything from bookkeeping to production, never keeping up with orders.

He searched in vain for an ideal financial backer but by 1873, at the age of sixty-one, he had wearied of travails and was ready for retirement. A buyer for his baby food enterprise was not long in materializing, and Nestle sold the venture for one million Swiss francs. Conditions of the sale included the food processing plant, equipment, and rights to the Nestle name and trademark nest, Nestle being German for "little nest".

Henri Nestle made a complete severance from his company. He was never a shareholder of the new company nor involved in any operations. He led a quiet life until dying in 1890. He left no heirs.

Peter Paul

Peter Paul Halajian was a familiar figure to early commuters up and down the Naugatuck Valley in turn-of-the-century Connecticut. Every day he would walk up and down the train platforms hawking his homemade candy from a basket.

Halajian came to Naugatuck from Armenia in 1870, and began

work in a local rubber company. He was paid per piece, so when he reached his quota, usually in the early afternoon, he would rush off to join his two daughters in operating a fruit stand. By the early 1900s Halajian had two small shops, one in Naugatuck and another down the road in Torrington.

He advertised his wares on crude handbills distributed through the Valley:

> *"Peter Paul has very good food*
> *You don't throw any down the chute*
> *His delicious ice cream your dreams will haunt*
> *The more you eat it, the more you want*
> *Ice cream soda the year round*
> *No better soda was ever found*
> *His homemade candy will make you fat*
> *To Peter Paul, take off your hat."*

In 1919 Peter Paul and five Armenian friends put up a thousand dollars each to found their own candy business, Peter Paul Inc. The partners and their wives all dipped chocolate by hand in a fifty by sixty foot loft on Webster Street in New Haven. They worked at night because there was no refrigeration and the owners wanted to sell their candy when it was as fresh as possible the following day.

The first candy was a Konabar, a gooey concoction of nuts, fruit, coconut and chocolate. After about a year of experimentation Peter Paul introduced their trademark candy in 1922—the Mounds bar. A Mounds was a drift of snowy white coconut inside dark bittersweet chocolate. The Mounds bar was a number-one seller for many years, sustaining Peter Paul profits.

Arthritic and blind, Peter Paul Halajian died in 1927. Almond Joy was developed after World War II, giving Peter Paul Inc. the most powerful one-two sales punch in candydom, allowing the company itself to remain one of the very few nationally known candy-only firms in the United States.

Reese's

For the first thirty-eight years of his life, Harry Reese of York County, Pennsylvania survived through a succession of menial jobs before he landed a job managing one of Milton Hershey's dairy farms during World War I. Inspired by Hershey's great success, Reese struck out on his own. He moved to nearby Hummelstown, Pennsylvania and began boiling a mixture of caramellike molasses and coconut. His Johnny Bar failed, but his Lizzie Bar was successful enough for Reese to move back to Hershey and buy a plant on Chocolate Avenue. It was 1923; Reese was forty-four years old.

On the suggestion of a former customer in Harrisburg, Reese began tinkering with a special peanut butter wrapped in milk chocolate. Reese originally sold his peanut butter cups in five-pound boxes to be used by candy wholesalers in assortments. But by the 1930s he shifted to penny sizes for individual sale, and it wasn't long before the entire factory was devoted to manufacturing Reese's Peanut Butter Cups.

Harry Reese died in 1956 at the age of seventy-seven, leaving the company in the hands of his six sons. In 1963 his company was purchased by his old employer and neighbor, Hershey's. It was the first significant outside acquisition by the candy giant. Today the Reese's Peanut Butter Cup is the most popular candy bar in the United States and Canada. It is made the same way Harry Reese made it three-quarters of a century ago.

ussell Stover

All this thing really needs, thought Russell Stover, is a better name. Christian Nelson had been struggling with his inspiration for more than two years. While moonlighting from his job as a school-teacher in 1919, Nelson tended to a small grocery in Onawa, Iowa. It was there he hit upon the idea to somehow combine chocolate and ice cream.

Nelson had the darndest time trying to get the chocolate to stick to the ice cream. One day he ran into a candy salesman who told him that cocoa butter improved the clinging ability of chocolate. It worked. Nelson called his confection the "I-Scream" Bar. His first batch of five hundred sold out in no time at the annual Onawa Firemen's Tournament.

That was enough to convince Nelson. He quit his jobs, filed for a patent, and went out to spread the word of the new "I-Scream" bar. By 1921, after repeated failures, Nelson was reduced to racking balls in a pool hall for twenty dollars a week when he met with Russell Stover, a superintendent for an Omaha ice cream company.

Stover, then thirty-three years old, liked the product and readily agreed to form a partnership with Nelson. But the name had to go. Stover named the chocolate-covered ice cream an "Eskimo Pie." The early Eskimo Pie was a small one and a half ounce stickless bar, and it was an immediate sensation. At one point that summer 250,000 bars were put on the market, and they sold out in less than a day.

The partners set up a national distribution office in Chicago, and in less than a year over fifteen hundred licenses to make Eskimo Pies had been issued. By the spring of 1922 sales were averaging a million pies a day, and Nelson was reaping thirty thousand dollars a week in royalties.

But the success quickly melted. Royalties went unpaid and imitators freely infringed on the patent. The partners were spending four thousand dollars a day in legal fees just to defend the patent. Stover became so infuriated over the situation he sold his share of the business to Nelson for thirty thousand dollars.

At this point Stover switched directions. Coming to the chocolate and ice cream Eskimo Pie from an ice cream background, he left to pursue the chocolate business. Using his Eskimo Pie money he headed to Denver, where he opened his first candy store. For the second time Stover set up a national distribution, this time for boxed chocolates.

Stover left his business in Kansas City during World War II to serve as chairman of the Washington Commission of the National Confectioners Association. In the years after the war, he ceded his presidency and retired to Miami Beach, where the "Eskimo Pie King" died in 1954.

Wrigley

There are several ways to build a successful product. One can improve upon an existing product or invent a totally new product. However, William Wrigley, Jr. chose the toughest route of all. He took a bad habit and converted it into a worldwide obsession.

Wrigley legitimatized chewing gum by advertising. He became the largest advertiser of any single product. "Advertising," he once said, "is like running a train. You've got to keep on shoveling coal into the engine. Once you stop stoking the fire goes out and the train will gradually slow down and come to a dead stop." By the time of his death at age seventy in 1932, Wrigley had spent $100,000,000 in advertising. The growth of his company never slowed down.

Wrigley was the eldest of eight children born to a Philadelphia soapmaker in 1861. At the age of eleven he fled home for New

York to seek his fortune. He sold newspapers and slept on park benches, and quickly lost his zeal for independence. He returned home to his parents and schooling.

A school prank backfired on the curly-haired Wrigley, and he was expelled from school to work in his father's little soap factory. The labor was hard and Wrigley begged his father for a chance to peddle soap on the road. Selling soap across the countryside from his wagon, Wrigley was successful but found the work dreary. In 1880 he set out for a new mining boom in Leadville, Colorado.

He made it as far as Kansas City when his money ran out. Working as a waiter and counterman in a doughnut shop, Wrigley saved enough money to buy a supply of rubber stamps, which he sold at enough profit to return home to the soap factory.

Now he stayed eleven years before wanderlust seized him again. This time with a wife of five years Wrigley left for Chicago— the new metropolis of the West—in 1890. He had thirty-two dollars and one carload of soap when he established William Wrigley Jr. and Company.

Competition was keen, but Wrigley found some success with a shipment of umbrellas he gave away to retailers as a premium. He hired a salesman who had worked with baking powder. Wrigley added the baking powder to his line with good results.

No one knows how Wrigley became interested in chewing gum. He ordered his first batch in September, 1892 as an inducement to buy his baking powder. Jobbers found they could sell the free gum better than the baking powder so Wrigley decided to sell chewing gum. His first product was the long-forgotten "Wrigley's Vassar."

The gum was mixed like dough, rolled, cut into sticks, and packed by hand. Wrigley changed the product by making chicle, a juicy extract from tropical trees, his main ingredient. Growth was slow. He began advertising with trademark arrows and elves, and gradually his gum gained acceptance. On two occasions he collected the names of every telephone subscriber in Chicago and sent each a package of chewing gum.

In 1902, Wrigley came to New York with $100,000 to attempt a large-scale advertising campaign—which failed. Another attempt failed, until in 1907, despite a general economic recession, he broke through with a $250,000 national campaign. His name and products became firmly established in American culture.

Chewing gum factories were established in London, Berlin, Toronto, and Sydney, as well as Brooklyn. Wrigley gum packages eventually bore wording in thirty-seven languages, as output reached 40,000,000 sticks a day, always selling for five cents a pack.

During World War I, when Wrigley discovered some retailers were selling his gum for as much as a dime, he took out extensive ads proclaiming his gum cost five cents and anyone selling it for more was a wartime profiteer. In 1919 Wrigley's ads proclaimed, "5¢ before the war, 5¢ during the war, 5¢ after the war."

In the 1920s the chewing gum business was less of a challenge for Wrigley. He became sole owner of Catalina Island, twenty-five miles off the California coast, and developed it into a sporting resort. He undertook development projects in Arizona as well. In Chicago he built the white terra cotta Wrigley Building, opening up Chicago to business north of the famed Loop.

Wrigley dabbled in coal mining, transportation, hotels, ranching, and the motion picture industry, but his great passion was baseball. He purchased the Chicago Cubs in 1924 and spent over $6,000,000 making the team one of the model franchises in the National League. His team won the National League pennant in 1929, but never won a World Series Championship in his lifetime.

In 1925 Wrigley turned the presidency of the company over to his son Philip to spend more time with baseball. Wrigley's control over the gum empire did not wane until his death, however. As chairman of the board he was asked what would happen if his board disapproved of one of his decisions. Wrigley replied, "Then we'll get a new Board of Directors." His son recalled that stock-holder meetings rarely lasted beyond a reading of the last meeting's minutes and Wrigley's asking for a motion of adjournment.

Wrigley's death came in the depths of the Depression, which he combated by providing shelter in his Chicago buildings and feeding five hundred jobless men daily through the Salvation Army. The hard times had little effect on his business, however. "People chew harder when they are sad," noted Wrigley shortly before his death.

3
PART

From The Bottle

Anheuser-Busch

Georg Schneider, a German-born tavern owner, established the Bavarian Brewery in south St. Louis in 1852. The "Mound City" already had a rich beer tradition going back fifty years, and was clearly the leading malt city in the Midwest, ahead of Chicago and Milwaukee. The Bavarian Brewery was one of many neighborhood breweries.

From its inception, Schneider struggled with the enterprise. In 1857 he brewed five hundred barrels but was constantly on the lookout for a financial savior. In 1860 Eberhard Anheuser, a successful soap and candle manufacturer, bought the Bavarian Brewery with his friend William D'Oench.

Still the neighborhood brewery struggled. In 1864, D'Oench withdrew to return to his drug and chemical trade. Anheuser couldn't operate two diverse businesses like soap manufacturing and malt brewing by himself and sought help. He didn't have to look beyond his family.

In 1861, Lilly Anheuser had married a twenty-one-year-old German immigrant who was working as a "mud clerk" checking cargo along the Mississippi River. Shortly after their marriage, Adolphus Busch enlisted in the Union army as a corporal, but served only three months before he learned he had been bequeathed a portion of his wealthy father's estate.

Busch returned to St. Louis to open a brewers' supply store, the same business the family had conducted in Germany. In 1865 Busch merged his business with his father-in-law's Bavarian Brewery as equal partners. Within a year the brewery's output of

Anheuser beer doubled to eight thousand barrels.

The trade grew steadily, with the enthusiastic Busch often acting as his own sales force in the local saloons and beer gardens. Anheuser and Busch also employed "beer collectors," whose duty was to make monthly rounds to every restaurant and beer garden in St. Louis and buy Anheuser beer for the house.

Anheuser's participation in the enterprise declined through the 1870s as Adolphus Busch searched for the perfect brew. In 1876 Busch brewed a light Bohemian beer with rice as a supplemental grain. He called the new beer "Budweiser," after a Bohemian brewer named Budweis.

At the same time Busch became the first brewmeister to pasteurize his beer so it could withstand any climatic change. Busch was now able to bottle beer, and "St. Louis Lager Beer" began appearing in saloons in Denver and elsewhere. In 1878 he undertook a major plant expansion for the newly named Anheuser-Busch Brewing Association.

In 1880 Eberhard Anheuser died after a two-year illness, having lived long enough to see his tiny brewery on the banks of the Mississippi grow into a national concern. Adolphus Busch always invested in new technologies to find the most economical and expeditious way to manufacture malt. In 1881 he purchased three massive fifty-ton ice machines to turn his brewing operation into a year-round business.

He always bottled his own beer, and soon wasn't able to buy enough bottles fast enough. He studied manufacturers on both sides of the Atlantic before founding the Busch Glass Company. Transportation was always a problem, and Busch amassed a fleet of 850 railroad cars to move his beer.

By the 1890s, Busch was advertising extensively. His favorite medium was freshly painted beer wagons, advertising Busch considered more dignified than large billboards. He used playing cards, calendars, corkscrews, and knives as promotional materials for his fourteen beers. He distributed thousands of historical lithographs advertising his products. The Anheuser-Busch brewery grew to occupy forty acres. It required more than twenty-two hundred men to operate. Busch was brewing over three thousand barrels a day. It was the world's largest brewery.

Busch traveled extensively, and took an interest in other matters

besides brewery work. He served for a time as president of the
South Side Bank and the Manufacturers' Railroad Company. Most
of his business activities ceased after he contracted dropsy in 1906.

In 1911, Busch celebrated his fiftieth wedding anniversary in a
style the nation's papers trumpeted as "unprecedented in its elab-
orateness in the world's history." The value of the floral tributes
alone exceeded $50,000. Busch presented his wife with a crown
studded with gold, diamonds, and pearls valued at $200,000.

Busch died in 1913 in his native Prussia, on the eve of World
War I. His son Augustus took over and the company patented the
world's first diesel engine for the brewery, which was quickly adapted
for military use. Anheuser-Busch rode out of Prohibition with the
introduction of the world-famous Clydesdales in 1933, to resume
its position as the world's leading brewery.

Bacardi

Don Facundo Bacardi was a prosperous wine importer and merchant
in Cuba. He had emigrated from Spain at the age of fourteen, and
married a daughter of a French Bonapartist fighter in 1843. They
raised four children as Bacardi built his influence in Santiago de
Cuba. But rather than relax in comfort, Bacardi became intrigued
with improving the harsh rum favored by buccaneers and Spanish
adventurers in the area.

Rum is created by fermenting a drop of yeast in molasses, a
byproduct of sugarcane processing, and continually transferring
the culture to larger vats as it grows. As a major supplier of sugarcane, Cuba provided Bacardi with tons of cheap molasses with
which he could experiment. For many years he toiled in search of

a smoother, mellower rum.

Bacardi perfected his rum, augmenting his personal stock of liquor. But the distinctive taste of Bacardi's rum did not stay sequestered under his roof for long. Friends persuaded Don Facundo to undertake the laborious task of producing his rum commercially. He invested $3,500 in a dilapidated tin-roof distillery, better suited as a home to its colony of fruit bats than to distilling rum. On February 4, 1862 Bacardi began selling rum from his ancient stills and fermenting tanks.

Bacardi's rum went to market in bottles dressed in labels bearing a bat insignia, a suggestion of Don Facundo's wife. That bat trademark remains on Bacardi bottles today. Bacardi's rum was awarded a gold medal of recognition at the Philadelphia Centennial in 1876, and a few years later Don Facundo stepped down from the business. Assisted by his three sons and a son-in-law, Bacardi was able to keep his production process a family secret. Even today Bacardi, which is the world's most popular rum, is in the hands of the family.

Coors

Adolph Coors, born in 1847 to poor working parents, was charting his future as an apprentice brewer when the Prussian War tore apart his homeland. Rather than serve King William I, he stowed away on a ship bound for America in 1868. Caught in midjourney Coors was permitted to work off the cost of the journey in Baltimore. He labored as a bricklayer, stonecutter and fireman for a year before making his way west to Naperville, Illinois, hiring on as a brewery foreman for the Stenger Brewery.

He saved his money and worked his way to Denver on the railroad in April of 1872. While surveying the economic climate, he toiled through the summer as a gardener and then purchased a partnership in the bottling company of John Straderman. By the end of 1872 he was the sole owner, bottling beer, ale, porter, cider and seltzer water.

Still, he dreamed of brewing a quality beer. On Sundays, his only day off, he walked through the town of Golden, to which he was attracted by the rich Clear Creek Valley with abundant clear cool streams, formulating his brewing plans. He discovered an abandoned tannery on the banks of the river—the ideal site for his brewery, with many clear springs on the property. Coors knew that water is the most basic ingredient in beer.

One of his customers, Jacob Schueler, raised eighteen thousand dollars to invest in the "Golden Brewery" in 1873. In less than a year, the tannery turned brewery was returning a profit. By 1880 Coors was brewing enough premium beer to buy out Schueler.

Now Coors concentrated on solidifying his business. He traveled widely, studying the competition. Coors maintained an overwhelming concern for the high quality of his beer, constantly expanding the brewery and improving the product. By 1900 the Golden Brewery had survived a national Depression, devastating flood, and the growing threat of Prohibition.

Prohibition hit Colorado in 1914. Coors dumped seventeen thousand gallons of beer into Clear Creek. The brewing equipment turned out several food products, including a near-beer called Mannah. Malted milk became a sideline business which lasted until 1955. Coors shifted much of the factory to the production of cement and high-quality porcelain products.

Adolph Coors did not live to see the end of Prohibition. He died in 1929, but the business foundation he laid allowed the Adolph Coors Company to survive. Of the 1,568 breweries operating in 1910, Coors was one of only 750 to reopen in 1933.

allo

On a dusty day in Modesto, California in 1933, Joseph Gallo, Jr. became deranged and shot his wife. He turned and chased his sons through the fields of his small vineyard with a shotgun. The boys escaped and Joseph Gallo turned the gun on himself.

Ernest Gallo was twenty-three and Julio Gallo twenty-two at the time of the family tragedy. They decided to use their small inheritance of six thousand dollars to produce their own bulk commercial wine. They faced enormous odds. The country was paralyzed by the Depression, and seven hundred wineries were competing for the shrinking market.

And they didn't know how to make wine.

Julio went to the Modesto Public Library and checked out several materials on winemaking. He would make the wine. Ernest would manage the business, sell the wine, and keep the books. It was to be a dynamic pairing. Julio was an easygoing sort who loved good times and making wine. Ernest was a grim, tough businessman who would gain a reputation as the toughest client in advertising, at one point changing agencies seventeen times in thirty years.

Making the wine themselves, the Gallos were able to go to market at half the going rate of one dollar. Ernest traveled east, signing up enough distributors to sell the entire first year's production. The Gallos pocketed thirty-four thousand dollars profit in their first year.

All the profits went back into the business as banks snubbed the brothers. Until 1938, the Gallos sold bulk wine to bottlers, but that year they brought out their first wine under the Gallo label. This was far more profitable for Ernest and Julio.

Ernest Gallo was a pariah among Napa Valley vintners who carefully crafted high-quality, distinguished wines. Gallo considered them "wine snobs" and attacked the low end of the market with cheap sherries and muscatels. He built stainless steel vats which eliminated bacteria from the romantic old wooden vats, and his winery took on the appearance of an oil factory.

In the 1950s, Ernest noticed that ghetto blacks bought 40-proof port white wine and cut the sweet taste by mixing in lemon juice. He directed Julio to mix white port and citric acid to develop a wine he called "Thunderbird." Gallo directed a massive advertising campaign directly at ghetto blacks with a catchy jingle: "What's the word? Thunderbird. How's it sold? Good and cold. What's the jive? Bird's alive. What's the price? Thirty twice."

Thunderbird launched an entirely new wine business—mass marketing. Gallo sold 2.5 million cases in less than a year. But his success came at a price. Gallo was left with a tainted image as the paper-bag drink of choice for winos. He followed with "Ripple," and the Gallo image suffered more.

The Gallos continued to introduce new wines. They added carbonation to a sleepy old apple wine that barely registered on company books. Boone's Farm sales jumped from 30,000 cases a year to 720,000 cases a month. Gallo was soon controlling eighty-eight percent of this new "pop wine" market. As competitors jumped in, Gallo stopped all advertising at the height of the "pop wine craze." He made even more money on each case as the fad died away.

In the 1970s, the Gallo brothers were selling one out of every three bottles of wine purchased in America. Ernest moved into premium wines, for the first time. Experts praised the new wines but only heavy advertising could overcome the unsavory Gallo image. Case sales for premium wines tripled.

Ernest Gallo was totally unprepared for the explosion of wine coolers in the 1980s. This was his market—low-priced pop wines. But he missed it. The new California Coolers with wine and fruit juices tapped into many trendy markets: young, affluent, fitness, and female. California Cooler had a five-year head start but really no chance against the Gallos.

Gallo introduced Americans to Frank Bartles and Ed Jaymes. In real life they were an Oregon farmer and a Santa Rosa building contractor. In commercials the actors pitching the wine coolers became so popular that when they "asked for your support" viewers sent donations to the company. In a year, Gallo's Bartles & Jaymes were the market leaders.

Ernest and Julio Gallo guided America's most popular winery for nearly sixty years. The fortune that was built on family tragedy climbed over $700,000,000.

uinness

In 1722 a new, dark beer brewed with roasted barley began appearing in pubs around London. It was a heavy, sweet ale and was quickly popular among the laboring classes, particularly porters—hence its name. But when thirty-one-year old Arthur Guinness joined the ranks of Irishmen brewing beer in 1756, he wasn't particuarly interested in dark beers.

He leased a brewery in Liexlip, just west of Dublin. The ambitious Guinness sold his brew locally, but was thwarted in his attempts to sell his beer abroad by Ireland's restrictive export tariffs on beer. He searched acrossed the Irish Sea in Wales, but found no suitable existing brewery. Meanwhile, Irish brewers were being squeezed out by English imports flooding the island under favorable English tax laws. There were some seventy breweries in Ireland when Arthur Guinness starting working in brewhouses in his late teens. Fewer than half that number operated by the mid 1750s.

Returning to Ireland, Guinness settled just outside the walled city of Dublin in a small ale brewery at St. James Gate. He leased the brewery on December 31, 1759 for an extremely reasonable rate: "a dwelling house, a brewhouse, two malt houses, and stables" for forty-five pounds sterling each year. The lease was to be honored for nine thousand years. The document was still in force more than two centuries later.

There had been a brewery on the site at least as far back as 1693. It lay on the main road to Dublin from the corn-growing districts of central Ireland, and water from the river Poddle coursed through the property. For his first twenty years, Guinness brewed ale and table-beer, all the while railing against the unfair trade situation with England. In 1777, partly assisted by testimony from Guinness, the Irish House of Commons repealed many of the restrictive regulations.

In 1778 Arthur Guinness brewed his first porter. By 1799, only four years before his death at the age of seventy-eight, Guinness was selling only porter. The St. James Gate brewery would grow to be the world's largest without ever advertising, greatly assisted by thousands of physicians' testimonials about the benefits of Guinness: as a cure for insomnia, debility, constipation, digestive disorders, nervousness, and even as an aid to nursing mothers.

Heineken

Gerard Adriaan Heineken was looking to get into the beer business. In 1863, he convinced his wealthy mother that there would be fewer problems with alcoholism in the Netherlands if the Dutch could be induced to drink beer instead of gin. His mother bought De Hooiberg ("The Haystack"), a brewery that had been operating since 1592. At the age of twenty-two Gerard Heineken began running the largest brewery in Amsterdam.

Heineken proved to be an astute brewer and businessman. Sales multiplied within a few years and in 1867 he started work on a sprawling new brewery. Six years later, work was started on a brewery in Rotterdam. In 1873, Heineken developed a new cooling technique for wort that eliminated a brewer's traditional dependence on seasonal ice. Heineken commenced year-round brewing.

Heineken traveled throughout Europe in search of better raw materials. In 1879 he hired a former student of Louis Pasteur, Dr. Elion, to work in the Heineken's laboratory—unique in the brewing world at the time. Dr. Elion developed a specific yeast cell— yeast which yields the alcohol in beer—which came to be known as the Heineken A yeast. Still the primary ingredient in Heineken today, the new yeast gave Heineken excellent consistency in its expanding range of breweries.

The pinnacle of Gerard Heineken's career came four years before his death, when the gold medal of honor was awarded to his brewery during the Paris World Fair of 1889. At the time Heineken was selling two hundred thousand hectoliters of beer each year, while the average Dutch brewery sold only three thousand hectoliters.

Heineken began exporting beer after just twelve years of operation, establishing a long tradition in the opening of new markets that led it to be the most widely exported beer in the world. In 1914, Dr. Henri P. Heineken, the founder's son, took control of the brewery. Traveling by ocean liner to New York City, he met Leo van Munching, the ship's Dutch bartender. Impressed by his knowledge of beer, Heineken offered van Munching a position as the company's importer in New York City, a relationship that endures to this day. In 1933 when Prohibition ended in America, Heineken was the first foreign beer to be sold. It remains America's top-selling imported beer.

Hires

For Charles Hires, a trifling matter like a honeymoon was no reason to stop his obsessive experimenting with root beer recipes. He spent the first days of his married life tinkering with an assortment of roots, herbs, and berries, including juniper, spikenard, wintergreen, sarsaparilla, hops, vanilla beans, ginger, licorice, deer tongue, dog grass, and birch bark.

Root beer traces its origins back to colonial times. For those who didn't want to dig their own roots, a few pharmacies began to market packets of roots in the early 1800s for brew-it-yourself beverages. Hires, a descendant of Martha Washington, became interested in root beer as a sixteen-year old pharmacy student at Jefferson Medical College in Philadelphia in 1866.

Two medical professors assisted him in developing a formula for a beverage he sold at the soda fountain of a drug store where he clerked. He dreamed of his own soft drink business, but there didn't seem much chance of that happening.

One day Hires was walking down Spruce Street in Philadelphia and watched an excavating crew digging out a cellar. Thinking fast, he told the contractor he could dispose of the troublesome soil in the basement of his drug store a few blocks away. Hires had recognized the soil being carted from the worksite as potter's clay, valuable in removing grease stains from clothing.

He rolled out the soil, sliced it into cakes and wrapped it in tissue paper. Hires' Potter's Clay was soon for sale in stores throughout Philadelphia. Hires netted almost seven thousand dollars from this venture, which he plowed into manufacturing his soft drinks.

He hit upon an especially tasty combination of sixteen roots and berries and set out to market his "root tea"—so named in deference to Pennsylvania's growing temperance movement. Friends scoffed at this plan, praising the drink but despairing the name. They convinced Charles Hires that "root beer" would project a more robust image.

The first Hires Root Beer came in packets and sold for twenty-five cents. The packet was designed to be mixed in five gallons of water. Hires rented a booth at the Philadelphia Centennial Exposition in 1876. Response to his refreshing samples was so strong he started offering his powders by mail, using the beverage industry's first advertising. "A delicious, sparkling and wholesome beverage," he raved in *Harper's*.

Hires knew the future of soda pop did not lie with home brewing, and in 1893 he pioneered the bottling of soft drinks. Before the end of the century, over three million bottles of Hires Root Beer were spewing from plants across the United States, Canada, and Cuba. Hires ads proclaimed that the tasty beverage "gives children the strength to resist the enervating effects of the heat, bridges the convalescent over the trying part of a hot day, and helps even a cynic see the brighter side of life."

In 1898 Hires began the manufacture of condensed milk, building a chain of twenty-one factories scattered throughout the country. He sold the milk business to Nestle in 1917 and retreated from active participation in the day-to-day affairs of the root beer operation. Hires's chief hobby in the latter part of his life was deep sea fishing. In 1937, as he packed to go on an extended fishing trip, Charles Hires was felled by a stroke. He died at the age of 86.

Jack Daniel's

Jasper Newton Daniel was called Jack around his house, when he was called anything at all. The last of ten children, the runt of the family—never standing more than five foot five inches tall or weighing more than a hundred twenty pounds, young Daniel felt snubbed in the busy family and left home at an early age to live with a Tennessee neighbor. Later, he moved to live and work on the farm of Dan Call. On the farm, Call blended whiskey distilling with maintaining a Lutheran ministry. In 1862, Call chose the church over his moonshine business, and sold his still to thirteen-year old Daniel.

Daniel peddled whiskey to both sides throughout the Civil War, hiding his cargo under bales of hay on dangerous fifty-mile excursions to Huntsville, Alabama. After the war ended, Daniel bought a tract of land in 1866 to build a distillery. He located his new plant about four miles from Lynchburg, Tennessee at Cave Spring in "the Hollow," an area known for its pure limestone water. The water was free from iron and a constant fifty-six degrees. His process of mellowing the liquor and filtering it through charcoal quickly proved popular.

Daniel was a shrewd businessman who created an image for his distillery based on his personality. He wore a mustache and goatee and sported a planter's hat and knee-length frock coat, evidently even while performing manual labor around the distillery. He never appeared in public unless in full regalia.

As liquor laws changed in the postwar period, Daniel registered his business as the first registered distillery in the country, hence Jack Daniel Distillery No. 1. "Belle of Lincoln" and "Old Fashioned" were early brands, but his greatest sales came from "Old Time No. 7", an esteemed "Tennessee sippin' whiskey." "No. 7" took first place in an international taste test during the 1904 St. Louis Exposition. In the 1880s, Daniel's nephew encouraged him to market in bottles as well as wholesale barrels. Daniel developed his distinctive square bottles because, after all, legend has it, he was a "square shooter."

Jack Daniel retired in 1907, turning ownership of the distillery over to a nephew. He never married and lived with his sister and a brother-in-law his entire adult life. He died in 1911 from complications owing to a 1905 toe injury—which happened when he angrily kicked a safe that refused to open. After the toe problem, he had to have the leg amputated.

Miller

Frederick Miller arrived in the United States as an experienced brewer of modest means. He toured America in search of the ideal site to establish a new brewery, eventually choosing Milwaukee for its abundant supply of water, fine grain, and skilled craftsmen. He bought a tiny, wooden brewery in the Menomonee River Valley in 1855, and it became Fred Miller's Plank Road Brewery.

Miller set to work applying the methods he had learned as a

brewmaster in Riedlingen, Germany. His first year, the Plank Road Brewery produced three thousand barrels of beer. Miller's beer was popular enough to stand out among the many other Wisconsin breweries.

With every opportunity, Miller modernized his operations. He established one of the first bottling lines. By 1883, the renamed Menomonee Valley Brewery was selling eighty thousand barrels a year and unable to keep up with demand. Five thousand of those barrels were going into bottles. Miller's bottling operation was bigger than many breweries.

In 1888, Frederick Miller died. He was sixty-three years old. His sons and a son-in-law took control of the brewery. Their first act was to change the name of the brewery to the Frederick Miller Brewing Company in honor of the efforts of the founder.

Molson

John Molson was born in Lincolnshire, England in 1763, and orphaned in 1772 at the age of eight. His share of his parents' estate was placed in receivership, and young Molson was sent to live under the strict guardianship of his grandfather. At the age of seventeen, he suffered a debilitating illness that doctors could neither diagnose nor treat. A sea voyage was prescribed.

Molson chose Canada as an exciting destination of opportunity, but the sea journey to Montreal was anything but therapeutical. England was simultaneously at war with France and the British colonies in America, and the seas were awash in warships. Several times the ship was swamped, and the captain often spent entire days in his cabin drunk. In midvoyage, Molson and his party were forced to transfer to another ship.

Montreal in the 1780s was a frontier town of eight thousand, mostly French and mainly involved in the fur trade. Molson scouted the community for possible enterprises and became intrigued with a malting house started by a friend, Thomas Loyd. There had been other breweries tried in Montreal, but the French drank only wine and spirits. All the other breweries had closed.

Still, starting up a brewery was inexpensive, there was little labor involved, and the profit margins were substantial. And locally brewed beer was not subject to duties and taxes. When Loyd brewed and sold fifty hogsheads of ale late in 1782, Molson decided to join him in January of 1783.

The circumstances are unclear, but by January, 1785 Molson was sole owner of the brewery. He had purchased four hundred acres of land north of Lake Champlain, which became Vermont after the Treaty of Paris ended the American Revolution. At some point, Molson apparently traded his land for Loyd's share of the brewery.

Molson closed the brewery and sailed home to England to settle his inheritance and study English breweries. He returned to Montreal with brewing equipment and a supply of high quality barley seed, which he distributed free to local farmers. He also brought with him a small book, *Theoretical Hints on an Improved Practice of Brewing*.

Molson's first output that winter was eighty hogsheads, or forty-three hundred gallons. In 1787 Molson said, "My beer has been almost universally well liked beyond my most sanguine expectations." It was also the only beer available. By 1791, when the Constitutional Act separating Quebec into Upper Canada and Lower Canada was effected, Molson was a leading member of the Montreal business community.

Molson, despite being English in the French-dominated Lower Canada, gradually expanded his brewery through the end of the century. Output grew to more than fifty thousand gallons annually. In 1797, Molson entered the lumber business. He sold two million board feet in two years but made little profit.

Molson's next venture outside brewing took place in 1809, when he entered a partnership to finance the building of a steamship. For years Molson had watched sailing ships fight the swift current of the St. Lawrence River from his brewery on the river's bank. He set out to commission a steamship.

The *Accommodation* took ten passengers on its maiden voyage on November 1, 1809 as Canada's first steamer. The venture lost money, but pioneered the waterway for Molson's future fleet.

In 1814, Molson signed a partnership with his three sons ensuring the brewery would remain in family control. With his time freed from the everyday duties of running the brewery, Molson eagerly diversified his interests. He was elected to represent Montreal East in the Canadian Parliament, serving from 1816 to 1820 and advancing the establishment of the Montreal General Hospital.

Molson built the Mansion House, Montreal's finest hotel, which included a public library and post office. It burned down but he quickly rebuilt it, adding Montreal's first theater next to the hotel. He invested heavily in Canada's railways, and served as President of the Bank of Montreal from 1826 to 1830.

Molson died in 1836 at the age of seventy-two, while a member of Canada's Legislative Council. In his will he stipulated that his portrait, painted in 1811, should hang in the brewery for as long as the Molson family retains control, but if "the brewery ever pass into the hands of strangers" the portrait must be removed. It still hangs in the Molson brewery today.

Paul Masson

In 1878 a *Phylloxera* plague attacked European vineyards, decimating the grape harvests. All cures were ineffective. The remedy was in America, where the toughness of the root-bark of wild vines withstood parasitic infestations.

Nineteen-year old Paul Masson, from the Burgundy wine-growing region of France, staked his future on California. Many of his countrymen were already there. After a drought in 1863, many California cattle ranges were planted in grape vines. Masson reasoned he could get part-time work and finish his education.

Which is exactly what happened. He joined the vineyard of Charles LeFranc who, with two daughters and no sons, no doubt welcomed a husky, broad-shouldered man bred of vintners. Masson enrolled in nearby Santa Clara College.

By the 1880s, California was on the verge of overproduction. A grower needed extremely high quality wine to stay in business. The best wine required the best grapes. as well as the best equipment. Masson decided early on to be a champagne master.

Masson sailed to France to buy the finest equipment available. He returned for a splendid harvest—ten thousand bottles in 1884. The output doubled in 1885, and tripled in 1886. Masson's first champagne was a hit in 1887. From then on, no wine left a Paul Masson cellar for at least three years while it aged.

Masson married one of the LeFranc sisters and the winery became the LeFranc Masson Wine Company. In 1892 his father-in-law died and he introduced the first "Paul Masson Champagne . . . 'Special Dry' and 'Extra Dry.'" It was a champagne in the great French tradition, made from dark pinot grapes.

Masson, with an inventory of millions of bottles undergoing natural in-bottle fermentation, claimed a large share of the American luxury market with the famous names of France. In 1900 he returned to his homeland for the first time in twelve years to enter his Pinot Champagne in open competition—and won. In 1905 Masson began dynamiting the foothills around Los Gatos to plant the first full Pinot Vineyard in America.

The flamboyant Masson, famous for his sybaritic lifestyle, was known around San Francisco as "Duc de Cognac." His continued honors for Paul Masson Champagne brought California wines respect around the world. Masson never missed an opportunity to entertain and serve his wines—even if it wasn't his party.

In 1918 wineries began to disintegrate with the advent of Prohibition. Only six wineries in the United States were licensed to make wine for sacramental and medicinal purposes. Paul Masson was one of the six. The price of grapes, however, soared—as millions of European immigrants bought them to make legal home wines. Since grapes didn't ship well cheaper grapes were planted.

After his wife's death in 1932, Masson began to lighten his administrative burden by selling the original LeFranc property. In 1936 he sold his prized LaCresta hillside vineyard to Martin Ray, a young stockbroker who carried on Masson's zealous operations under the Paul Masson name. The new ownership was still presenting Masson with gold medals until he died in 1940 at the age of eighty-one.

Perrier

Dr. Louis Perrier was a French physician and entrepreneur. That his name should be recognizable across America is a fluke of commercial and social history. In 1903, Perrier and English aristocrat St. John Harnsworth joined forces to purchase the historic natural spring in Vergeze, France. Emperor Napoleon III stated in 1863 that the spring waters of Vergeze should be bottled "for the good of France."

This the partners did, selling the sparkling waters in green twenty-three-ounce bottles. Perrier advertised his drink as "the champagne of bottled waters" and sold it for nearly a dollar a bottle. Accordingly, Perrier was available only in gourmet and specialty-food shops for decades and decades.

Then fitness and health consciousness hit America in the late 1970s. From 1980 until 1989 the bottled water industry grew from an eighty million dollars business to one accounting for almost three billion dollars in sales. Perrier spent the most money the earliest in the boom, and became so popular many people assumed Perrier invented bottled water. Suddenly everyone knew Louis Perrier's name.

 chweppes

All his life it seemed like Jacob Schweppe had people deciding his career path for him. Now, stranded in England as his homeland dissolved in revolution, Schweppe would make the call himself.

In 1752, when Schweppe was twelve, his parents considered him too delicate for work on the family farm in Witzenhausen, Germany and allowed a travelling tinker to care for him. Schweppe showed such a proclivity for mending pots with his skilled hands that the tinker returned him to his parents with advice to send him to a silversmith. The silversmith convinced his parents to turn him over to a jeweler. So Jacob Schweppe went to Geneva and became a jeweler.

An amateur scientist, Schweppe devoured all the news he could find on the experiments of Joseph Priestly, who was working with gas and water. Schweppe's own efforts with carbonated water were not satisfactory to him, so he offered his artificial mineral waters to doctors to give to poor patients.

Finally he perfected his carbonation system with a compression pump, and demand for his mineral water spread. Schweppe continued giving away his water to rich and poor. He was, after all, a researcher.

Many people insisted that he take money for his water, so he started charging a nominal fee in 1780. Schweppe finally quit the jewelry business and became the first manufacturer of artificial mineral waters. The soft drink industry was born.

After ten years the little business was firmly established when a friend and sales employee wanted to also make mineral water and sell it along with Schweppe's. He had only seen the machine in operation, so he described the apparatus for well-known engineer Nicolas Paul to build him one. Paul did so but built a better machine for himself to compete with Schweppe. Rather than engage in a fight, Schweppe became partners in 1790 in the firm of Schweppe, Paul & Gosse.

The range of mineral waters expanded, and the partners decided to start a factory in London. His partners, both younger than himself, convinced the fifty-two-year old Schweppe to leave his family and launch the product in London.

Schweppe met with little success. He was forced by economics to set up in a particularly nasty quarter of London. In 1792 there were many inferior mineral waters on the market, and Schweppes was no novelty. He was selling virtually nothing, not even to doctors who usually preferred his product.

Schweppe wanted to come home. Besides the desultory business climate, revolutionary fervor was sweeping through Europe. His partners persuaded Schweppe to stay in England. At considerable personal expense he sent for his daughter Collette, the only survivor among his nine children.

Suddenly a letter arrived from the partners calling him back. The partners were bickering, sales were dropping. Schweppe had had enough. He dissolved the partnership, surrendering the business he had built for ten years in Geneva. Now, in 1793, Schweppe was free to run his artificial mineral water business as he wished.

He introduced an egg-shaped bottle to hold his aerated waters. The bottle design remained in use for over a hundred years. Its shape insured the bottle would be kept on its side so the cork would stay saturated, sealing in the precious gas. Each cork was tarred and held in place with a string.

Schweppe gained the endorsement of Erasmus Darwin, grandfather of Charles. He began referring to his product as "soda water," and recommended it for complaints of kidneys, bladders, and indigestion. Schweppe's Seltzer was touted for its pleasant taste and as a mixer with liquor. It also helped fever and hangovers.

By 1798 Schweppe was clearing the handsome sum of twelve hundred pounds a year. His English fame had eclipsed his Geneva

business, which collapsed among the bickering remaining partners shortly after the dissolution. He sold three quarters of his
company to three men from the island of Jersey for £2250, retaining
an eighth for himself and an eighth for his daughter.

Schweppe retired the next year in 1799. Napoleon had
annexed Geneva, making Schweppe a French citizen. He traveled,
dabbled in agriculture, and tended bees until his death in 1821 at
the age of eighty-one. His daughter sold the last of the family's
share of Schweppes in 1824.

Smirnoff

Peter Smirnoff distilled his first vodka in Russia in 1864, continuously filtering his pure grain alcohol through hardwood charcoal
for eight full hours. By 1877, Smirnoff's vodka had won him his
first double eagle, Russia's highest commercial honor, as the best
product in his industry. Two more double eagles quickly followed,
and in 1886 Peter Smirnoff became the purveyor to the court of
His Imperial Majesty, Czar Alexander III.

As the royal distiller, Smirnoff's sales soared; he was rumored
to be producing one million bottles of vodka a day by 1900. But as
his affiliation with the Imperial Court made Smirnoff wealthy it
also doomed the firm when the government was overthrown in the
Revolution of 1917. Vladimir Smirnoff was one of the few family
members to escape the carnage. He settled in France where he
attempted to recreate the secret family distilling process.

Meanwhile, a Smirnoff supplier, Rudolph Kunett, had sought
refuge in America. Upon learning of Vladimir Smirnoff's efforts,
he purchased the American rights to the product for $2,500 and

introduced the first vodka to the United States in 1934. Five years
later it seemed he had struck a poor bargain. No one in America
was buying vodka, not even displaced Russians. It was considered a
lethal potion which delivered particularly bad hangovers.

When Vladimir Smirnoff, a fourth generation family member
in the vodka business, died in 1939, Kunett unloaded the vodka
rights to G. F. Hublein and Company for $14,000 and a job. The deal
included the last two thousand bottles in Kunett's Connecticut distillery. The bottles were filled and labeled, but there were no vodka
corks left in stock. To clear the bottles out of the closing distillery
Hublein president John Martin corked them with Smirnoff's
whiskey corks, left over from a failed attempt to market Smirnoff's
whiskey. It was no wonder the purchase of Smirnoff's was routinely
referred to as "Martin's folly."

Martin shipped the remaining vodka to a salesman in the South,
assuming that would be the last he heard of the name Smirnoff. The
salesman sampled the delivery and found the "whiskey" to be col-
orless and tasteless. He advertised it on his route as "Smirnoff's
White Whiskey. No Taste. No Smell." And sold out. As John Martin
later said about the sales ploy, "It was rather ingenious, but totally
illegal."

What Martin discovered through his salesman was that people
weren't drinking the vodka straight and chilled as it was traditionally consumed in Russia, but mixed with other drinks. Martin
quickly repositioned vodka to Americans as a drink mixer. Today
Smirnoff's is the biggest selling liquor in the United States.

uengling

There is no documentation to verify what the Yuengling family business was in Germany, but when David G. Yuengling, an immigrant from Wurtemburg, Germany, arrived in America in 1828 at the age of twenty-one he immediately looked for a place to start a brewery. It is not unreasonable to deduce that the Yuengling brewing tradition stretches back past America.

Yuengling headed for the eastern Pennsylvania coal country, and in 1829 opened the Eagle Brewery on North Centre Street in the rolling Appalachian foothills. The new brewhouse was not two years old before fire consumed it. In 1831 Yuengling rebuilt the brewery a few blocks away on a mountainside, where tunnels gouged from the rock provided natural cold temperatures necessary for aging and fermentation. That brewery stands today, and Yuengling is officially recognized in the *National Register of Historic Places* as America's oldest brewery.

David Yuengling was among the first to brew lager beer. That first year he produced six hundred barrels of beer and ale. The malt was transported from Philadelphia by way of the Schuylkill Canal and the final brew was delivered throughout the region by horse-drawn wagons. David Yuengling's reputation was such that many noted nineteenth century brewers learned their art in the Mahantongo Street brewhouse.

By the time his son joined him in 1873, David Yuengling was brewing twenty-three thousand barrels a year. He died in 1873 at the age of seventy, having started a family business that would stretch continuously into the fifth generation.

4 PART

In The Medicine Cabinet

Bausch & Lomb

1849 was a big year for John Jacob Bausch. He made a wrenching decision to leave his homeland of Germany and come to America. He met his future wife and got married. He lost two fingers to a buzz saw, met his partner—and discovered his life's work.

Bausch was born in 1830, one of seven children; they lost their mother when Bausch was six. Germany was a poverty-stricken land suffering from a series of crop failures. Bausch's older brother turned wood to eke out a meager living, and decided to try his hand at spectacle manufacture. John Jacob helped his brother with the grinding and polishing and became interested in the activity.

Somehow in 1848 young Bausch heard of a job in an optical shop in Berne, Switzerland. He went to Berne on foot, occasionally catching a ride in a passing stage, carrying his life's belongings in a knapsack. He got the job and started out at thirty-six cents a day. It was a good start, but Bausch was overwhelmed by the poor times and oppressive poverty. It was a lawless age of political upheaval. Reluctantly, in 1849 he decided to come to America.

He found the same conditions in his new country. Upon landing in New York he was immediately advised to leave and seek better opportunities. Bausch went to Buffalo where he worked as a cook's helper before borrowing five dollars to go to Rochester. He was married before the year was out and shortly afterwards his hand became twisted through a buzz saw where he was working as a wood-turner.

Henry Lomb, a Rochester friend, brought him food while he recuperated. Unable to continue woodworking, Bausch sent home to his brother for optical materials, which he peddled around Rochester. He met minor success, and borrowed sixty dollars from Lomb to open an optical shop in 1853. Bausch began grinding lenses by hand.

By 1861, after eight years of hard work, Bausch's business debts about equalled his resources, not counting the thousand dollars he owed Lomb. Lomb, aged thirty-two, volunteered for the Union army and rose to the rank of captain.

During the war, Bausch found a piece of vulcanized rubber lying in the street. He took it home and adapted it into frames, which included the first known nosepiece. He acquired exclusive rights to make optical products from the hard rubber.

When the Civil War ended, Bausch & Lomb formed the Vulcanite Optical Instrument Company, which became Bausch & Lomb Optical in 1868. With Bausch's vision and drive, the company grew and diversified. Lomb was not a practical mechanic and had nothing to do with the factory, but he worked well with the employees.

Bausch's son returned from Cornell in 1875, and perfected the microscope. In 1893 they purchased the patents for field glasses. Bausch & Lomb supplied the lens for the first Kodak camera. At the time of his death, Bausch & Lomb was one of the largest manufacturers of optical equipment in the world. He had lived long enough to see the culmination of a complete optical business for both personal and scientific needs.

Bayer

Friedrich Bayer was born in 1825, the only boy among six children. His father was a weaver, his ancestors dyers. As a young man he served a chemical merchant apprenticeship and set out to start his own business in natural dyes in 1848. By 1860, he owned five acres of land and two houses on the property.

Up until 1856, all color dyes had been produced from vegetable and animal materials. That year, coal tar dyes were discovered, and the balding Bayer immediately realized the enormous potential of these synthetic dyes. From the black, sticky mess could come all the colors of the rainbow.

Bayer and his partner Johann Friedrich Weskott, a master dyer, began to search for their own artificial dyes. They tagged their little side business "The Laboratory in the Kitchen" as pans bubbled on stoves with gooey tar. By late 1862, they had created a bluish-red dye they named fuchsine after the flowers of the fuchsia.

In 1863 the general partnership of Friedr. Bayer et Compagnie was formed to produce aniline dyestuffs. Bayer did the sales and marketing and Weskott handled production. Both men were cautious enough to retain their old firms. On paydays, Bayer personally handed each employee his wages. The first payroll of a company that would one day employ over 150,000 people included one chemist, one foreman, and four laborers.

Competition grew steadily, and Bayer & Company produced different color dyes. In 1865 they acquired shares in the first American coal tar dye factory in Albany, New York. The firm gained notoriety when it scored a silver medal in 1867 at the Paris World Exhibition.

Bayer pioneered employee relations in 1873, when the company started a Worker's Relief Fund as a health plan for workers. By that time Friedrich Bayer was becoming increasingly aware of his own health. In 1877 the sons of the founders became partners. Bayer died on May 6, 1880—seventeen years before the invention of the product by a company chemist that would make his name a household word: aspirin.

Breck

Two pivotal things happened to John Breck at an unusually early age. First, he was made fire captain of the Chicopee, Massachusetts Fire Department in 1898 at the age of twenty-one, becoming America's youngest fire chief. Less happily, he was also going bald by that time.

Distressed by his premature hair loss, Breck began studying hair care and attending chemistry classes at Amherst College in between fighting fires. At the time, Americans washed their hair—if they did so at all—with multipurpose bar soap. Shampoos were known in Europe, however.

Breck earned his doctorate and did succeed in developing a liquid shampoo. He sold some bottles to friends and through word-of-mouth, but the handsome young firefighter–doctor was more interested in arresting his own hair loss. Doctors assured him there was no winning this battle but Dr. Breck quit firefighting in 1908 and moved to Springfield, Massachusetts to open a scalp-treatment center.

He continued to sell Breck Preparations, mostly his shampoo, to local hairdressers. Breck had introduced the modern shampoo to America. For twenty years, he continued his research into hair treatment and distributed his hair-care products in Massachusetts. In 1929 Breck teamed with a Boston-based beauty supply dealer to form the John H. Breck Corporation. Sales the first year hovered around ten thousand dollars.

In 1930, Breck introduced the first pH-balanced hair shampoo. In 1933, he developed special shampoos for dry and oily hair. All three were packaged in elegant gold-foil boxes, and indeed Breck products were sold exclusively in beauty salons until 1946. To help promote his products, the first "Breck Girl" appeared in print in the January issue of *Modern Beauty Shop*. The advertising campaign was one of America's longest and most well-known, launching the careers of Cybill Shepherd, Cheryl Tiegs, Kim Basinger, and others.

John Breck turned the company over to his son Edward in the 1930s, and the Breck Corporation remained in family hands until 1963. For all his work in the field of hair care, John Breck never found a cure for his own baldness.

olgate

When William Colgate went into business, he had the toughest competitor of all—his own customers. Colgate set out to sell soap at a time when seventy-five percent of all American soap was made at home. One day was set aside in a housewife's week to make soap from accumulated cooking fats. Colgate had to convince American women that not only was his soap cheaper and better, but that they weren't bad housewives if they didn't brew their own soap.

Colgate's father Robert had arrived in America in 1800 to take title of a farm and began to manufacture soap and candles. Nineteen-year-old William tried his own hand at making soap in Baltimore in 1802, but his business survived only a year.

Colgate resurfaced in New York in 1806, opening the doors to William Colgate & Company at 6 Dutch Street. He arrived at 7 A.M. and waited anxiously for customers. Finally around noon an elderly gentleman walked in and, after critically eyeing the new soap for what seemed like an eternity, bought a two-pound bar. Colgate had his first sale.

Colgate asked his customer where the soap could be delivered. It was an unheard of practice at the time to deliver bars of soap, but Colgate had decided it would be his policy. He closed shop an hour early, made the delivery, and won a customer for life.

In the early days Colgate, was soapmaker, buyer, salesman, bookkeeper, and delivery man. He knew his biggest weapon in selling soap would be fragrance. Homemade soap smelled awful, and he thought if he could develop a scented soap pleasing to the senses he could win over reluctant housewives.

It worked. Housewives began making excuses for why they couldn't make their own soap and had to buy Colgate's. "Just tell your family you didn't have the ingredients this week," Colgate would smile. His business prospered.

In 1847 Colgate built a pan for boiling soap that held forty five thousand pounds in a single batch—a world record. His business associates scoffed; they said he could never generate enough orders to keep such an enormous pan operating. Two years later, Colgate had to move to even larger quarters across the river in Jersey City, New Jersey.

Colgate set aside a good portion of his income for religious benefactions. He fathered eleven children, passing the business onto his sons after his death in 1857. In 1908, some thirty years after the introduction of the world's most famous dental product— Colgate Tooth Paste, which was sold in jars—five Colgate brothers turned what had been a family business for 102 years into a public company.

Dr. Scholl's

Nobody cared about feet. Physicians ignored them, shoemakers were oblivious to them, even their owners just accepted the inevitability of corns, bunions, and fallen arches. There were not even standard shoe sizes; you could buy either wide or narrow. It wasn't until the Civil War that Americans actually enjoyed right

and left shoes. This was simply not acceptable to William Mathias
Scholl.

Born into an active La Porte, Indiana farm family of thirteen
children in 1882, William took personal responsibility for shoeing
the large brood. He designed his own shoes using a sturdy waxed
thread. At sixteen, Scholl took his peculiar talent to a local shoe-
maker, where he apprenticed for a year. He moved to Chicago,
working as a salesman by day and attending Loyola University and
the Chicago Medical School at night.

The young physician immediately applied his lessons to—by
his way of thinking at least—the monumental malaise surrounding
foot care in the country. He patented an arch support "Foot-Eazer"
in 1904, and began manufacturing foot products under the "Dr.
Scholl's" patent name in 1907. William Scholl became a one-man
foot care industry.

He wrote manuals on foot care for physicians and more general guides for the public. He set up a podiatric correspondence
course for shoe store clerks. He led a coterie of consultants who
canvassed the country delivering medical and public lectures on
proper foot care.

Dr. Scholl would walk into a client's office, casually produce a
skeleton of a human foot from his pocket and toss it on the desk.
Having gained everyone's attention, he would proceed to describe
the anatomy of the foot and demonstrate the value of his Foot-Eazer.

For Scholl, there was never an end to his mission to deliver
America from foot problems. He complained that for every person
he saw walking properly he saw another fifty who weren't. His remedy was to walk two miles a day, briskly with "head up, chest out,
toes straight forward."

His advertisements were scandalous for the day—naked feet!
In 1916, Scholl sponsored a Cinderella Foot Contest, bringing
nationwide attention to feet. Thousands of women scurried to
local shoe stores on presumably perfect feet. What they discovered, as Scholl had hoped, was the disparity between their own feet
and the American ideal.

The resulting quest for perfect feet led to such demand for Dr.
Scholl's yellow-and-blue packages that they were given their own
sections in many stores. Scholl could certainly stock the shelves:
over the years he was to be credited with more than a thousand
foot aids.

A lifelong bachelor, Scholl practiced his specialty in Chicago from 1905 to 1949. In 1912 he founded the Illinois College of Chiropody and Orthopedics, later renamed the Scholl College of Podiatric Medicine. He remained active in the operation of the Scholl Manufacturing Company until his death in 1968. He liked to boast that he never forgot a foot.

Gillette

The man whose idea was to change the face of half the world's population was King C. Gillette, a tall, distinguished-looking traveling salesman and a good one. Gillette was pulling down as much as six thousand dollars a year before the turn of the century, a very good wage for the time. But he was obsessed with an idea. Although untrained mechanically, he was determined to invent something—preferably an item people would use, throw away, and buy again.

To aid his discovery, Gillette systematically went through the alphabet listing every conceivable disposable material need, searching for that one big idea. It came to him one morning in his fortieth year in 1895 in Brookline, Massachusetts: "On one particular morning when I started to shave, I found my razor dull, and it was not only dull, but it was beyond the point of successful stropping. As I stood there with the razor in my hand, my eye resting on it as lightly as a bird settling down on its nest—the Gillette razor was born. I saw it all in a moment, the way the blade could be held in a holder; the idea of sharpening the two opposite edges of a thin piece of steel thus doubling its service; and with a handle equally disposed between the two edges of a blade. All this came as though the razor were already a finished thing and held before my eyes."

It all seemed so simple. Immediately, Gillette wrote to his wife, visiting in Ohio: "I have got it; our fortune is made." But five years passed with nothing but a crude model. He toiled with clock springs, a hand vise, and files. Toolmakers and cutlers told him he could never make sharp wafer-thin steel blades. Engineers advised Gillette to drop the radical idea.

One Massachusetts Institute of Technology professor agreed to collaborate with him in 1901. Gillette later wrote, "William Nickerson was the only man in the world who could have perfected the razor." Nickerson had already invented the push-button system for elevators. By 1903 the two men had a razor ready for market. Desultory first year sales were fifty-one razors sold for five cents apiece, and 168 blades.

How phenomenal would be the growth of the Gillette safety razor?

Gillette had sold blocks of stock to raise five thousand dollars. One Pittsburgh bottler bought five hundred shares for $250 to curry favor as a possible supplier, but he considered the stock of no value and forgot about it in a file drawer. Four years later Gillette had to track him down to buy back the stock for $62,500. By 1908, five years after the introduction of the safety razor, Gillette sold thirteen million disposable blades.

Gillette searched for a trademark seeking a label as "internationally recognizable as the dollar bill with Washington's face." It was decided to use the picture of the boss. Gillette's familiar visage of heavy mustache, wing collar, stick pin, and wavy black hair was printed on blade wrappers. Eventually it would be printed more than one billion times, making Gillette instantly recognizable wherever he went.

In World War I, Gillette sold 4,180,000 razors to the government at cost, indoctrinating millions of men just reaching shaving age to the razor. Afterwards Gillette sold the razor as a break-even item. Manufacturers gave away Gillette razors with any conceivable product—candy, marshmallows, gum, tea. The company made its money on blades.

Gillette served as president until 1931. When he retired, the man who searched relentlessly for a time-saving product people could use, throw away, and buy again had sold over six billion steel razor blades.

Johnson & Johnson

A man laid out on a nineteenth-century operating table faced a worse chance at survival as a man riding in a cavalry charge. Germs and sterilization were unknown when Robert Johnson left the Pennsylvania countryside as a sixteen year-old in 1861 to apprentice in a Poughkeepsie apothecary.

Johnson worked in New York as an importer and salesman of drug products until 1873, when he entered into a stormy partnership with George Seabury. Their relationship was strained further when Johnson brought his younger brothers, James and Edward Mead, into the Brooklyn pharmaceutical firm.

By 1886 the three brothers were ready to start their own medical products company. On a train ride through New Jersey James Johnson spotted a "To Let" sign on a four-story red brick building in New Brunswick, New Jersey. Johnson & Johnson, with fourteen employees, sprouted from the fourth floor of that old wallpaper factory.

James Johnson designed and built the machinery. Mead Johnson handled sales and advertising. Robert Johnson was president, financier, and guiding leader. He owned forty percent of the business, with each of his brothers holding an equal thirty percent share.

The first catalog of Johnson & Johnson products was offered on June 1, 1887. Fourteen of the thirty-two pages were devoted to Robert Johnson's medicated plasters, which utilized India rubber. From the dawn of civilization, people sought healants in roots, herbs, and plants. Sawdust plasters were devised as a way to keep medications in close contact with the skin.

Johnson was an early advocate of Joseph Lister's theories on germs and their role in disease. He actively promoted the use of antiseptic, sterilized surgical dressings. With the help of Fred Kilmer, owner of the nearby Opera House Pharmacy, Johnson & Johnson published an influential booklet called "Modern Methods of Antiseptic Wound Treatment." The booklet was proclaimed as a major scientific work educating the public on germs and the vital importance of heat sterilization in surgery. And, of course, the back of the booklet contained descriptions of Johnson & Johnson sterilized bandages, sutures, and other products. Eventually four million copies of the booklet would be distributed around the world.

Sales grew steadily. Robert Johnson was constantly looking for new health care products to wear the trademark Johnson & Johnson red cross. Salesmen, known as "travelers," were often trained physicians who brought back ideas from discussions with clients. If the product materialized it was often named for the discover: "Dr. Simpson's Intranasal Tampon," for instance.

Baby powder came to the company in 1890 when a physician wrote to the company that one of his patients complained of skin irritation from a medicated plaster. Kilmer, by now the head of company research, suggested sending him a small tin of Italian talc to help relieve the itching. Soon the powder was included with certain plasters, and then sent to mothers as part of maternity and obstetric kits for home births.

Robert Johnson, tall and stout with penetrating brown eyes, worked in every facet of the business, even presiding over the daily ritual of opening the company's morning mail. In 1890 he developed "First Aid Kits" for railroad workers who were frantically connecting America. The Railway Station and Factory Supply Case was a large wooden box designed to "prevent an extension of the injury rather than its treatment." Johnson's "first aid" concept was adopted by thousands of first aid training programs throughout society.

Johnson & Johnson's heat sterilized bandages and absorbent sterile cotton gauze dressings served on the battlefields of the Spanish-American War in 1898. In the aftermath of the devastating Galveston hurricane of 1900, Johnson & Johnson replaced all damaged company goods at cost. After the San Francisco earthquake Johnson canceled all druggist invoices under a hundred dollars to keep their products flowing to the needy.

Robert Johnson atypically left his office early on January 31, 1910, complaining of not feeling well. He died a week later from Bright's disease, an acute kidney ailment. James Johnson took over for his brother, saying, "My brother's policy is my policy."

Mennen

Gerhard Mennen arrived in America from Germany in 1871, and went to work in the New Jersey swamps outside Hoboken as a surveyor. Shortly thereafter he contracted malaria, and through the course of his recovery he became intimately versed in the druggist trade. He found a job in an apothecary and studied pharmacy at night. By 1877, Mennen had a profession in his new country at the age of twenty-one.

The next year he bought a small drugstore on a wooded street in downtown Newark for a few hundred dollars. In the fall of 1878 he introduced his first product: Mennen's Sure Corn Killer. Advertising of the time was crude at best. Mennen hired a horse and wagon and banjo player and traveled from town to town in half-hour stands. The entertainment was interrupted by Mennen's lecture on corns and a brief exhortation to buy a bottle of his elixir at local drugstores. He made no attempt to sell his potions on location.

With his business growing, Mennen then turned his attention to worried mothers whose babies suffered from prickly heat and chafing. The customary powder of the day was a mixture of corn starch and chalk that was harsh and only exacerbated the problem. Mennen developed a pleasing, aromatic powder from talc, and also created a convenient cardboard shaker with a spin-wheel cover for sprinkling. Borated Talcum Infant Powder appeared in 1889.

Mennen's powder was selling well in his own store, but response from ads in medical journals was disappointing. Mennen returned to the wagon, handing out samples of America's first talcum powder during performances by minstrel players in Mennen's Talcum Show.

Mennen imprinted his portrait on the cap to inspire trust, and added a smiling baby to the front. Fifty cents of every dollar he earned went back into advertising. Billboards at the time were used only to announce seasonal circus arrivals and theatrical productions. Mennen bought the space in idle times. The Gerhard

Mennen Chemical Company became one of the largest advertisers of the era.

The success of the business encouraged Mennen to take a family vacation to Europe in 1901, where he developed a lethal carbuncle on his neck and underwent an emergency operation. A week later he contracted pneumonia and died, at the age of forty-five. Mennen's widow continued the momentum of the company, and when his son Joseph Mennen took over a decade later the family business was a leader in shaving creams and skin lotions.

Phillips

Most businessmen believe the best way to spread the name of their products is through advertising. Charles Henry Phillips was the anti-advertiser. He believed that the products which flowed from his laboratory should gain favor and prestige through their own merit. Accordingly, most of Phillips apothecary products disappeared. The one that did not, Milk of Magnesia, made his name famous.

Phillips came from England to engage in the retail drug business in Elizabeth, New Jersey. Pharmacists at the time were chemists who concocted their own remedies and many dreamed of inventing that one break-out product. Phillips moved to Glenbrook, Connecticut in 1849 to establish his own laboratory.

For a quarter-century Phillips built a reputation as a provider of treatments for chronic diseases and nutrient supplements with such cumbersome names as Phillips' Palatable Cod Liver Oil Emulsion and Phillips' Phospho-Nutritive and Phillips' Phospo-Muriate Quinine Compound.

In 1873 Phillips received a United States patent for the invention of Milk of Magnesia. Magnesia had long been known as a laxative, but it was difficult to administer in its known powder form. Phillips suspended magnesium hydroxide in water, making the treatment palatable. The name was registered in the *Trade Mark Journal* in 1880, two years before its inventor's death, making Phillips' Milk of Magnesia one of America's oldest brands.

The stomach treatment was roundly endorsed by physicians and dentists and, just as Phillips believed, the merit of Milk of Magnesia has gained it a place in American medicine cabinets for over a hundred years.

Schick

Shaving, in one grisly form or another, has always been with us. The first shaving implements of which we have any record were made approximately 2000 B.C. They were little more than sharp shells and flints. Throughout history men gouged and hacked at their faces for various reasons.

The Egyptians regarded a clean-shaven face as a symbol of status. Alexander the Great required his soldiers to shave their beards less they be grabbed as handles in sword fights. The first barber appeared in Rome in 300 B.C. using bronze and iron to provide a less than smooth shave. And then, for two thousand years, there were no advances in shaving.

King Gillette changed shaving forever with replaceable blades, and then came the Schick Dry Shaver in 1928. The original idea for a shaving instrument which could operate without water, soap, and scraping blade first occurred to Colonel Jacob Schick while on Army duty in Alaska. The prospect of blade shaving in minus-forty degree temperatures would undoubtedly start any man's mind racing.

Schick, a career Army officer, had come to Alaska after a colorful career. An Iowan, Schick grew up in the southwest where he supervised the building of a New Mexico railroad spur at the age of sixteen for his father's coal company. In 1896 he enlisted in the army, serving with the first expedition to the Philippines.

On his second tour of duty in the Philippines in 1905, Schick contracted dysentery, which hospitalized him for a year. On the advice of physicians, Schick was transferred to Fort Gibbons, Alaska. The cold climate helped restore his health, and Schick played an active role in laying out more than a thousand miles of telegraph lines in the interior of the territory.

On a hunting trip Schick sprained an ankle so badly he was unable to walk. A slain moose provided food and frozen stream water supplied water until he was able to walk again. During his forced idleness, he worked out a system for shaving without lather or water. He sent his blueprints to an American company but they were rejected.

Schick retired from the army in 1919. Over the next several years he marketed many inventions. None met any real commercial success, but two, the "Pencilaid" and the "Pencilnife"—devices for sharpening pencils—did provide him enough capital to resume experiments with his dry shaving system. At one time his wife Florence mortgaged the family home to raise ten thousand dollars to enable Schick to continue tinkering.

Up until that time, there had been no electric motor small enough and powerful enough to drive a shaving head and fit within the case of a shaver. The impulse motor Colonel Schick developed for this specific application was the most powerful of its size in the world. He patented his new electric razor in 1928.

But why would millions of satisfied Gillette blade shavers want to switch? Potential investors were happy with their blade shaves and apparently so too were consumers. Schick sold his interest in the Magazine Repeating Razor in 1930.

Schick did not give up on his razor. He set up a factory in a small loft in Stamford, Connecticut and started turning out a few shavers a day in 1931. He sold the razors in New York City for twenty-five dollars each—an astronomical price in the heart of the Depression.

He realized a small profit the next year and poured the money back into national advertising. For the next few years Schick advertised his new shaver with whatever money he could find. Despite the hard times, Americans responded to the new advance in shaving comfort. Within five years Schick had one million electric razors in use.

The Colonel died of cancer in 1937, in the midst of a suit against patent infringers. Judge Manton, a Justice of the Supreme Court of Appeals in New York, handed down a decision voiding Schick's patents. The judge was later to be found guilty of taking bribes in rendering many dishonest decisions, including the Schick case, the highest ranking juror so convicted to that time. But the damage was done. Some sixty companies, many of dubious standards, raced into the electric shaver business, and electric shaving earned a bad reputation which persisted until a post-World War II resurgence.

Smith Brothers

Serendipity named them Trade and Mark, and their images have been commercially reproduced more times than any others. They were so successful they spawned a spate of cheap imitators such as the "Schmitt Brothers" and the "Smythe Sisters." They are the Smith Brothers.

James Smith was a Scot who emigrated to Quebec, Canada for fifteen years before migrating to Poughkeepsie, New York, where he opened a restaurant. He sold candy as a sideline, with his oldest son William hawking the confections so successfully he was known around town as "Candy Boy." Legend has it that one day a peddler stopped in the restaurant, and not having the money for a meal, swapped a cough drop recipe for some food.

Whatever the origins, by 1852 James Smith & Sons Compound of Wild Cherry Cough Candy was on the market "for the Cure of Coughs, Colds, Hoarseness, Sore Throats, Whooping Cough, and Asthma." The claims were later toned down, but if there was any-place that needed such a remedy, it was the bitter, windswept Hudson Valley.

James Smith died in 1866 and the Smith brothers, William and Andrew, inherited the business. The next generation concentrated more on the cough drops than the restaurant. They converted a barn on the edge of town into the first cough drop factory, and sold their Smith Brothers cough medicine in glass countertop jars.

To discourage counterfeiters, the brothers molded the initials "SB" on each drop—and began advertising the fact. To further thwart imitators they developed a trademark based on their own bearded visages. To announce their government protection they printed the word "TRADEMARK" on the label where it was divided; the "TRADE" by chance appearing under William's picture and the "MARK" resting under Andrew. The labels were pasted on the glass jars.

In 1877 the Smiths produced one of the first "factory-filled" consumer products by selling their black licorice and cherry cough drops in small packages—each adorned by Trade and Mark. In their lifetime, William and Andrew Smith saw production of their cough drops soar from five pounds a day to five tons. The business would remain in family hands until 1963, but the only Smiths anyone ever knew were Trade and Mark.

Upjohn

In the late 1880s, pills prescribed by doctors were so hard a hammer couldn't crack their protective shells. Such pills not only did not dissolve in the stomach; they were often passed by the patient without any medicinal benefit whatsoever.

In 1885, thirty-two-year old Dr. William Erastus Upjohn patented a tedious process which would revolutionize the drug industry. Dr. Upjohn's new "friable" pill crumpled under the pressure of a thumb. The patent didn't reveal Upjohn's process, which remained secret for decades.

Upjohn, a graduate of the University of Michigan, had been practicing medicine in rural Hastings, Michigan for a decade when he introduced his friable pill. In 1886 he formed the Upjohn Pill and Granule Company in Kalamazoo with his brother Henry. Henry died a year later of typhoid fever, but two other brothers, Frederick Lawrence and James Townley, soon joined the business.

Upjohn's first price list featured 186 pill formulas. He was a tireless promoter of his products. He developed the graphic image of a thumb crushing a pill, which became a widely-recognized trademark. He appeared at the 1893 Chicago World's Fair handing out souvenirs at his exhibit in front of an enormous bottle filled with colored pills. By 1900 Upjohn was selling two thousand items.

By that time medicine in tablet form, even more digestible than Upjohn's pills, began to appear. Upjohn formed a Tablet Department and sought a new company star to replace the friable pill. Company chemists developed a tasteless laxative they called "Phenolax." Upjohn suggested Phenolax would work better as a flavored tablet, and in 1908 the pink, mint-flavored laxative hit the market. By 1914 the company was selling a hundred million Phenolax tablets a year.

Squabbles among the brothers led W. E. Upjohn to buy out his brothers in 1910 with money borrowed from banks. For several years, despite the phenomenal success of Phenolax, Upjohn scrambled to meet his obligations. In 1913 he began the evolution into a research-based pharmaceutical firm with the hiring of Dr. Frederick W. Heyl from the University of Wyoming. The first product from the research team was an oral digitalis in 1919, quickly followed by Citrocarbonate, a pleasant acid alkalizer, and Characol, a cherry flavor cough syrup.

Upjohn turned over most of the daily operations of the business to others in the 1920s. He spent most of his time in his later business years guaranteeing a family successor in the pharmaceutical firm. His son briefly became president, but died of an embolism in 1928. Eventually an Upjohn nephew took over the company.

An avid gardener, Upjohn grew 650 varieties of peonies at his Kalamazoo estate and authored a book on flowers. He shortened the workday at the Upjohn Company in the summers, partly so employees could water lawns and tend home gardens.

To enhance the increased leisure time of his employees, Upjohn donated funds for the Milham Park Municipal Golf Course. He built a seventeen-acre park and was instrumental in the local cultural and religious community. He served in Kalamazoo city politics for a time, and in 1926 organized the W. E. Upjohn Civic Trust.

During the Depression, Upjohn bought twelve hundred acres to be converted into a farm where the jobless could work individual farm plots. In 1932, after a late autumn visit to Upjohn Richland Farms, he came down with a chest cold which rapidly progressed to pneumonia. He died soon after at the age of seventy-nine. "Hearts and flags of the city were at half-mast," reported the newspapers as Kalamazoo mourned its "first citizen."

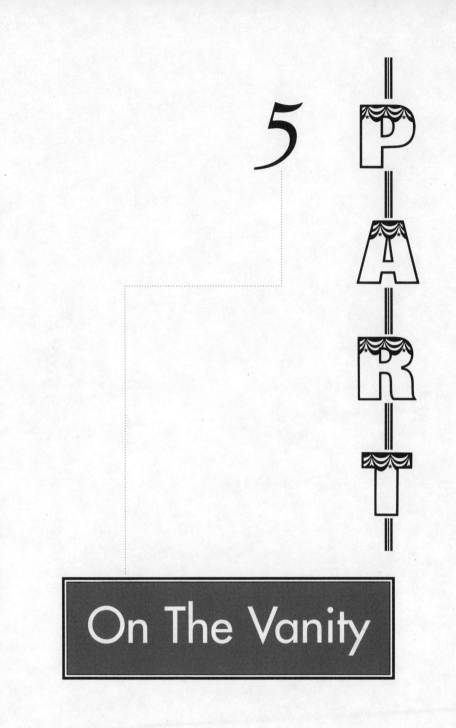

5

PART

On The Vanity

Chanel

Coco Chanel was ready to introduce a new perfume, an unorthodox scent created by a chemist on the Riveria. A fortune teller had once told her that five was her lucky number, so she called her fragrance simply Chanel No. 5. It made Coco Chanel a millionaire many times over.

But perfume, although it made her famous across the world, was only a sidelight for Chanel. Her influential fashions freed twentieth century women from rigid bone corsets with an uncluttered, casual look. Among her innovations were jersey dresses, trenchcoats, turtleneck sweaters, bellbottom trousers, bobbed hair, sailor suits, and costume jewelry.

Chanel's life, much of which couldn't be distinguished from fiction, was appropriately turned into a Broadway musical in 1969, thirteen months before her death. When asked what she thought of Katharine Hepburn—then sixty—in the starring role, Chanel, who was herself eighty-six, replied scathingly, "She's too old."

Chanel was born in a dour mountainous region of southern France in 1883. She was baptized Gabrielle Bonheur—Gabrielle Happiness. Her mother died of tuberculosis when she was six and her father abandoned his four daughters. Coco was sent to live with strict aunts, where she helped raise horses to sell to the French army.

Before her sixteenth birthday, Coco escaped her aunts by persuading a young cavalry officer to take her away. Chanel became swept up in a world of high society when her French officer turned

out to be an heir to an industrial fortune. The two were inseparable for the next ten years.

By 1911, Chanel was ready to make her own mark on society.
She started selling hats in a haphazard fashion from a tiny Parisian
shop. Over the next few years, she became a force in the fashion
world by disdaining the elaborate and grotesque hats that were in
fashion for simple and attractive hats. She began to impress
wealthy and influential women with her originality in her shop at
31 rue Cambon.

"Women are not flowers; why should they want to smell like
flowers?" she commented when introducing Chanel No. 5. Women
responded, and she eventually would have twenty-four hundred
people in her workrooms. Women around the world knew her name.

It was a tossup as to what caused more of a sensation in the
1920s: Chanel's fashion creations or her social life. One winter she
came back from Cannes with bronzed skin and other women, who
had always considered paleness the mark of a lady, began to seek
tans. When Chanel had her expensive jewelry copied so she could
wear it without being stared at, costume jewelry was born. When
Chanel went to Venice she outfitted herself in comfortable slacks
that bulged slightly at the bottom and the fashion world went wild
for bellbottoms.

She kept a small suite at the swank Ritz hotel. One night some
gas in her hot water heater exploded, spraying her with soot. An
impatient woman, Chanel cut her long black hair so there would
be less to shampoo. Later that night when she appeared at the
opera, she set off an immediate fashion craze.

In the late thirties the fashion world deserted Chanel for other
designers and when World War II broke out Chanel shut her cou-
ture house at 31 rue Cambon. She spent time at the Ritz and in
Switzerland as she receded from public view for fifteen years.
Chanel returned, fiery as ever, on February 5, 1954, showing a heavy
navy jersey and a sailor hat. Critics were lukewarm but women
bought it, and the suit evolved year after year with increasing success.

The suit was a hallmark of Chanel design. Although she
dressed the world's most famous women and reveled in luxury herself, she was the constant democratizer of fashion. She claimed
that her most important task was to make women look young.
"Then," she said, "their outlook on life changes. They feel more
joyous."

lizabeth Arden

When Elizabeth Arden died in 1966, estimates of her age ranged from eighty-one to eighty-eight. She had built an industry based entirely on illusion, and the mother of the beauty treatment business never missed an opportunity to create a similar aura around her own life.

Elizabeth Arden was born Florence Nightengale Graham in Ontario, Canada, the daughter of a Scotch-English teamster. For the first thirty years, she toiled in a succession of mundane jobs around Toronto, the last as an office assistant to a dentist. In 1908 she came to New York as a treatment girl in a salon, working for tips.

She learned massage and studied elementary formulas for cosmetics. In a few years, Graham was ready for her own salon. Searching for a more glamorous name, it is said she selected "Arden" from a favorite Victorian novel, although there is nothing in her background to suggest she would have favored such literature.

She surely took "Elizabeth" from a mentor for its mellifluous sound. She was soon to steal more than her name. Headstrong and indulgent of no opinion other than her own, Arden resolutely built her business. A second salon quickly opened and others were planned.

When chemists told her that a fluffy face cream—"like whipped cream"—was an impossibility, she pressed the subject until Cream Amoretta was ready for market in 1914. It became the basis of her cosmetics fortune. Creating cosmetics was an Arden specialty, and she tried them all on herself. Hers was the final decision on every aspect of the business—the color of the package (pink was a trademark), the mood of the advertisement, the naming of the perfume.

Arden entered the treatment business at the ideal time—respectable American women were beginning to use rouge and lipstick, previously only the accoutrements of harlots. She traveled to dozens of salons in Europe to expand her product line. She was a pioneer of advertising beauty products in fashion magazines and newspapers.

Arden at first used sybaritic salons to introduce her beauty products, but by 1915 she began to realize that bulk sales were where her future profits lay. She opened a wholesale department to promote her line in department stores and drug stores. More than three hundred scented Elizabeth Arden cosmetics were available around the world.

In a highly competitive follow-the-leader industry, Arden was an innovator. In 1934 she transformed her Maine Chance Farm in Mount Vernon, Maine into a beauty retreat for women. At the height of the Depression, women doled out $750 a week for exercise, beauty treatments and general pampering. A second Maine Chance Farm opened in Phoenix in 1947.

Mixing with her prominent clientele, Arden was introduced to horse racing. She developed an intense passion for racehorses, which she often selected for their handsome looks alone. She directed her trainers to forego traditional rubbing liniment for Elizabeth Arden skin tonic. Her unconventional methods helped; in 1947 her stable produced the Kentucky Derby winner, Jet Pilot.

There was little time in Elizabeth Arden's life aside from her rich patrons and fast horses. Two emotionless marriages ended in divorce. Childless, the business she created and controlled with consummate skill was left in disarray by her passing. After her death her estate was saddled with thirty-seven million dollars in taxes.

Estée Lauder

Josephine Esther Mentzer was born in Queens, the youngest child of Hungarian immigrants. Her father had led a privileged life in his homeland, but possessed few marketable skills in early twentieth century America. He opened a small hardware store, above which the family lived. At school a teacher decided to "add a little Romantic French" to her harsh-sounding name and called her Estée Mentzer.

One day her Uncle John Schotz came to New York to visit. He was a skin specialist and set up a makeshift lab in the basement. Estée would watch with fascination as he mixed his secret magic cream potions that made her face feel "like spun silk." Soon she was creating her own creams and testing them on high school friends.

Estée Mentzer married Joseph Lauter in 1930, while she was in her early twenties. His name had been "Lauder" in Austria but was mangled by immigration officials. The couple changed it back. After her marriage, Estée spent every spare moment cooking up "little pots of cream for faces" which she sold to local beauty shops.

She began giving free demonstrations at resort hotels in the summer and wealthy homes in the winter. Soon she was running a beauty concession on the fashionable Upper East Side. As her social contacts expanded, so did her business. Estée's singleminded approach to business strained her marriage, and the couple divorced in 1939. Estée Lauder went to Miami Beach to sell cream to vacationers.

An illness to their eldest son reunited the Lauders, who remarried in 1942 and began selling the creams as a family business. In 1946 Estée Lauder, Inc. was formed with Joseph and Estée Lauder as the only employees and a line of four basic skin care products. Estée finally convinced Saks Fifth Avenue to place a big order. They converted a restaurant into a factory, boiling and sterilizing the creams on the old stoves, and managed to fill the orders. The creams sold out in two days.

Other major cosmetic giants sold in drugstores and beauty salons where turnover was high. The Lauders didn't have a sales force, so they sold exclusively to department stores, giving the Estée Lauder line a status. She traveled the country in the late 1940s and early 1950s promoting her cosmetics while her husband managed the plant.

At every store she selected and trained the sales staff herself. These were the people who would be walking ads for her products.

Customers always received small samples with every Estée Lauder purchase, a trademark that would be widely copied. By 1953, Estée Lauder counters were in prestigious stores across the country.

She now introduced her first fragrance, which she named Youth Dew. Up to that time, perfume was a classic gift for men to give to women. Lauder called her fragrance Youth Dew so women would buy it themselves. Priced at $8.95, Youth Dew soon accounted for 80 percent of Lauder's business at Saks and was still selling well thirty years later.

In 1967, Lauder pioneered men's toiletries with Aramis, and was quickly the leader in mens' trade. She turned over a great deal of the operations to her son Leonard in 1973, but continued to develop new scents, building on her reputation as "one of the best noses in the business."

Lauder turned to the social whirl with royalty and celebrities as she promoted herself and her products through the society pages. Sales grew to over one billion dollars. By 1993, more than one of every three department store cosmetics and fragrances were Estée Lauder products.

Jergens

Cold creams and lotions have been around since the second century, but it took a lumberjack to bring them onto American vanities. Andrew Jergens came to the United States from the Netherlands and by the time he was twenty, in 1880, he had saved an investable sum of five thousand dollars from his work as a lumberjack.

He bought into a one-kettle soap business in Cincinnati, where he and his new partners manufactured a fragrant toilet soap. In

1894 he brought his brothers Herman and Al into Andrew Jergens & Company. In 1901 Jergens acquired the product that made him a household name, although he had no idea he was buying it.

Jergens bought the Robert Eastman Company, hoping to add its line of perfumes to its product mix. Along with the sale came Charles Conover, an Eastman chemist who had developed a smooth white lotion that reached the marketplace as "Jergens Benzoin And Almond Lotion Compound." The luxurious lotion, whose recipe was kept secret for more than fifty years, was soon Jergens's best seller, despite no advertising beyond word of mouth.

When national magazine advertising began in the 1920s, Jergens began an ascent to national prominence. In the radio age Jergens sponsored the popular Walter Winchell show for sixteen years, and his familiar sendoff—"with lotions of love"—elevated Jergens to a name synonymous with lotion.

Kimberly-Clarke

In 1872, four young men between the ages of twenty-eight and thirty-five invested seventy-five hundred dollars each to manufacture paper in Neenah, Wisconsin. They were three hundred miles west of the nearest important paper mill, and they figured they could become the primary supplier to the growing western newspaper market. They selected Neenah for its location next to the fast-flowing Fox River, and set out to make quality printing paper.

From the beginning expansion was always a priority. All earnings were ploughed back into the business. In 1874 the partners bought out the only local mill. John A. Kimberly and Charles B. Clarke handled the management of the operation, and Frank C.

Shattuck and Havilah Babcock supervised merchandising and milling. The business prospered.

At the time linen rags, straw, and jute were the chief sources of supply for paper mills. In the 1880s wood pulp supplanted the traditional sources, and the company moved into the tree business. New technologies generated specialty papers as papermaking became a chemical process.

By 1906 John Kimberly was the only remaining partner, and he incorporated the Kimberly-Clarke Corporation. With cotton in short supply, company technicians developed Cellucotton—a fluffy, absorbent material used in surgical hospitals in World War I. After the war, Kimberly sought a way to reduce his burgeoning inventories for Cellucotton.

First came Kotex, a new feminine napkin. In 1921 Kimberly-Clarke introduced Kleenex Cleansing Tissues as a substitute for the unsightly cold cream towel. A glamourous magazine campaign showing Hollywood and Broadway stars removing makeup with the new paper tissue kick-started sales. But unexpectedly consumers wrote the company praising the tissue as a disposable handkerchief.

At his death in 1928, still the president at the age of ninety, John Kimberly and his management were still undecided how to best promote their popular product. He would not live to see Kleenex pass from a Kimberly-Clarke product into common use and the dictionary.

Mary Kay

Mary Kay Ash was a victim of the worst kind of sexism. She would take men out in the field, train them expertly, and return to the office to find her trainees become her supervisors—at twice the salary. "They have families to support," she was told. But *she* had a family to support too.

Mary Kay Wagner had married fresh out of a Texas high school when she was eighteen. Ben Rogers was the "Elvis Presley of Houston," she liked to say. He played guitar and sang for the Hawaiian Strummers. They were married for eight years with three kids when Ben was drafted into the army in World War II. He never came home.

Mary Kay had been alone before. Back in the early 1920s when she was seven, her father came down with tuberculosis and could no longer work. Her mother put in long hours in a café and instilled self-reliance in little Mary Kay, who took care of her father and the family home. Now she filed for divorce and got a job as a part-time secretary.

To get more income she joined Stanley Home Products, giving house party demonstrations. She enjoyed the work and talking to the people, but nobody seemed to be buying much. What was she doing wrong?

She borrowed twelve dollars for round trip train fare and three days in a hotel for the company's annual sales convention in Dallas. She saw the "Queen of Sales" crowned and accept a lovely alligator bag as a reward. Mary Kay was hooked. She would be "Queen of Sales" next year, she promised herself. And she was. But her gift was an underwater flashlight. She vowed that if she were ever in the same position, she would give away prizes that truly motivated. She left Stanley in 1953 for a better job at World Gift Company.

Mary Kay rose rapidly through the company to become national training director. She developed business in forty-three states for the Dallas-based firm but chafed at her treatment in the male-dominated company. Still, she was making $25,000 a year, a good living even if it should have been better.

In 1963 an efficiency expert warned World Gift that Mary Kay's power in the hierarchy was too great. This was too much. Rather than accept a reassignment she retired. Remarried by this time, she went home to become a housewife and write a book on selling for women. As she listed her ideas she decided to start her own selling business.

Her product came from a home demonstration for Stanley ten years earlier. She had noticed that all the women at this party had flawless skin. It turned out one of the ladies was a cosmetologist who made skin creams from material similar to that used to tan hides. Mary Kay became a regular customer, and when the cosmetologist died in 1961 she bought the formula from the woman's heirs, not as an investment but to assure herself a continued supply of the face cream.

She took five thousand dollars of her own money and made plans to open a small boutique. But just before the opening her husband died of a heart attack. Aside from her personal grief, Mary Kay also was left without a business partner. She persuaded her twenty-year old son Richard to take a 50 percent pay cut from selling insurance and manage her business while Mary Kay trained the sales force. Mary Kay Cosmetics formed on September 13, 1963.

She took the home party technique from Stanley and called them "beauty shows." She called her sales people "consultants" and paid the highest commission in the direct sales field—50 percent. Most importantly, she concentrated her line in skin care products, where Avon, her major competitor, would be weakest.

Mary Kay innovated the concept of no fixed territories; if a woman's husband was transferred she could sell wherever she went. This fostered not competition—as would be expected—but a cooperative attitude among the consultants. The real competition was for Mary Kay bonuses.

Her revival-meeting-style annual convention in Dallas became legendary. Over four days of product introduction, training, and most importantly, recognition, Mary Kay could give away scores of coats, trips, jewelry, and of course, trademark pink Cadillacs. "Women *need* praise," she said, "and so I praise them. If I criticize I sandwich it between layers of praise."

Her sales force is among the most motivated anywhere, although the average consultant makes only about two thousand dollars a year in her part-time work. The company motto remains: "God first, family second, career third."

Mary Kay Ash borrowed ideas from other direct selling companies before her. Her true legacy was in creating a successful company for women, by women.

ax Factor

The problem was that faces would show up red or green; they reflected costume colors. The technology for color films was developed in 1937 but the makeup used in Hollywood for black-and-white films simply wasn't working. It was Max Factor, who was responsible for every other makeup innovation in Hollywood up to that time, who came up with the solution.

Max Factor was born in Russia in 1877. He became an apprentice to a wigmaker when he was fourteen, and by the time he was twenty young Factor was running his own makeup and hair goods shop in his hometown of Lodz. Business was good, good enough that in 1904 Factor brought his wife and three children to St. Louis where, with a partner, he took a booth at the St. Louis World's Fair.

Within a year his partner had pilfered most of the profits, but Factor was able to raise money for another makeup, perfume and hair-products shop in downtown St. Louis. All the while, he was hearing tales of the new motion picture industry growing in Los Angeles. At the time no cosmetics manufacturer dominated the film business, and in 1908 Max Factor headed to the frontier town of Hollywood, California.

The first Max Factor studio was in the Pantages Theater. At first he served as West Coast agent for other cosmetics firms while formulating and testing his own theatrical makeup. In 1914 he perfected the first makeup designed for movie use, and leading actors and actresses began seeking him out for advice on how to avoid looking ghastly white on the silver screen.

Factor's work with the movie industry led to such innovations as false eyelashes, the eyebrow pencil and a powder brush. In the 1920s Factor introduced "color harmony" in the movies. For the first time, makeup items were created to harmonize with hair, eyes, and skins of blondes, brownettes (a Max Factor term), brunettes, and redheads.

At first his products were used only in the movies, but actresses soon began to use the makeup off-screen as well. Eventually non-actresses adopted the product, and in 1927 "Color Harmony Make-up" was made available to everyday women. That same year talking movies were introduced with highly sensitive film and hot set lighting. A whole new makeup was required, and Max Factor's Panchromatic Make-up earned him a special award from the Academy of Motion Picture Arts and Sciences.

In 1929, after two decades of work in Hollywood, Factor decided to enter the general cosmetics world. It was the ideal base from which to nurture an international empire. Factor's clients were the most famous and glamorous people in the world. Jean Harlow, Claudette Colbert, Ginger Rogers, and others insisted that they be made up for the camera by Max Factor and no one else. And Factor made certain the world knew about it.

He staged lavish publicity extravaganzas which were well-reported in newspapers and movie reels around the world. Women everywhere wanted to look like their favorite movie actresses. Within twenty years Max Factor would be the leading American cosmetics company in the international market.

With the advent of color films, Factor once again needed to develop a suitable theatrical makeup. He formulated "pancake makeup" which restored flesh to actors' faces and in 1938 the first color movies made their appearance. The new pancake formula was introduced to the public with full-page color advertisements in *Vogue*. Within months there were sixty-five different imitations of Max Factor Pancake, but Max Factor outsold all sixty-five combined.

It was Max Factor's final contribution to the movie industry. He died in 1938, having ushered movie stars from wan, chalky black-and-white films through sound and finally into full color.

ond's

Pond's Cold Cream has been the leading facial cleanser in America for almost a hundred years, one of the longest runs of commercial success for any product. Unfortunately for its discoverer, his career was not nearly so long.

Theron T. Pond worked as a chemist in Utica, New York, selling drugs from his apothecary shop. In his spare time he worked in a small lab in the back of the store with an extract he obtained from the bark of a witch hazel shrub, known to alleviate pain from wounds. After distilling the extract, he combined it with pure grain alcohol and aged it in oaken barrels for up to five years.

Pond's Extract drew raves from local physicians, and in 1849 he formed the T. T. Pond Company with two partners from Utica. By 1852 illness forced Pond to sell all interests to his partners and he died shortly afterwards, never to profit from the company that bore his name.

cott

As America charged into the twentieth century, the standard of living was rising rapidly. Indoor plumbing, for over a hundred years reserved for royalty and the rich, was becoming within the reach of home owners and hotels. As outhouses gave way to "the smallest room in the house," the Scott Paper Company saw an obvious need to produce a product known as "toilet tissue."

Toilet paper had been around since pre-Civil War times in packages of individual sheets. The product never caught on. People couldn't understand why they would want to waste scarce clean paper when out-of-date catalogues and yesterday's newspapers could get the job done—and supply ample reading material.

Scott's tissue paper came in small rolls, wrapped in plain brown paper. It was the ideal product at the right time. But there was a problem. The strict Victorian mores of the day proscribed overt advertising of such an unmentionable product as toilet tissue.

The fledgling business took a different tack. They purchased "parent rolls" of paper, which they converted into perforated rolls of toilet paper, and sold to independent merchants under private labels. At the peak of its private label venture Scott produced more than two thousand different brands for its customers. Still nobody knew the Scott name.

E. Irvin and Clarence Scott had come from Saratoga County, New York to Philadelphia, where they pooled their meager resources to form the Scott Paper Company in 1879. The original business of Scott was "coarse" paper goods, including such items as bags and wrapping paper.

Anonymously, they built their business until Arthur Hoyt Scott, Irvin's son, urged the senior partners to concentrate on a few of its own name brands. His philosophy was to make only a few high quality products, sell them at as low a cost as possible, and keep a high profile with advertising. In 1902, Scott Paper made its first acquisition, buying the Waldorf trademark from one of its customers. Waldorf is still in distribution today, the nation's oldest name-brand toilet tissue.

Legend has it that the paper towel joined the Scott Paper team in 1907 from the desire of a Philadelphia schoolteacher to replace an unsanitary cloth towel used daily by her students. One roll of paper arrived from their supplier excessively heavy and wrinkled. The roll was rejected for toilet tissue and scheduled to be sent back to the mill. A member of the Scott family rescued the roll, suggesting it be perforated into small towel-sized sheets.

Sani-Towel debuted in 1907 as the first disposable "paper towel." Hotels, restaurants and railroad stations were the only customers for years. Housewives were more interested in economics than convenience, and continued to wash their cloth towels. In 1931 Sani-Towel became ScotTowels; a roll of two hundred sheets retailed for a quarter. The paper towel was on its way to becoming an American household staple.

By that time the Scott brothers had faded from their leadership positions. Rising demand for their disposable paper products had forced the innovation of new papermaking methods. The Scotts had built the largest and most efficient tissue manufacturer in the world.

6

PART

In The Yard

Burpee

Nowhere is a seller's reputation of more paramount importance than in the seed business. To the consumer, an ill-bred seed looks exactly like the blue-ribbon winner. Not until it actually grows months later will the buyer know if he has made a good bargain.

Washington Atlee Burpee never forgot the need to win his customer's trust. He wrote relentlessly in his catalogs about the need for a seed merchant's honesty. At times he even argued against the selling of his own seeds.

At the turn of the century a craze swept America for growing ginseng root to sell to the Chinese trade. Burpee detested such get-rich-quick plotting, and angrily fired off a missive in his 1904 catalog admonishing his readers about ginseng root. The plant was devilishly difficult to grow, he wrote, and if it was that easy to make millions of dollars selling ginseng root he would be doing it. But if his customers still wanted to buy ginseng root seed—now knowing the truth—he could sell it in good conscience.

Burpee came to seeds from his days as a poultryman. He became an avian specialist by the age of fourteen, and in 1874, when he was ready to begin the study of medicine at the University of Pennsylvania, Burpee was actively selling and exhibiting fancy breeds of chickens, geese, turkeys, and pigeons. He had already published the first of many authoritative information bulletins, "The Pigeon Loft, How To Furnish and Manage It."

Burpee withdrew from the University of Pennsylvania medical program after one year because he couldn't stand the suffering of patients. In 1875 he offered a line of fowls and livestock by mail order in the sixteen-page "W. Atlee Burpee's Catalogue of High Class Land and Water Fowls." Seeds were probably first offered as feed for birds. Almost immediately he issued a separate seed catalog he called "Burpee's Farm Annual."

Burpee offered a dollar's worth of vegetable seeds for twenty-five cents, and pushed his introductory deal by offering a twenty-two dollar sewing machine to anyone buying three hundred twenty-five-boxes. But for the most part he sold his seeds from his Philadelphia area home at premium prices.

Gardens were much more an integral part of American life in the late 1800s than they are today. Not only food and beauty sprouted in the family garden. Garden plants provided medicines, cosmetics, useful household items, and even fuel.

Burpee loved seeds and assumed his customers were waiting breathlessly for his new pronouncements. He put his personal seed beliefs on special pink pages in the front of his catalogs. It was a chatty catalog, often written in flowery longhand, that educated and excited the reader.

He further informed the public with information bulletins. In the early days he wrote the bulletins himself, but by the 1880s the seed business had grown so large he had others write the educational pamphlets by offering cash prizes for essay contests. Some were quite extensive: "How and What to Grow in a Kitchen Garden of One Acre" ran 198 pages.

Burpee also sponsored prizes for growing contests and naming new plant varieties grown on his Fordhook Farm in Doylestown, Pennsylvania, north of Philadelphia. He conducted trials on thousands of vegetables and flowers at Fordhook. Plant breeding was of supreme importance to Burpee, who was always seeking the ultimate seed.

In 1905 Burpee received a letter from a California lima bean grower stating he had discovered two new bush lima beans on his property that were so excellent that he was auctioning them to the nation's seedsmen. Burpee paid a thousand dollars for each seed. When he had grown enough to sell bush lima seeds in 1907, Burpee spent six pages glorifying the seed in his catalog.

The bush lima seeds were headliners in Burpee catalogs for decades. Golden Bantam corn, introduced by Burpee in 1912, remains a prized ear of corn. Iceberg lettuce is a produce staple.

Perhaps W. A. Burpee's most enduring success was Burpee's Surehead cabbage which was found growing in Europe and first sold in 1877.

W. A. Burpee was exceedingly conservative in his personal habits. He refused both electric lights and telephones at his Fordhook Farms home for years. He did not own a car until a year before his death in 1915, when a liver ailment claimed the world's largest seed merchant at the age of fifty-eight.

After his death his family, who continued the business, perpetrated a campaign to name the American marigold, Burpee's favorite, as the country's national flower. Their efforts failed, and America continued without an honored blossom until Ronald Reagan elevated the rose to national flower in 1986.

Coleman

"What the average man needs is not a gasoline buggy or a good nickel cigar but light to read and work by." Especially a man with bad eyes like William Coffin Coleman, who spoke those words to explain the motivation behind the Coleman lantern.

Coleman was the son of schoolteachers who migrated west from New England in 1871, the year after his birth. Despite having no money, Coleman entered the University of Kansas to study law. He survived on canned tomatoes, brown sugar, and day-old bread but his funds ran out when Coleman was still one year short of his law degree.

He started selling typewriters and began making calls in the dusty coal town of Brockton, Alabama. As he walked down the board sidewalks, he saw a brilliant light in a drugstore window, a glow so bright that even he, with his bad eyes, could read comfortably.

The illumination was not from Mr. Edison's marvelous new invention, but emanated instead from a gasoline-powered flame.

Coleman thought that this new light could replace smoky oil lights and flickering gas lights on America's farms, western towns, and everywhere electricity had not yet reached. He invested all his money buying samples of the new Efficient Company lamp which burned gasoline under pressure. He took his new product line to Kingfisher, Oklahoma. It was January 1, 1900.

At the end of his first week, he had sold only two lamps. What was wrong? No one ever believed more vehemently in his product. Asking around, he discovered that months earlier a predecessor had sold dozens of gasoline lamps in town that glowed brightly for a few days and then clogged with uncleanable carbon deposits. Coleman knew his lamp was better, but how to prove it?

He would not sell lamps but light. He would become a one-man utility company. He leased his lamps for one dollar a week. No light, No pay. The Kingfisher merchants couldn't refuse that deal. The lamps were reliable and sales boomed. The Hydro-Carbon Company was born.

He sold a two thousand dollar interest in his business to two brothers-in-law and used the money to purchase the patent rights to the lamp, which he renamed the Coleman Arc Lamp. He moved to Wichita, where in 1905 Coleman Arc Lamps lighted the first night football game under artificial light as Fairmount College ground out a victory.

In 1909 he invented the Coleman table lamp. It was portable and could be carried anywhere. By adding bug screens the lamp could be used outside, and in 1914 the first of over thirty million Coleman gasoline lanterns, usable in any weather, was built. The Coleman Lantern was named an essential product in World War I, and Coleman sold one million to the government so farmers could work around the clock. The Coleman lantern went to the South Pole with Admiral Byrd.

President Roosevelt launched massive rural electrification projects during the Depression, and Coleman's traditional markets disappeared. He took the company into oil heaters and gas floor furnaces, although ventures into home appliances failed. In World War II, Coleman developed a compact stove for field use, and after the war rode the wave of expanding interest in outdoor recreation with insulated coolers and jugs, tents, and sleeping bags.

In 1949 *The Saturday Evening Post* carried an article on William Coleman under the headline, "The Company That Should Have Gone Broke." But Coleman had always shown an innate ability to cope with change. At the time of his death in 1957, his company was the leading manufacturer of camping products and a major supplier to the mobile home industry.

John Deere

The life expectancy of a blacksmith shop in the early nineteenth century was roughly akin to that of a wagon wheel shouldering a two-ton load through a rutted mountain pass. If the cinders from the iron filings didn't spark a fire, the intense heat from the forge constantly jeopardized the wooden structure.

In 1831, twenty-seven-year old John Deere realized a lifelong dream when he opened his own blacksmith shop in Leicester Four Corners, Vermont. Deere had begun apprenticing as a blacksmith ten years earlier for thirty dollars a year. By 1825 he was an experienced journeyman with a reputation across the countryside for his fine-tined pitchforks.

Deere's quality work attracted an investor, Jay Wright, who helped set him up in his own shop. But shortly after he opened for business the small shop burned to the ground. He started again and again the shop burned. Frustrated, Deere gave up and took a job repairing iron parts of stagecoaches.

When Deere again tried to start a blacksmith shop, Wright filed a writ to recover money lost in the original venture. Thus stymied in business, Deere left Vermont in November 1836, leaving his family behind in Rutland.

Deere left with only a few tools and $73.73, making his way West by canal boat and stage. He headed for Grand Detour, Illinois, where other Vermonters had settled by an odd bend in the Rock River. The prairie land here was rich and the water power plentiful.

It was hard to figure that in less than one year, from these unpromising beginnings, the young Vermont blacksmith would create the foundations of the largest agricultural machinery manufacturer in the world.

In Illinois Deere found his smithing skills immediately in demand, and he was able to rent some land and erect a small shop. He was kept busy seven days a week hammering, welding, casting, and assembling farm implements. When time allowed, he peddled some of his handmade goods to merchants.

The prairie soil was rich, certainly, but it did not release its bounty willingly. Farmers using cast iron plows had to carry paddles and stop every few yards to wipe the blades clean of the black, sticky soil. Deere reckoned that a steel plow might help the situation.

In 1837 he fashioned a plow that would "scour" the soil from a discarded sawblade. Deere polished the surface with thousands of cutting strokes. It did the job perfectly. The plow literally "sang" as it sliced through the black gumbo soil. The next year Deere quit general blacksmithing and started making plows exclusively. He turned out ten that first year, and made enough profit to construct a house and send for his family.

After that Deere could sell all the plows he could make: forty in 1840, seventy-five in 1841 and one hundred in 1842. By 1843 Deere had settled his debts in Vermont and began buying steel directly from England. By now there were many steel plow manufacturers. Deere expanded his business with a relentless devotion to quality. "I will not put my name on a plow that does not have in it the best that is in me," he vowed.

In 1846 Deere despaired of Grand Detour's future with regard to transportation and shifted his factory to Moline, Illinois. He took on partners, and for the first time steel was made for the specifications of his plows. Deere, Tate & Gould manufactured over two thousand plows a year.

The partnership did not thrive. Tate wanted standardized

plows; Deere wanted to improve constantly. The partnership dissolved in 1852. Deere did not suffer, however. The years before the Civil War were halcyon years of innovation for John Deere & Co.

After the War, Deere, now in his sixties, sold off most of his holdings in his company, retaining a quarter share. He farmed around Moline and served as mayor for a year in 1873, keeping order between the increasingly hostile Prohibitionists and anti-temperance factions. Deere died in 1886 at the age of eighty-two, still renowned as the creator of the "plow that broke the prairies."

cott's

In 1868 the home lawn was regarded merely as ground cover, not a thing of beauty. Grass was used to keep down dust and protect children and horses from mud. Quality was of no concern. Each fall stable manure laden with undigested weed seeds was spread through neighborhoods. Grass, if manicured at all, was groomed by the sharp teeth of sheep.

Orlando Mumford Scott harbored a white-hot hatred of weeds. To him, weeds were the sin of neglect. He despised the weeds that grew on his Marysville, Ohio farm and set out to develop an inexpensive weed-free grass seed. But if weedy lawns weren't enough for Scott to overcome, he had to change the attitudes of homeowners. Many Americans *liked* the look of their weedy, uncut natural lawns.

Scott, who operated the Union County elevator after his discharge from the Union Army, considered farmers too complacent. He recognized the costly toll extracted by weeds, even if farmers didn't. Weeds represented the biggest cost in farming by far—

much greater than the cost of a good seed. Weedy seed, no matter how cheap, was expensive in terms of extra work and time.

Working in a period before state and federal regulations when mediocrity had no limitations, Scott waged a one-man war against weeds. Clean, high quality seed was his battle cry. With care in selection and skillful cleaning, Scott produced nearly weed-free seed. Scott's Farm Seeds were 99.91 percent weed free.

In the 1880s, hand-pushed rotary mowers began appearing in American stores. Homeowners started coming around to the white-bearded Ohio seed merchant's way of thinking with regard to manicured lawns. Slowly, the lush green lawn gained stature as a luxury item.

With his sons Dwight and Hubert, Scott started a mail order business for his weed-free seeds in 1906. Beautifully produced shelter magazines like *House Beautiful* and *Better Homes and Gardens* began displaying luxuriant lawns. Scott's quality seeds blended from around the world were the best way to make a new yard look like the magazines.

In 1916, without solicitation, Scott received an order for five thousand pounds of seed from Brentwood in the Pines Golf Club on Long Island, opening this market to the company. Five years later, one in five golf courses used Scott seed. Then the Scotts sold grass seed to club members for their home lawns.

The Scott's complete line of lawn care products began with the introduction of Turf Builder, the first fertilizer specifically for grass in 1928. O. M. Scott had lived long enough to see the lawn gain status on par with the automobile.

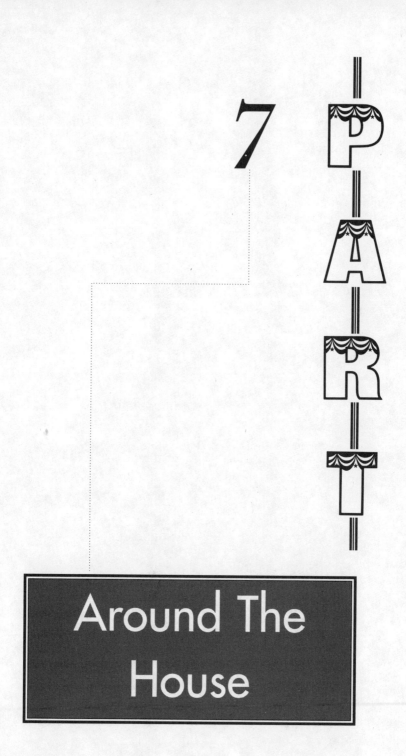

7 PART

Around The House

ndersen

In 1870, sixteen-year old Hans Andersen arrived in Portland, Maine to start a new life. Bringing with him his only possessions—a set of drafting tools and a diploma from night school in Copenhagen—his goal was to get to the Midwest. Heading west, he purposely sought work from employers who did not speak his native language so he would have to learn English. Andersen learned his first three English words while helping a team of field hands clear tree stumps: "All together boys."

He ended up in Spring Valley, Minnesota, and by his early twenties, he began operating a lumber yard. Shortly thereafter, he was hired by the largest sawmill in LaCrosse, Wisconsin to dispose of a huge surplus of lumber that was the result of low demand during the Depression of the 1880s. Hans harbored retail experience that served him well in this endeavor. He was so successful that when the project was complete, he was able to buy his own sawmill in St. Cloud, Minnesota.

In 1886 Andersen learned of another major lumber surplus—about one million board feet—just south of a town, called Hudson, Wisconsin. He began managing the sawmill in town and brought along some of his best men from St. Cloud. But when fall came, the mill's owner insisted these laborers be laid off during the slow winter months. Andersen refused and resigned on the spot. He started his own retail lumber yard and hired the men to work for him.

At the time, there existed no accurate window frame on the market. So, the Andersen Lumber Company began to manufacture standardized window frame units made of durable white pine. By standardizing a few basic dimensions, the company gained the advantage of mass production. These window frame units were made with such precision they surpassed the quality of any frame available to home builders at the time of their introduction.

The actual manufacture of window and door frames began in earnest in 1904. By 1912, production reached 132,455 frames. Andersen developed the "two-bundle" method of packaging knocked down window frame units. Eleven sets of both horizontal and vertical members, packaged separately, could be assembled in a variety of combinations that fit together perfectly without cutting or trimming.

In 1913 the Andersen Lumber Company moved into a new 66,362 square-foot facility in what would become Bayport, Minnesota. The next year Andersen died, at the age of sixty, with the family business established as the leading innovator in the window business.

Armstrong

By 1860, twenty-four-year-old Thomas Armstrong had saved up three hundred dollars from his job as a clerk in a Pittsburgh glass factory. He was due to be wed that year, and it seemed a fine stake upon which to start a married life. But instead, Armstrong took the money and invested in a one-room shop run by John D. Glass, who cut out cork bottle stoppers. He did, however, hold onto his day job, stopping by the cork shop in the evenings to cut cork by hand.

Each piece of cork sold by John D. Glass & Co. had to be cut and shaped by hand. It was tedious and slow, and it was equally impossible to deliver cork of uniform quality to customers. In 1862, again with the support of his wife, Armstrong invested a thousand dollars in an unproven machine that cut cork. He quit his clerk's job and jumped into the cork business full-time.

Armstrong now needed to expand his market greatly to recoup such a large investment. Cork was the only way to plug the bottles of the day, more and more of which were containing the new pharmaceuticals and alcoholic beverages that were appearing everywhere on the market. But at the time cork was sold locally, so buyers were able to inspect and choose the cork they wanted. It was a policy of "buyer beware."

Armstrong knew that to ship his cork to distant markets he needed a way to insure its quality. In 1864 John Glass died, and Armstrong brought his brother into the firm as partner. He pioneered brand-name recognition in the cork industry by stamping "Armstrong" on all his bags of cork. The name carried with it a money-back guarantee.

During the Civil War, Armstrong made bottle stoppers for the Union Army. He was singled out for praise for fulfilling contracts at the agreed price with top-grade corks. The favorable publicity and Armstrong's groundwork for national distribution led to a large drug contract after which the company leapt forward.

In 1878 Armstrong stopped buying cork from importers and set up direct purchasing lines with cork suppliers in Spain and around the Mediterranean. By 1890 Armstrong was the world's largest cork manufacturer—with 750 employees, all of whom Thomas Armstrong could address by name.

Into the twentieth century, Armstrong's only raw material was cork. But cork harvesting was a seasonal activity, and the fluctuations in supply led to fluctuations in price and profit for Armstrong. More ominously, there was a growing fervor in America to ban the sale of all alcohol—which would mean the elimination of one of Armstrong's biggest markets.

The product line in the early 1900s included insulation, cork board, gaskets, and flexible coverings. But the year 1908 simultaneously saw a death and birth for the company. Thomas Armstrong died in Pittsburgh, ending the founder's reign and the company's ties to the city.

Meanwhile in Lancaster, Pennsylvania, the Armstrong Cork

Company produced its first linoleum flooring. Linoleum, made from cork flour, mineral fillers, and linseed oil pressed onto a burlap backing at high temperatures, was not a new product. But Armstrong was the first to look past its utilitarian uses and add colors suitable for every room in a house. Future generations of Americans who knew the Armstrong name would never see an Armstrong cork.

Bissell

Is it more improbable that the Bissell name is known at all or that it is still known today? There were carpet sweepers patented two hundred years before Melville Bissell brought his first mechanical sweeper on the market in 1876, and his sweeper itself should have been swept away with the popularization of the vacuum cleaner fifty years later. But people are still "Bisselling," just as they did a century ago.

Melville and Anna Bissell sold crockery in Grand Rapids, Michigan. The fragile glass and china arrived in their shop packed tightly in sawdust-stuffed crates. Invariably the dust would spill on the floors and rugs, irritating the Bissells' allergies. Among the many carpet sweepers available at the time, Melville Bissell selected the "Welcome" to pull the allergy-inflaming dust from his rugs.

A lifelong tinkerer, Bissell found his new carpet sweeper lacking and set out to make a few improvements on his own. His model used floor wheels and angled bristles to fling debris up into a removable compartment. He was quite satisfied with his new invention, and when several patrons inquired about the device, the now clear-eyed Bissell converted the second floor of the crockery store into a carpet sweeper assembly area.

The timing was right in America. New scientific research into the dangers of germs and filth spurred a new devotion to house-cleaning. Still, the spread of the Bissell name from a small crock-ery store in Grand Rapids to every household in America was not achieved without dedicated missionary work, mostly performed by Anna Bissell. While her husband supervised the shop as its capacity grew to thirty machines a day Anna Bissell visited shopkeepers, many over and over, until she was able to win in-store demonstra-tions and displays for the Bissell sweeper across Michigan.

Early product information stressed the mechanical marvels of the Bissell sweeper, touting product innovations to homemakers who just wanted clean rugs. When a young company bookkeeper persuaded the Bissells to emphasize the cases constructed of "golden maple, opulent walnut, and rich mahogany" sales soared. When Bissell introduced a limited edition sweeper crafted from rare ver-milion wood from the jungles of India, the advertising emphasized how the wood was dragged by elephants to the banks of the Ganges River. Bissell sold more sweepers in six weeks than it had the previous year.

In 1883 the Bissells moved into a new five-story brick factory which was gutted by fire almost immediately. Melville Bissell mort-gaged his entire personal fortune, including a team of prized harness horses, to rebuild and meet orders. The rushed production resulted in defective sweepers, which Bissell recalled at an astronomical loss of $35,000. But the revolution in American housecleaning was in full force, women were happily "Bisselling," as carpet sweeping came to be known, and the firm withstood these reversals.

In 1889, Melville Bissell contracted pneumonia and died at the age of forty-five. Anna Bissell assumed the presidency, becoming one of America's first female corporate executives. She had been deeply involved with the company from the start, and now she aggressively set out to make Bissell an international phenomenon, not just an American institution. As the Bissell carpet sweeper col-onized the world it even received a product endorsement from Queen Victoria—and the Bissell rolled across the rugs in Buckingham Palace.

Anna Bissell guided the company into the 1920s, leading the fight against the insurgency of the new electric vacuum cleaners. No longer was the mechanical sweeper the only convenience in the closet. But the Bissell has survived, dodging obsolescence as a quick-cleaning adjunct to its more powerful neighbor for use on small messes.

Black & Decker

The names Black and Decker are instantly recognized by any homeowner who ever built his own workshop. But consider the products that S. Duncan Black and Alonzo G. Decker set out to make when they pooled twelve hundred dollars in 1910: a milk bottle cap machine, a vest-pocket adding machine, machinery for the United States Mint, and a cotton picker.

The two partners opened a small machine shop in Baltimore in 1910 to make these specialty machines. The next year their first ads for the Black & Decker Manufacturing Company began appearing in *Manufacturers Record & Horseless Age*. But the course of their company was soon to change forever.

After much tinkering, Black and Decker patented a pistol-grip drill with a trigger switch and universal motor, and in 1916 introduced the first portable half-inch electric drill. In 1918, the company opened product service centers in Boston and New York, and added sales representatives in Russia, Japan, Europe, and Australia. Sales passed one million dollars.

Black & Decker expanded their line to add other power tools with the unique pistol grip. An electric screwdriver was introduced in 1922, and an electric hammer in 1936. Black & Decker was an innovator in consumer education to teach the public about their new power tools.

They purchased two Pierce Arrow buses to use as classrooms

on wheels. In 1929, a specially outfitted six-passenger Travel Air monoplane was used as a flying showroom. And in 1932, one of the first industrial movies, a sixty-minute sound production, was used to sell Black & Decker tools.

Black served as president of the firm until 1951, and Decker succeeded him for the next five years. The two men had taught the world about power tools, selling more portable machine tools than anyone else. But why stop there? In 1971, a Black & Decker Lunar Surface Drill removed core samples from the moon.

raun

In his apartment in Frankfurt, Germany in 1921, Max Braun began turning out small electronic components which bore his name. But while all of Braun's creations disappeared anonymously into the assemblies of bigger machines, he had a dream for a consumer product—an electric foil shaver.

Braun carried a prototype shaver with him constantly, making subtle alterations for years until he had a product which met even his demanding standards. Braun put his revolutionary electric foil shaver, the world's first, on the market in 1949. It ushered in the popularity of electric shaving around the world.

Max Braun died unexpectedly in 1951, leaving the business to his sons, Arthur and Erwin. To the founder "form always followed function," and in 1955 when Dieter Rams came on board as chief designer he elevated the credo to an art form. Today, more than forty Eurostyle Braun appliances are maintained in the collection of New York's Museum of Modern Art.

arrier

Willis H. Carrier grew up on a farm in Angola, New York, a boy of mechanical inclinations. He graduated from Angola Academy in 1894, but lacked the money and entrance requirements to pursue an advanced education at nearby Cornell University. He continued studying, however, and in 1896 he won a scholarship contest that paid for Cornell tuition.

Carrier was still only halfway home to his dream. He now borrowed money for a tutoring school to prepare for competition exams to win a university scholarship for board, room, and books. Carrier won the necessary extra money, but his years studying electrical engineering in Ithaca were fraught with money worries.

After graduation in 1901, Carrier began work with Buffalo Forge, earning ten dollars a week working with fans, heaters, and temperature control. He studied water content in the air and devised a system for dehumidifying the air using an ammonia compressor. On a foggy day in Pittsburgh, where he waited on a railway platform on his way to a business appointment, Carrier conceived the methods of affecting air temperature by changing its moisture content. His idea of "dewpoint control" became the basis for the air conditioning industry.

In 1904, Carrier was ready to patent his process. His "Apparatus For Treating Air", a method of dehumidifying air by *adding* water, was such an advanced concept that his first few sales were not for temperature reduction but for cleaning air in ventilating systems. Meanwhile, Carrier was promoted to the head of engineering and research at Buffalo Forge at the age of twenty-nine.

Carrier Air Conditioning Company of America, owned by Buffalo Forge, was established in 1907 with J. Irvine Lyle as sales manager. Lyle introduced cooling systems into industry after industry. By 1914, Carrier had installed over three hundred air conditioning systems in factories across the country. But with the advent of World War I, Buffalo Forge decided to confine its operations to traditional manufacturing activities. Carrier Air Conditioning was shut down.

On June 26, 1915, Carrier and Lyle and five other young engineers formed the Carrier Engineering Company. Despite limited capital, the new firm closed more than forty contracts in the last six months of the year. Willis Carrier was kept busy in the field selling, advising, and supervising. He had time to file only two patents in 1915, his smallest output in years.

To grow, Carrier needed to find a simple refrigerating system to run warm water through a pipe and turn it cold. By 1923, he introduced centrifugal refrigerating machines to do just that. Comfort air conditioning was at hand. Carrier's first installation of the new process was in Hudson's Department store in Detroit, but his big breakthrough in comfort advertising came in movie theaters. Successful air conditioning systems were installed in Texas and spread to Broadway. No longer did entertainment emporiums have to shut down on excessively hot days.

Carrier continued to improve the efficiency of his air conditioning systems. In 1928 he introduced the residential "Weathermaker" and sold his first individual units to small retailers. In 1930, after many aborted tries, Carrier began air conditioning railroad cars. In 1932 Carrier introduced The Atmospheric Cabinet, the world's first room air conditioner, and finally in 1939, Willis Carrier cooled the last remaining hot spot in America—the skyscraper.

America's massive military output in World War II was made possible in part by Carrier Air Conditioning. Irvine Lyle died in 1942, at the age of sixty-eight, while Willis Carrier devoted himself to what he later referred to as his greatest engineering achievement—a wind tunnel simulating freezing high altitude conditions to test prototype planes.

After the war, Carrier suffered a heart ailment that left him bedridden. He remained as Chairman Emeritus and a constant consultant to Carrier engineers until his death in 1950 at the age of seventy-four.

Colt

It was not unusual for boys in frontier America in the nineteenth century to be entranced with firearms; Samuel Colt happened to be more precocious than most. Born in Hartford, Connecticut in 1814, Colt was discovered at the age of seven dismantling and assembling a gun. At fifteen he was expelled from Amherst Academy in Massachusetts when a Fourth of July demonstration of an underwater mine he built went awry and inundated invited guests with muck rather than destroying a raft.

Colt returned to Ware, Massachusetts to toil in his father's silk mill, but he soon talked his way onto a merchant ship bound for India working as a hand. By the time he returned home a year later, the sixteen-year-old Colt had fashioned a white-pine model of a multibarreled, repeating pistol. He handed his wooden gun to a Hartford gunsmith named Anson Chase, who he hired to create a handgun capable of firing several bullets in succession—the dream of gunmakers for over two hundred years.

Colt raised money for his venture by traveling the countryside giving demonstrations of nitrous oxide, calling himself "the celebrated Dr. S. Coult of London and Calcutta." The most famous six-shooter in history was financed by laughing gas. Chase was hired to build one pistol and one rifle. The first pistol exploded; the second wouldn't fire at all. Colt fine-tuned his design, and by 1836 had secured French, English, and American patents. He was twenty-two.

Colt and several investors went into business in Paterson, New Jersey as the Patent Arms Manufacturing Co., making rifles, carbines, shotguns, and muskets. As chief salesman, Colt won a demonstration for a repeating musket for the US Army, but won no converts. Undaunted, he left for Florida, the site of the only ongoing United States military action in 1837—where army troops battled the Seminole Indians. The men in the field proved more receptive to Colt's rifles than the brass back in Washington. Although he sold several hundred weapons over the next few

years, Colt was never able to land a contract with the United States
Army and the Patent Arms Manufacturing Company went bankrupt in 1842.

Colt drifted back into underwater mines. In 1843, he laid the
first submarine cable connecting Coney Island and Manhattan.
The following year the entire Congress adjourned to watch Colt
blow up a five-hundred-ton ship. But his missionary work in Florida
for his repeating firearms was about to pay dividends. When
General Zachary Taylor headed west to lead the United States
Army against Mexico in 1846, he ordered a thousand repeating
pistols from Colt. Taylor had become converted while serving in
the Seminole wars in Florida.

Colt, no longer owning a factory, was forced to subcontract the
work out. In fact, he had no inventory left from his earlier venture
and owned no models of his revolver. He redesigned a new pistol
from memory, adding a sixth barrel on the suggestion of American
war hero Captain Samuel Walker, a friend and believer in Colt's
revolver. The new .44 calibre revolvers were known as Walker
Colts, but the captain was lanced in the Battle of Juamantla shortly
after the start of the war and his name disappeared from the gun.

Colt supervised the manufacture of each of his pistols, and
eventually moved into his own sprawling factory on the banks of
the Connecticut River in Hartford. The brick armory was designed
in the shape of an "H," and was topped by a stunning blue dome
encrusted with gold stars. By 1851 he had supplied the United
States Army with six thousand revolvers. That year he also won a
patent lawsuit that ensured no other company could make repeating firearms based on his designs. When Colt traveled to London
to display his revolvers at the great Crystal Palace Exhibition he
opened an armory in London, the first American manufacturer to
do so.

In 1855, Colt's Patent Arms Manufacturing Company was
incorporated, with ten thousand shares of stock with a par value of
a hundred dollars each. Colt owned 9,996 of the shares. He lived
highly, at one time buying five thousand dollars worth of Havana
cigars to bring back with him from Cuba. He built the monarchial
Armstear, one of the most spectacular private estates in America,
but his maniacal work pace left him little time to enjoy it.

Colt was typically up at five, checking on the farm and his

brickworks. After breakfast he was in the armory overseeing every aspect of his fifteen hundred-man operation. When the Civil War began, Colt was running the largest private armory in the world. Colt's Patent Arms Manufacturing Co. would turn out nearly 400,000 revolvers for the Union Army from 1861 to 1865, but Samuel Colt did not live to see the impact of his invention on America. He died suddenly of a massive stroke in January of 1862. He was only forty-eight, and with a personal estate valued at fifteen million dollars he was one of the wealthiest men ever to live in the United States to that time.

Fuller

The man whose name meant successful selling in the twentieth century was self-described as "devoid of a salesman's personality." He never had a practiced line of sales patter and, hailing from Nova Scotia, his speech was peppered with "oots" and "aboots" rather than "outs" and "abouts."

Alfred Carl Fuller came to selling brushes because no one else would hire him. After leaving the family farm in 1903 for Boston, the eighteen-year old Fuller struggled to find his place in the world. He moved in with his sister and her husband and was a most undesirable boarder: he brought with him seventy-five dollars, no discernible skills, and no prospects.

Fuller landed a job as a trolley conductor, but after eighteen months, eager to prove he could be a motorman, he commandeered a trolley, failed to negotiate a switch, and was fired. He tried life as a gardener and groom, but was dismissed in a short time. A stint as a deliveryman for his brother-in-law ended after two months. Fuller had demonstrated a knack for forgetting pick-ups and leaving packages at the wrong address.

He came to brushes because it seemed so simple. A brother had peddled household brushes before he contracted tuberculosis and died. Six days before his twentieth birthday, Fuller went to his brother's former partner to ask for a chance to sell brushes. He -sold six dollars worth on his first day and was off.

Although brushes were constantly used, nobody seemed to be paying much attention to their manufacture. Fuller's customers made suggestions for new brushes, but neither his employer or other suppliers would deviate from their traditional line of top-sellers. Fuller soon realized that these specialized brushes could "be made in fifteen minutes out of a few cents worth of materials and sold for fifty cents."

In 1906, after only a year in the brush trade, Fuller used $375 in saved capital and pieced together a small workshop in his sister's basement. He planned to sell from samples for future delivery, making only what he had already sold on his tiny hand-operated wire-twisting brush machine.

The formula, simplicity itself, was parlayed to success by Fuller's indefatigable ways. To Fuller, selling was merely a mathematical proposition. Ring enough doorbells and you will eventually have more orders than you can handle. Fuller possessed an honest, unsophisticated approach, a neat appearance, and an unassuming attitude. But he learned early on that a quality product—and its demonstration—sold itself. His first week out he cleared $42.15 in profits.

Soon Fuller was in Hartford, Connecticut with its long avenues of big, old Victorian residences filled with dust-catching grillwork, steam radiators, and elaborate woodwork. His Capitol Brush Company, soon to be renamed Fuller Brush, now featured one laborer and one salesman—and a backlog of orders.

In 1908 Fuller brought home a wife, a Nova Scotia girl he had courted over the glove counter at a Boston department store. There was no time for a honeymoon, and the couple briskly expanded the business. A chance newspaper ad in 1910 for agents brought a flood of orders, and soon Fuller had a national network of 260 dealers, most of whom he had never met.

Each dealer paid for his sample kit and advanced the money

for his first order. When he delivered the order, he collected the amount due and sent the proceeds to Hartford, less his commission of fifty percent. Fuller delivered nothing until he had received cash. Within ten years sales vaulted from thirty thousand dollars a year to over a million.

In 1922 the *Saturday Evening Post* coined the phrase "Fuller Brush Man," and launched the army of Fuller representatives into the popular lexicon. A veritable gold mine of free publicity in editorials, cartoons, and jokes followed. In 1948 Columbia Pictures released a paean to Fuller Brush with the release of *The Fuller Brush Ma* starring Red Skelton. Skelton prepared for the part by taking a sample kit and making some calls. Unrecognized, the Hollywood star rang up four sales to the ten housewives he called on.

The star of Fuller Brush was always the free sample. "Without the free sample I couldn't possibly make a living. It's the best merchandising device ever uncovered," said one Fuller Brush dealer. Fuller Brush men were revered for their professional ability to gain access to a home. One salesman persuaded the household staff of the presidential residence at Hyde Park to admit him inside. Franklin Roosevelt bought thirteen dollars worth of brushes.

Fuller became affectionately known as "Dad" throughout his company, but his own family life was not as successful. He was divorced in 1930. Remarried two years later, Fuller began to indulge in the arts and music and wound down his business activities. He retired in 1943, turning the door-to-door business over to his son Howard.

Under Howard's aggressive leadership, the company flourished in expanding suburbia, topping $100,000,000 in sales by 1960. But times were changing. When Alfred Fuller died in 1973, one month short of his eighty-nineth birthday, strangers were no longer welcome in the home, two-income houses were deserted during the day and the Fuller Brush Man, now seventy-five percent women, were Fuller Brush representatives.

Glidden

In 1875, a group of middle-aged men banded together to form a varnish-making business in Cleveland. Glidden, Brackett & Co. brought together the talents of Francis Harrington Glidden, Levi Brackett, and Thomas Bolles. That the Glidden name survived is a testament to his outlasting his partners, becoming The Glidden Varnish Company in 1894.

In the early days, the partners produced a thousand gallons of varnish each week, and delivered it to customers across Cleveland in a horse and wagon. For the first twenty years of the business, only industrial varnishes were manufactured, coatings for furniture, pianos and carriages. In 1895, with his partners retired, Glidden took off after the growing, new consumer market for varnishes and paints. The company introduced Jap-A-Lac in sixteen colors for use in the home.

Glidden was one of the first manufacturers of the consumer age to realize the influence of women, traditionally the commanders of the home, in the purchasing process. He advertised in *Ladies' Home Journal* and *Housekeeping Magazine*, with depictions of women finishing chairs and tables and window casings. Glidden's aggressive advertising propelled his varnish beyond Cleveland into New York and Chicago and even Canada.

Francis Glidden had built a two million dollars business when he sold the company in 1917 at the age of eighty-five. When the Glidden Company introduced the first water-based paint in 1949, the prominence of the Glidden name was assured.

Hoover

In 1908, William Henry Hoover operated a harness and leather goods factory in New Berlin (now North Canton), Ohio. The infant auto business was seriously threatening the future of Hoover's horse collars, and he was looking to expand his company. On a hot summer day, Hoover met with James Murray Spangler on his front porch to discuss a cleaning contraption Spangler had sold his cousin, Hoover's wife.

Vacuum cleaners were a boon to sanitation and health in the early 1900s, but they were cumbersome and required two people to operate. Spangler was an aging sometime inventor working as a janitor to clear debts. He developed a portable cleaning device to minimize dust that rose from the carpets he cleaned every night—dust that aggravated his asthma.

Spangler attached a creaking electric fan motor atop a soap box and sealed the cracks with adhesive tape. A pillow case billowing out the back served as a dust bag. Hoover and his wife were both impressed with the new machine, but not many homes had electricity in 1908.

Hoover bought the patents anyway, and started the Electric Suction Sweeper Company. He set aside a corner of his leather goods factory for the production of suction sweepers, turning out six cleaners a day. James Spangler, his debts now relieved, became Hoover's superintendent of production.

The first Hoover advertisement appeared in the *Saturday Evening Post* on December 5, 1908. The ad described the simple premise of the suction sweeper: "A rapidly revolving brush loosens the dust which is sucked back into the dirt bag." The ad went on to further state that "repairs and adjustments are never necessary." Finally, readers were offered a free ten-day trial at home.

Hundreds of homemakers took Hoover up on his offer. He shipped the suction sweepers through local dealers who received a commission if the cleaner was purchased. If not, the dealer could keep the vacuum cleaner for in-store demonstrations. Thus began the national network of loyal Hoover dealers.

Hoover then organized an army of door-to-door demonstrators. The sales power of the skilled demonstration was Hoover's secret weapon. No one could deny that his portable vacuum cleaner, which embodied all the basic principles of today's vacuums, was effective and time-saving. Research and innovation followed. In 1926, Hoover patented an agitator bar which beat the carpet before brushing it. When he died in 1932, the horse and William Hoover's leather fittings were long since departed from the American scene, but Hoover vacuums were established as the American standard for cleaning.

Jacuzzi

It must be the name. Candido Jacuzzi did not set out to make his name synomous with laid-back California luxury. Jacuzzi did not invent the whirlpool; it was others that made his soothing-sounding name generic. His business roots were much less romantic.

Candido Jacuzzi was born in northern Italy in 1903 and emigrated with his family, fifteen strong, to the United States early in the century. The family settled in Berkeley, California, becoming machinists. Candido, the youngest of seven brothers, would never complete grammar school.

The first Jacuzzi Brothers, Inc. product was an airplane propeller known as the Jacuzzi "toothpick." America's first military planes sported the specialized propeller in World War I. After the war, the brothers designed the Jacuzzi J-7, a cabin-style monoplane. There followed a breakthrough development of submersible pumps that opened markets worldwide to Jacuzzi. Factories sprouted in

Canada, Mexico, Brazil, Chile, and Italy. More than 50 industrial patents are held by the Jacuzzis.

In 1943, Candido's fifteen-month-old son contracted rheumatoid arthritis, leaving the boy crippled and distorted with pain. The boy received regular hydrotherapy treatments at local hospitals, but Candido could not stand to see his son suffering between visits. He realized that the water pumps Jacuzzi Brothers was making could be adapted to give his son whirlpool treatments at home.

In 1948, Jacuzzi designed an aerating pump that could be used in a bathtub. The unit sat right in the water and could be moved from one bathtub to another. Over the years, other sufferers heard about the home relief provided by the portable whirlpool and Jacuzzi manufactured some for special orders.

In 1955, the firm decided to market the Jacuzzi whirlpool bath as a therapeutic aid, selling it in drugstores and bath supply shops. To generate a little publicity for the unknown product, portable Jacuzzis were included in the gifts showered on contestants on TV's *Queen for a Day*. It was pitched as relief for the worn-down housewife, but when Hollywood stars like Randolph Scott and Jayne Mansfield—who were decidedly not worn-down—began offering testimonials, the Jacuzzi started to acquire its legendary allure.

The Jacuzzi became a symbol of the sybaritic lifestyle. Hundreds of thousands of Jacuzzi portables were installed, both indoors and outdoors, at recreation centers and private homes. But the whirlpool bath was still mostly a sidelight at Jacuzzi Brothers. By far the bulk of their revenues came from sales of water pumps, marine jets, and swimming pool equipment.

Candido Jacuzzi, who had worked his way up as sales manager and general manager, was forced to resign as president of the firm in 1969 when he was indicted on five counts of income tax invasion, triggering a series of hardships that clouded the final years of his life.

Rather than face trial, Jacuzzi fled the country, splitting his time between Italy and Puerto Vallarta in Mexico. In 1975 he suffered a stroke that left him paralyzed. He was able to return home to Scottsdale, Arizona, but before his death in 1986 Jacuzzi was dealt the cruelest blow of all—the sale of Jacuzzi Brothers in 1979, prompted by family squabbling.

Johns Manville

Just as fire has always fascinated man, so have materials that can be set ablaze without burning. The asbestos story in America is the story of two men: Henry Ward Johns and Charles Branton Manville.

From his childhood, Johns was captivated by the heat and fire resistant properties of asbestos. Fires were common tragedies in the 1800s, extracting a heavy toll on human life. When he reached the age of twenty-one in 1858, Johns left his West Stockbridge, Massachusetts farm and came to New York to start a small business as a jobber of roofing materials.

Ten years later, Johns received his first patent for an asbestos product. He gave it the cumbersome name "Improved Compound For Roofing And Other Purposes." He developed a new pipe covering, and in 1874 asbestos was discovered on nearby Staten Island. Johns's business success spread.

He hired a travelling salesman named Reed, who before getting his first commission check had secured so many orders for asbestos roofing that he had to be recalled because the factory couldn't keep pace. For all his excellent work, Reed's reward was a factory job.

Charles Manville worked in the grocery trade in Neenah, Wisconsin for most of his life. In 1878, at the age of forty-four, he set out for the South Dakota gold rush. He returned to Milwaukee four years later, poorer for his troubles.

He began the manufacture of steam pipe and boiler covers. In 1886, he found a mixture of wool felt and blue clay that was a superior insulator and went into a successful business with his three sons. Manville bought Johns's business west of Ohio in 1897, one year before Johns's death. In 1901, the two companies consolidated under the leadership of the respective founders' sons. Thomas Manville was the first president of the new Johns Manville.

Thomas Manville would introduce thirteen hundred items made of asbestos, earning the title "Asbestos King." He ran the company as a one-man show. *Fortune* reported in 1913, "Manville took little advice, borrowed no money, dickered with no competitor." Manville boasted that he "never spent a nickel on laboratories or chemists." But he sold the heck out of asbestos, increasing sales to forty million dollars a year when he died suddenly of heart disease in 1925. His father outlived him by two years, dying at age ninety-three in 1927.

Johnson

For much of his lifetime, Samuel Curtis Johnson migrated from town to town in the Midwest. He was born on Christmas Eve, 1833, the eldest of 11 children. His family moved every few years. Appropriately his first job was with the Chicago, Milwaukee, and St. Paul Railroad. Never able to obtain a proper education in his youth, Johnson decided to enroll at Oberlin College in Ohio at the age of twenty-four.

A year later he was on the move again, working for the Kenosha, Rockford & Rock Island Railroad in Kenosha, Wisconsin. When he married shortly thereafter, he began investing half of his monthly hundred dollar salary in the railroad. The line went bankrupt and Johnson lost his entire savings.

For the next thirty years, Johnson's career was undistinguished as he drifted in and out of a variety of jobs. In 1886 he hired on with the Racine Hardware Company, selling decorative parquet floors. Johnson bought his employer's company that year and began selling and installing parquet floors on his own.

After his customers spent so lavishly for their special floors, Johnson soon found himself fielding questions on the best way to care for the inlaid floors. He knew that fancy European parquet floors had been maintained with beeswax for centuries. Johnson began mixing his own waxes, and starting in 1888, every floor his company installed came with a free can of Johnson's Prepared Paste Wax.

Although other waxes and polishes were available, it was Samuel Johnson who gained a wide reputation as a wood-finishing expert. By 1898, Johnson was selling more wax and paste than parquet floors. Although waxed floors are not the priority they were one hundred years ago when expensive wood required extra care, it is still Johnson's wax, manufactured with the same secret formulation, that gets the job done.

Kohler

John Michael Kohler did a brisk business selling products from his foundry in Sheboygan, Wisconsin to immigrants passing through the city on their way west. He sold enameled tea kettles and flat-rimmed kitchen sinks. He also made an enameled iron vessel that farmers used as a combination hog scalder and watering trough.

Sensing an emerging market for household products, Kohler designed and cast four ornamental iron feet. He welded them to his hog scalder and, in 1883, put the first Kohler bathtub on the market. That first bathtub, so the legend goes, sold to a local farmer in exchange for one cow and fourteen chickens.

The Kohlers had been cheesemakers and dairy farmers in the Austrian Alps until the family came to America in mid-century. The Kohlers settled in rural St. Paul, Minnesota, where there is still a Kohler dairy selling Kohler milk. John, however, left the family farm to peddle goods in Chicago.

On a sales trip along Lake Michigan, Kohler met a young woman named Lillie Vollrath in Sheboygan. By 1873, the twenty-nine-year old Kohler was married and buying out his father-in-law's interest in a small foundry and machine shop. Kohler directed twenty-one employees in the manufacture of plows, road scrapers, hitching posts, cemetery crosses, garden settees, and any ironwork a customer might need.

In 1880 the factory burned to the ground. Kohler rebuilt the plant, added an enamel shop, and started shifting production from plowshares to plumbing fixtures. As sales increased, he was able to indulge in civic interests. Kohler became part owner of the Turner Hall and the Sheboygan Opera House, two of the major cultural centers in the community. Kohler even put in one term as mayor of Sheboygan.

In 1899, Kohler moved his foundry from Sheboygan to a small village called Riverside four miles west of the city. Many hailed the move as "Kohler's Folly." They found if difficult to understand why a prospering foundry would locate away from its skilled work force, away from utilities, and away from city services and convenient transportation.

John Kohler would not live to see the full scope of his vision realized. He died before his new plant was in full production. Three months later fire destroyed the factory and the company was forced to move back to Sheboygan.

Kohler's sons returned the business to Riverside to reestablish the family factory, devoted now solely to plumbing products. A small cluster of employees' homes grew up around the Kohler factory. In 1912, by popular vote of its residents, the village of Riverside was incorporated and its name was changed to Kohler.

John Michael Kohler had always dreamed of building a model city. It was a dream he passed on to his family, and they would not let it die.

Mason

Food preservation in early America was at best a short term proposition. Fruits and vegetables were stored in cellars, buried in pits lined with charcoal, baked sawdust, chopped straw, or corn husks. Dried fruits and vegetables were the best winter fare available, and fall spelled the beginning of increasingly monotonous menus.

A French confectioner, Nicolas Appert, won a twelve thousand franc prize in 1810 for his theories that heat would preserve fruits, meats, fish, and vegetables by arresting the natural tendency of foods to spoil. For the next half-century, there was virtually no advancement in the salvation of the consumer's taste buds.

In 1858, John Landis Mason left the family farm in Vineland, New Jersey and moved to New York to work as a tinsmith on Canal Street. Holed up in a small rented room at 154 West 19th Street, the twenty-six-year-old Mason worked on the problem of an airtight jar, undoubtedly spurred on by the thought of the coming winter and its dreary diet.

In the middle of November, Mason took out his first patent for a mold which could turn out a glass jar with a threaded top. The threads would allow a metal cap to be screwed down, forming an airtight seal. Mason took out a second patent on his "improved Jar" on November 30, 1858, the date which glass jars carried for the next seventy-five years.

That winter Mason took on partners and moved his modest business to 257 Pearl Street. Mason and his partners crafted the tops on Pearl Street. The jars were ordered from glassblowers who had made the molds, each mold generally costing less than ten dollars, according to the specifications in Mason's patent. From these beginnings it is estimated that over a hundred billion jars have been made from Mason's creation.

The humble Mason jar is surely one of America's most important inventions, for it changed the dietary habits of a nation and spawned one of the country's great industries. Mason's jar proved to be a blessing to housewives on farms and cities alike. The chemically inert qualities of glass preserved fresh flavors. Clear, transparent jars permitted housewives to see contents at a glance. Easy to clean and reuse, Mason jars could be effortlessly stored by the hundred. Individual jars were often handed down from one generation to another.

The Civil War interrupted Mason's thriving new business. After the war, Mason reestablished his factory in New York. In 1873, he moved to New Brunswick, New Jersey. Here Mason became associated with the Consolidated Fruit Jar Company, which soon acquired rights to the first two patents. These patents expired in 1875, after seventeen years, and accordingly entered the public domain, free of protection. The next year Mason assigned his remaining rights on eight other jar patents to Consolidated.

John Mason busied himself with his new family—he had married in 1873 when he moved to New Brunswick and his new wife would present him with eight daughters—and dabbled in new inventions. He patented a folding life raft, a soap dish, a brush holder, and a sheet metal cap die, but never again devised anything as perfect in its utility as the Mason jar.

Daniel Maytag came to America in 1852 at the age of nineteen as a carpenter, but ended up operating a store in Cook County, Illinois. In 1866 he traded his store for open prairie land in Iowa. So it happened that ten-year old Frederick Louis Maytag tended the family farm while his father built barns, houses, and churches throughout the developing countryside.

To supplement his farm income, young Maytag supplied coal

to area schoolhouses. One dark night his horse stepped in a rut and snapped his foreleg. Maytag lost an entire winter's profits. He left the farm in 1880 to sell agricultural supplies for fifty dollars a month.

Maytag entered the manufacturing business in 1893 as half-owner of the Parsons Band Cutter and Self Feeder Company. In addition to farm implements, Maytag also became a leading manufacturer of buggies, and dabbled in early automobile experiments.

He began looking for new products to replace the firm's increasingly obsolete line of buggies. In 1907, he began selling a power washer with a gas engine for farm use. In 1909, Maytag bought out his partners and renamed the business the Maytag Company. Maytag now devoted all his energies to his washing machines. And they needed it.

The company struggled for more than a decade. By 1922, Maytag was sixty-five years old and owed large sums of money when the breakthrough came. Howard Snyder, a Maytag employee for fifteen years who had started as a serviceman, invented a gyrowasher with an aluminum tub. The new machine used a gyrator to create violent water action rather than rubbing, pulling, and twisting clothes.

The Maytag Company was eighth among sixty washing machine manufacturers when Fred Maytag traveled west to try and sell his new gyrowasher. He met little success until he finally convinced one dealer to carry the Maytag Aluminum Washer with "gyrofoam washing." That was all it took. The plant was soon swamped with orders.

Maytag sent sample machines unsolicited to a hundred dealers for demonstrations. Only seven returned it. On any dealer order over twelve machines, a Maytag salesman would travel to the store and work for thirty days with the dealer to sell them. Within eighteen months of the introduction of the gyrofoam washer, Maytag was the number one seller of washing machines in America, with more sales than the next four manufacturers combined.

Fred Maytag was now free to pursue his nonbusiness interests. He had been nominated for the Iowa State Senate back in 1893 but scoffed at the acclamation. He didn't campaign at all and lost handily. But in 1901 he actively campaigned for the Senate seat and won easily, serving until 1912. He was mayor of his hometown of Newton, Iowa and was the first director of the Iowa State budget in 1925.

He gave freely of his money, donating $250,000 to the Newton YMCA and building a park and public swimming pool. He also gave thousands of dollars to various Midwestern colleges. On his seventieth birthday, he distributed $132,000 to his employees. Fred Maytag retired to Beverly Hills where he died in 1937 at the age of eighty.

Oster

The fortunes of many of America's companies have been inter-twined with the country's wars. John Oster had built a solid business in the years before World War II, but government orders during the war not only exceeded any received before but pushed the company into new directions which would make Oster a "house-hold" name.

John Oster made his first hair clippers in 1924, working out of a basement with fifteen employees. At the time, hair clippers were heavy and indiscriminately used to clip animal as well as human hair. Women in the "Roaring Twenties" began bobbing their hair, and Oster's new lightweight clippers were ideal for the intricate hairstyles.

In 1928 Oster invented a postage-sized motor to power his hair clippers, the first portable electric hair clipper. Priced far below the hundred dollar professional models on the market, Oster's hair clippers became the standard in barber shops across the country. Oster faced four major competitors; he bought two of them and a third went out of business. With his reputation firmly established, Oster searched for other uses for his pint-sized motors. In 1935 he developed an "Oster massager," which was a big success in hospitals and sanitoriums.

Millions of American heads were shorn with Oster clippers during World War II, but the company also utilized its expertise in small horsepower motors to produce compact motors for mines and artillery. After the war, Oster realized that there would be a great demand for new, high-tech consumer products in American homes. He purchased the Stevens Electric Company, which had been making commercial drink mixers since 1922.

With refinements by Oster engineers, the first "Osterizer"—a practical food blender—appeared on the market in 1946. While housewives everywhere were chopping, slicing, and dicing food with their new portable blenders, the Oster line was expanding to include hair dryers, knife sharpeners, humidifiers, and ice crushers. By the time the Oster Company was purchased by the Sunbeam Corporation in 1960, John Oster had taken his miniature motors into every room in the house.

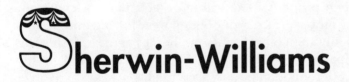

Sherwin-Williams

Nobody thought you could sell ready-mixed paint. Painting one's house was a very personal thing; the homeowner would always want to mix their own paints. Henry Alden Sherwin thought differently.

Sherwin was born in 1842 and raised in Vermont. He quit school at the age of thirteen and went to work in a store, spending his off-hours sleeping upstairs. For years, Henry listened to his uncle, a lawyer in Cleveland, rave about the bustling city by Lake Erie.

Finally, in 1859 Henry saved up enough money to go to Cleveland. Sherwin thrived in business. He worked as a bookkeeper for a wholesale grocery, and was soon offered a partnership. A religious man, Sherwin never reconciled himself to the fact that his firm sold liquor and he not only turned down the partnership but resigned his position.

In 1866, Sherwin invested two thousand dollars in a partnership of Truman Dunham & Company, a manufacturer of linseed oils. For three years Sherwin agitated for the company to take an active role in developing ready-mixed paints. Finally it was agreed that Sherwin would take what little paint business the firm had, and the other partners would take the linseed oil business.

In 1870, Sherwin found another partner in good-natured, fun-loving Edward Porter Williams. Williams proved to be a born salesman who spurred the company's growth, while Sherwin toiled meticulously to create a superior ready-mixed paint.

It took ten years. In 1880, Sherwin-Williams introduced its first ready-mixed paint. Henry Sherwin was convinced that his paint far surpassed any of the inferior canned paints then on the market. He had created a mill that ground color pigments fine enough to remain suspended in the oils that carried them. Sherwin-Williams paint would stay as fresh as the day it was mixed in the factory.

To overcome consumer resistance, Sherwin-Williams ready-mixed paint came with an ironclad warranty: "We guarantee that this paint, when properly used, will not crack, flake or chalk off, and will cover more surface, work better, wear longer, and permanently look better than other paints. We hereby agree to forfeit the value of the paint AND THE COST OF APPLYING IT if in any instance it is not found as above represented."

It didn't take much convincing for homeowners to abandon their linseed oil pots and turpentine jars in favor of a pre-mixed paint that covered their walls. Sherwin-Williams ready-mixed paints were an immediate success. The company began to sell only pre-mixed canned paints. Warehouses were opened in Newark, New Jersey and Boston to meet demand.

Sherwin quickly expanded his lines to turn homeowners into paint experts. He introduced surface preparations, primers, brushes, and cleanup materials. Meanwhile Williams concentrated on developing finishes for the powerful railroad industry, which led to the company's first plant outside Cleveland. In 1888, Sherwin-Williams started a factory in Chicago, destined to be the largest paint manufacturing plant in the world.

By the end of the century, Sherwin-Williams warehouses spanned the continent. The firm was taking steps to own and manufacture raw ingredients when Edward Williams died in 1903. Two years later the "Cover-the-Earth" trademark, a can of paint spilling across a globe, was adopted.

Henry Sherwin resigned the presidency in 1909 to serve as chairman of the board. He lived long enough to participate in his company's fiftieth Year Golden Jubilee before dying in 1916.

immons

Zalmon Simmons was a man whose imagination ran to telegraph companies and railroads. But his name survives, not in anything so grand, but surely something more important to most Americans: a good night's sleep.

Simmons started out in 1849 as a two–hundred–dollar–a–year clerk in a general store in Kenosha, Wisconsin. At the time the telegraph was new, and the country was dotted with little telegraph companies, most of which were making no money. The head of one such Wisconsin company owed Simmons some money and was about to sell his business to pay his bill. Simmons decided he might as well take over the business, cancelled the man's bill, and paid two hundred dollars for the telegraph line.

Simmons built up the Northwestern Telegraph Company, partly by letting the railroads use his lines free in return for allowing him to put his poles along their right-of-way. This proved particularly valuable in the rugged west, where poles were frequently toppled by storms and buffaloes.

This piqued his interest in railroads, and he eventually built the first cogwheel railway up Pikes Peak. The first bed business Simmons got into was the railroad bed business: he supplied clay ballast for railroads that ran across the Great Plains and frequently sunk in the mud during rainy periods. He became president of the Rock Island Railroad.

Simmons got into the bed business quite by accident. He had built himself a little factory in which he manufactured cheeseboxes for his dairy and wooden insulators for his telegraph lines. He met an inventor who showed him a woven-wire mattress, which was really a frame with strands of wire woven through it. The spring was crude, but an improvement over the wooden slats or ropes used to support mattresses of the day.

Simmons bought the invention and began making woven-wire mattresses in a portion of his cheesebox factory. The business went well, and Simmons put in a line of wooden beds, principally the old-fashioned folding bed, noted for trapping potential sleepers. In 1892 his factory burned down, and when it resumed operations Simmons dealt primarily in metal, especially brass, beds.

When Zalmon Simmons died in 1910 at the age of eighty-one, the metal bed was about to be supplanted by wooden bedroom furniture. But it would not matter to the Simmons company, as Zalmon Simmons II was guiding the business away from beds and into mattresses. When the Beautyrest hit the market in 1925, Simmons was exclusively in the mattress business.

inger

Isaac Merritt Singer was born in upstate New York in 1811. He ran away from his parents at age twelve to join a group of traveling actors. Singer remained an actor until he was twenty-four. After that he worked as a machinist and acted on the side. For years his means were small, and he despaired of ever inventing anything successful.

He patented a device for carving wood block type, and went to Boston in 1850 to sell the type to manufacturers. Their enthusiasm was decidedly restrained for his wood type, but one day while in the office of a prospective client he became intrigued with a broken-down sewing machine. Singer set out to familiarize himself with all aspects of the sewing machine.

What he learned was that sewing machines were available as early as 1790 in England. But since their inception, sewing machines had been horribly unreliable and in need of constant repairs. Singer set to work and quickly invented a reliable machine with a straight needle that moved up and down. He was granted a patent in 1851, and formed I. M. Singer & Company.

Singer's sewing machine was an immediate success, and also attracted the attention of Elias Howe—who had patented a sewing machine in 1846. Singer hired a lawyer named Edward Clark to defend him in exchange for a third of the business. The arrangement eventually became fifty-fifty, with Singer handling the manufacturing and Clark the finances.

Clark stymied the lawsuits and brought the men together to pool their patents by creating the Singer Machine Combination— the first patent pool in United States history. By arrangement, Singer and Howe each received five dollars from every sewing machine sold.

At first, the only market for the Singer sewing machines was professional tailors and harness makers. Seeking a way to bring the machine within reach of the American family, Clark introduced the first consumer installment payment plan. For many Americans, the sewing machine was their most expensive possession.

The Singer-Clark partnership came to an abrupt end in 1863, when certain unsavory details of Singer's personal life came to light—Isaac Singer had fathered twenty-four children by four women. Both men retained an equal share of Singer Company stock, but sold the rest to their employees.

Family troubles aside, the profits of the sewing machine business made Singer a wealthy man. Rather than ride out any scandals in America, Singer went abroad, settling in Tourquay—a well-known watering place in England—until his death in 1875.

Stanley

Frederick Trent Stanley always had a bit of the promoter in him. When he he was making suspenders during Andrew Jackson's presidency, he sent Old Hickory a pair to show him fine Connecticut craftsmanship. Jackson penned Stanley a testimonial to his fine suspenders. which Stanley was able to use to impress future customers.

But Stanley's flair for selling seldom seemed to carry his manufacturing efforts very far. Born in 1803, Stanley clerked for a time as a boy on a Connecticut River steamboat and migrated to North Carolina for three years to try his hand at country peddling. He crafted his suspenders for a bit, and in 1831 he teamed with his brother William to produce some of the earliest house trimmings and locks in America. This business sputtered along for a time until the Panic of 1837 crippled it fatally.

Frederick Stanley went to Mississippi at that point, out of the reach of his chroniclers. He next surfaced in 1843, back in New

Britain, Connecticut in a nondescript one-story wooden structure
that had once stood as an armory during the War of 1812. Here
Stanley would lay the foundations for the most famous toolworks
in America.

The Stanley Bolt Manufactory was one of hundreds of little
manufactories struggling to make a go of it, the majority of which
were one-man shops. The only thing setting Stanley apart was a single-
cylinder, high pressure steam engine shipped up from New York
and carted by ox to the little wooden shop. Stanley's was the only
automated shop in the region.

Stanley peddled his bolts by horseback and wagon across the
back country. His tiny business must have impressed his neighbors,
because in 1852 five friends pooled the staggering sum of thirty
thousand dollars to form The Stanley Works, with Frederick
Stanley as president. Losses the first year totalled $361.72, but sales
of wrought iron strap and hinges slowly elevated profits through
the decade.

Clearly the outstanding achievement of Stanley's presidency
was his recruiting of William Hart, a nineteen-year old "jack-of-all-
trades" when first hired in 1852. By 1865, Stanley was making hand
tools and hardware for the expanding West, but faced four strongly
entrenched competitors—all bigger and closer to cheap iron and
easy water transportation.

But The Stanley Works alone survived. Hart expanded production, increased efficiency and cut labor costs by twenty percent.
He packaged screws together with hinges for the first time. When
retailers were hesitant to accept the prepackaged hinges, he went
to stores and bought traditional hinges. Then he asked a clerk for
matching screws, all the while timing the transaction with a stop-
watch. When he pointed out the magnitude of the time savings his
hinge-and-screw package was an easy sell.

With Hart at the controls, Stanley veered toward civic service
and politics. He served as the first mayor of New Britain. But the
Depression years of the early 1870s left The Stanley Works in its
worst shape since its first year two decades earlier. Just before his
death, Frederick Stanley underwrote employee notes for money
borrowed from banks and, along with new cold-rolled steel hinges
pioneered by Hart—who succeeded him as president—insured
the company's success for the next generation.

teinway

Heinrich Engelhardt Steinweg was born the youngest of twelve children to a foresting family in Germany in 1797. His father and several brothers left to fight in the Napoleonic Wars, and only his father came home. Worse, while seeking refuge from marauding troops, Steinweg's mother died of exposure during a bitter German winter. Several years later, in 1812, Steinweg, his father, and three remaining brothers were working a hillside when a thunderstorm threatened. The family huddled inside a temporary shelter which was destroyed by a bolt of lightning. Only Heinrich Steinweg crawled out of the wreckage alive. He was the only one remaining from his family of fourteen. He was fifteen years old.

Struggling to support himself, Steinweg joined the Army. He was reputedly at Waterloo in 1815, serving as a bugler, and he stayed in the military until he was twenty-two years old. He had no musical training but built his first instrument, a zither—made with 30 strings stretched across a box—after the war. He longed to build instruments professionally, but was not willing to serve the required seven-year apprenticeship and turned to cabinetmaking instead.

Although it is not known for sure, it is generally assumed that Steinweg built his first piano at the age of thirty-nine as a gift for his wife, crafting it in his kitchen. In 1839, a Steinweg piano won a gold medal at the Brunswick, Germany trade fair. He sold the piano for three hundred marks and was in the piano business. With the help of three of his six sons, the Steinwegs were able to make ten pianos a year in Seesen, Germany.

Political upheaval was once again threatening Germany by mid-century. On June 29, 1850, Heinrich Steinweg landed in New York City, following the lead of his son Theodore, who had emigrated a year earlier. Theodore's letters, although clearly indicating that all things being equal he'd rather still be in Germany, convinced his family a less stressful life awaited them in America.

Father and sons worked in piano factories around New York,

but the family was not scraping for money after their successful German days. On March 5, 1853, Heinrich Steinweg opened his own piano factory. Aware of prejudices against Germans around New York, he began business as "Henry Steinway & Sons." Steinway was never completely won over by his adopted land; he didn't officially change his name until 1864, and German was always the official language in the factory during his lifetime.

The Steinways started in a loft on Varick Street. Their first piano sold for five hundred dollars; it is on display at the Metropolitan Museum of Art today. The eldest daughter, Doretta, was the company's best salesperson, and she often offered free lessons with the new piano. The firm's success was assured when a Steinway square piano won a gold medal at the New York Industrial Exposition of the American Institute. The first Steinway grand piano was sold in 1856.

By 1859, Steinway was making more than one piano a day. A new plant, swallowing an entire city block, went up off Park Avenue in 1860. With 350 men and steam-powered tools, Steinway's production increased to thirty square pianos and five grand pianos a week. The superior resonance of a Steinway piano was attributed to its overstrung bass strings on an iron frame. It quickly became the standard concert piano in America. In 1866, William Steinway built Steinway Hall, which was New York's premier concert hall until Andrew Carnegie built his palatial hall in 1890.

Henry Steinway endured the same tragedies with his offspring that he had with his brothers. Three of his sons died of illness within a short period in the mid-1860s. Henry himself passed away at the age of seventy-four in 1871, having started a legacy that fate had seemed determined to sabotage.

Tappan

W. J. "Bill" Tappan was well-known in the Ohio Valley in the 1880s. There wasn't a single door in the territory he had not knocked on trying to sell the iron stoves he cast in his foundry. Many of the farmers were poor, and Tappan often accepted payment in vegetables and grains because he felt folks should be able to cook on a good stove.

In 1891, after Tappan had stoked his foundry for ten years, a solar eclipse darkened the eastern half of the United States. He viewed the astronomical event as an omen, and changed the name of his entire company from the Ohio Valley Foundry Company to the Eclipse Company. Perhaps it was an omen meant specifically for Bill Tappan, because his Eclipse Stove was soon selling beyond the Ohio Valley and became one of the best-selling ovens in America.

Tappan went on to become one of the leading innovators in the American kitchen, becoming a name synomous with cooking. In 1920, the old Tappan cast iron stove gave way to sheet steel and the modern range. In the 1940s the company, name reverted back to the Tappan Stove Company and when it introduced the first commercial microwave oven in 1955, there was no need to take it door to door as Bill Tappan had done seventy-five years earlier. It was readily accepted as the quintessential American convenience.

Tupperware

When Brownie Wise received her first plastic Tupper "Wonder Bowl" it took her three days to figure out how to work the seal. Then, once she got the bowl sealed, she dropped it as she was putting it in the refrigerator. But instead of breaking the bowl bounced. And the stubborn seal kept the contents from spilling. The world was about to discover plastic.

Earl Silas Tupper became convinced that plastic was "the material of the future" when he worked with polymers in a DuPont chemical plant during the Depression. Born and raised on a rural New Hampshire farm, Tupper always fancied himself an inventor imbued with Yankee ingenuity. So he left DuPont to form the Tupper Plastics Company in 1938.

Nothing much happened for a few years, and then World War II forced the government to restrict distribution of critical raw materials. Tupper's experiments with plastics could only continue when he obtained some leftover material from his former employer, a chunk of rock-hard, putrid polyethylene slag. Tupper worked with the black slag until he developed a purifying refining process. He also pioneered an injection-molding machine which produced the first unbreakable plastic. The first of what would grow to be more than four hundred Tupperware products was a seven-ounce tumbler.

Some of Tupper's creations were busts. Americans would never see his plastic shoe heels, but they would come to know his food containers. Plastic was viewed with suspicion by consumers in the 1940s; quality was inconsistent and no one saw the urgency to switch from comfortable glass. It was Tupper's seal that broke down consumer resistance.

He modeled his airtight seal after a paint can, flaring the rim out slightly and molding the lid to lock onto it. When the air inside was "burped" out a partial vacuum was created and the food inside would not dry out in Americans' new refrigerators. This is what Brownie Wise discovered in her own kitchen.

Tupper first sold his containers through hardware stores and catalogs when the containers were introduced in 1945. He then began to tap into the popular home demonstration parties after World War II. Wise was a Stanley Home Products distributor when she started to buy Tupper's plastic containers from her whole-salers. When shipments were delayed one day in 1949, she called Tupper directly to complain. By the time he put down the phone he had made her director of a new home-sales program.

Wise was so energetic, so positive, so successful that Tupper pulled his products from store shelves and sold exclusively through direct sellers. In 1951, Tupper Plastics became Tupperware Home Parties. When Wise took over, there were some two hundred inde-pendent dealers in Tupper's sales system. Three years later there were nine thousand and twenty-five million dollars in sales.

Tupperware was strong and elegant in its simplicity. Tupper used only the best raw materials and adhered to the strictest toler-ances in his molds. Tupper was so exacting in his manufacturing specifications that he sold his products with a lifetime warranty. The only receipt a customer ever needed to replace a defective product was the name *Tupperware* on the container.

In 1958 Wise left the company, and Tupper sold the business to Rexall Drugs for nine million dollars. He retired to Costa Rica. By the time Earl Tupper died in 1983, it was estimated that Tupperware could be found in ninety percent of all American homes.

Yale

As more and more Americans began entrusting their money to banks in the early nineteenth century, it became incumbent on these new institutions to guarantee the safety of these deposits. Many tinkerers were working on an infallible vault lock. One was Linus Yale. Another was Linus Yale.

Linus Yale, Jr. was born in Salisbury, New York in 1821, where his father was an inventor of sorts—having produced a thresher, among other machines. Young Yale received a formal education, but followed an artist's muse after school. He scraped out a living as a mediocre portrait artist for nearly ten years. Meanwhile, in 1840, Linus, Sr. began to manufacture bank locks in Newport, New York.

Independently, Linus, Jr. began to work on locks as well. While his father created the association between the name Yale and locks it was the son's "Yale Infallible Bank Lock" which revolutionized the security industry. He improved his lock constantly, patenting in rapid succession the "Yale Magic Bank Lock" and the formidable "Yale Double Treasury Bank Lock."

At the time a "lock controversy" raged on the ultimate security afforded by bank locks. At the Crystal Palace Exhibition in London in 1851 it was demonstrated that the best English locks could be picked. Yale traveled to England and figured how to pick the celebrated Day & Newell "Parautoptic Bank Lock." When he returned to his Stamford, Connecticut factory he discovered how to pick his best Yale Double Treasury Lock. The experience led him to develop the Monitor Bank Lock, the first of the combination, or dial, locks.

Between 1860 and 1865, Yale undertook work on a small key lock for doors and storage chests. Keys of the day were clumsy and often weighed more than one pound. Yale crafted a flat key "Cylinder Lock" based on a pin-and-tumbler mechanism devised by the ancient Egyptians. With refinements, the lock was virtually pickproof.

Yale lacked the financial resources to mass produce his new security locks until he met Henry Robinson Towne in 1868. Although half his age, Yale found much to recommend the twenty-four-year-old Towne. Towne had graduated early from the University of Pennsylvania and was designing and installing naval engines while still in his teens in the Civil War. And he brought with him plenty of capital as the son of a wealthy foundry owner.

There would be no locks sold by the new partners, however. On Christmas Day 1868, Yale suffered a massive heart attack and died at the age of forty-seven. Although their business association lasted only a brief three months, Henry Towne had great respect for Linus Yale and saw to it that his name was stamped on every key blank the company stamped.

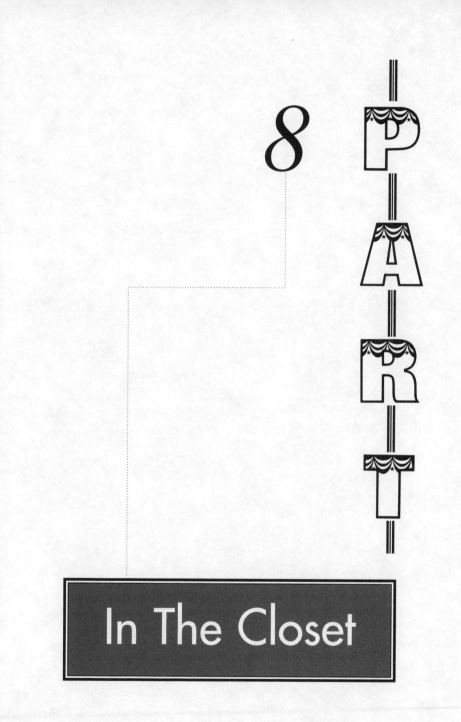

8 PART

In The Closet

Brooks Brothers

On the seventh of April, 1818, Henry Sands Brooks, then forty-five years old, realized the culmination of a dream when he opened a clothing emporium on the corner of Catharine and Cherry Streets in Manhattan. The son of a Connecticut doctor, Brooks had been a successful enough New York grocer to enjoy shopping junkets to Europe, where he indulged his taste for fancy clothes. Like every other merchant starting out, Brooks pledged "to make and deal only in merchandise of the best quality and to sell it at a fair profit only."

The business was not confined to retail selling, but also did a great trade among seafaring men in that part of New York. A grand tradition evolved when a seaman purchased an outfit: he was regaled with a hearty draft from a black bottle kept for this purpose beneath the counter.

Brooks brought his relatives—first his brother John and then his sons Henry and Daniel—into the business, which allowed the small shop to continue after his death in 1833. Men's clothing styles closely emulated English fashion trends, and like other clothiers Brooks offered as many classic London lines as possible.

Henry and Daniel envisioned the future of American dress. In 1845, at a time when most clothes were still tailor-made or sewn in the home, the Brooks brothers were the first to recognize the potential of ready-made clothing. They created the first ready-to-wear suit, an innovation that made fashion affordable.

In the 1850s, four younger brothers gravitated to the clothing business and the name officially became Brooks Brothers, by which time the Brooks tradition of clothing originals was firmly established. A sheep suspended by a ribbon was adopted as the official Brooks Brothers trademark. This symbol of British wool merchants dates back to the fifteenth century, when it was the emblem of the Knights of the Golden Fleece.

Brooks Brothers continued to adapt British styles to American wardrobes, introducing the foulard necktie in 1890 and the button-down collar shirt in 1896, inspired by English polo players who buttoned their collars against the wind.

It was the sack suit that cemented Brooks Brothers as the father of the classic American style of dress. Designed to flatter all body types, the sack suit was an immediate hit when it was introduced shortly before the turn of the century, replacing the tubular silhouette and padded-shoulder look that had been popular until then. The Brooks Brothers sack suit would become known as the first genuinely American suit, the quintessential business suit.

In 1915, shortly before Brooks Brothers's centennial, a new flagship store opened at 346 Madison Avenue in New York City, its current location. The store started by Henry Sands Brooks, who toasted sailors across the counter when they bought a suit, has been providing furnishings for men, women, and boys for 175 years.

Calvin Klein

Calvin Klein and Barry Schwartz were childhood friends growing up in the Bronx. Calvin always seemed to have a knack for knowing which combinations of clothes looked good. When Barry's mother took him clothes shopping, she always took Calvin along to hear his opinions.

Klein attended the Fashion Institute of Technology and began work in 1962 as a twenty-year old apprentice at twenty-five dollars a week. Schwartz went into the army, but his father was killed in a hold-up at his Harlem grocery store and Barry was discharged to run the store and support the family. He turned the grocery store into a profitable business. In 1968, he offered fifty percent of the business to his friend Calvin.

Klein was sorely tempted. After six years he had found little success. But he suggested they both come into his industry instead. Klein invested two thousand dollars and Schwartz ten thousand dollars to start Calvin Klein, Limited. A few weeks later, Martin Luther King was assassinated and rioting looters destroyed the Harlem store. Schwartz was in the fashion business full-time.

It was not a boom time in the world of fashion. The hippie generation was an era of dressing down, anti-fashion. One area where style was still in vogue was women's coats, and Klein concentrated his efforts there. He created a classic understated version of the trench coat, and personally wheeled his samples through the offices of Bonwit Teller, landing a fifty-thousand dollars order. Calvin Klein Limited was off.

Klein designed and Schwartz sold. When Klein launched a line of ladies sportswear, Schwartz wouldn't sell any popular Klein coats unless the buyer bought the sportswear too. While European designers still emphasized a layered look, Klein created clean, classic clothes that showed off women's bodies.

In 1975, Klein announced he would no longer use manmade fabrics, and introduced a designer jean. Jeans had been the lowest garment imaginable. They were popular as a uniform in the grungy 1960s and early 1970s, but as fashion came back jean sales fell off. Connie Dowling, a Bloomingdale's buyer, suggested that Klein make a stylish jean and market it as a high-fashion item emblazoned with his name.

Klein priced his new jeans at fifty dollars, twice the cost of traditional jeans. They were a hit, and when Klein launched provocative advertising campaigns they became a sensation. For many Americans, Calvin Klein jeans were the first designer item they ever owned.

Klein's quality and designs for the masses made America the fashion capital of the world. By the 1980s, European designers were copying American mass culture. Stores were selling over one billion dollars of Calvin Klein clothes as he became a celebrity.

Cannon

James William Cannon came of age in the Reconstruction Period in the South. His schooling ended when the Civil War ended. There was distress and destruction everywhere. The war-torn South was a total economic disaster area.

Cannon began clerking in a general supply store for bed and board, earning nothing but his keep. He clerked until he had developed a successful business buying and selling cotton crops. Then he opened a general merchandise store in Concord, North Carolina in 1877.

The South was still reeling from the devastation of the War. For ten years, Cannon watched poverty-ridden farmers come to his store and pay high prices for commodities imported from the North, particularly cloth manufactured out of cotton they had sold for pennies a pound.

Like other men of the day, Cannon realized that the South must have industry, not just agriculture. He studied the small mills around Concord with the idea of starting mills to provide employment and rupture the high-priced competition. With $12,000 of his own money and $75,000 from the sale of stock, he started Cannon Mills in 1887.

His product that first year was a cotton yarn; he then introduced a coarse grade of cotton known as Cannon cloth. In 1898, Cannon produced the first cotton hand towel manufactured in the South. He built a series of mills to produce the popular towels until 1905, when he purchased a six-hundred-acre farm to build a state-of-the-art factory to create his hand towels.

A rambling company town soon formed on the farm to house Cannon's twenty thousand employees. It was called Kannapolis—Greek for "loom city"—as Cannon grew to be the largest of the manufacturers of household textiles. Cannon was able to make it all work because of integrity and industry. He had never played as a boy, and never played as an adult. He had no hobbies, no form of recreation. He was not social, not public-minded, not inclined to publicity. "The less you say the less you will have to take back," said the man who presided over the mills until his death in 1921.

Much of the progress and development in household textiles is the result of Cannon's merchandising, advertising, and research. He planned a vast consumer advertising program—unheard of in the textile trade—but couldn't come up with a way for people who liked his products to ask for them by name before he died. It was left to one of his six sons to discover a way to sew the Cannon trademark to each towel and expand the immense textile business beyond even his father's vast vision.

Converse

It is a sad irony that the man whose name graces one of America's greatest athletic shoes was, for much of his life, sickly. Marquis Converse was born in Lyme, New Hampshire in 1861. Infirmities stalled his early business career, but he worked his way into a superintendent's position in Boston's Houghton & Dutton department store by his early twenties. The job was short-lived, however, as sickness forced him to resign.

In 1887, Converse co-founded a rubber shoe agency, but once again illnesses left him too weak to participate in the venture. This time he spent three years recovering. When Converse resumed his business activities, it was as a salesman. In 1908, at nearly fifty years of age, Converse started his own firm again.

By 1910, the Converse Rubber Shoe Company in Malden, Massachusetts was producing fifty-five hundred rubber shoes a day. In 1917, Converse introduced the high-topped canvas All Star, America's first basketball shoe. Charles "Chuck" Taylor was hired as one of sport's earliest player endorsers. In the days before professional basketball, Taylor starred for barnstorming teams across the country, playing and pushing his Converse shoes.

From his experiences on the court, Taylor designed sturdier soles for increased ankle support and traction. In 1923, Taylor's signature was sewn to an ankle patch. The highly recognizable shoe was adopted by the United States Olympic team in 1930. One year before he died in 1969 Chuck Taylor, a pioneer in sports marketing, was enshrined in the Naismith Memorial Basketball Hall of Fame.

Despite the success of the All Star, business was as much a daily struggle for Marquis Converse as was his health. By 1929 his firm had slipped into receivership. Two years later he dropped dead on the streets of Boston from a fatal heart attack. He had improbably lived into his seventieth year, but did not live to see the athletic shoe become a part of everyday fashion.

Endicott-Johnson

The man who was destined to have one of the largest payrolls in America didn't seem to be able to hold a job of his own. Henry

Bradford Endicott left his father's Dedham, Massachusetts farm in 1871 at the age of eighteen. In Boston he got work in a plumber's shop. Later he would allow that all he ever knew about the plumbing business was the extortionate prices one had to pay. When a state fair opened, Endicott went there instead of the shop. He was fired.

His job at a hardware store lasted ten days because he didn't like the way the customers were treated. Positions as an errand boy, porter, and woolen goods clerk all came and went before the year was out. Then Henry Endicott wandered into the leather district.

This he liked. When he was twenty-two, he used a legacy from his grandfather and a loan from his father, $2,900 in all, to open his own leather supply business. He prospered in this endeavor, and in 1890 he bought into a distressed Lester Brothers Shoe Company in Binghamton, New York.

Endicott sold enough boots to turn a small profit, but he was dissatisfied with his manager. A foreman applied for the job and stated confidently that he would work for nothing for one year if he did not show results. George F. Johnson would eventually become Endicott's partner.

With Johnson handling the manufacturing and Endicott the finances, the business grew rapidly. Endicott-Johnson became the first manufacturer to open its own company shoe stores. They built tanneries and achieved total integration of the shoe business.

They initiated an "Industrial Democracy" to manage their workforce, which would grow to over thirty thousand people under their command. Company towns of Endicott, West Endicott, and Johnson City sprouted in southern New York to house workers. An Endicott-Johnson employee was given an opportunity to acquire neat, clean homes at cost and enjoyed recreational facilities, health care, and libraries. In an era of unrest, Endicott-Johnson suffered not one strike. Endicott and Johnson initiated a profit-sharing scheme by which all profits went to the employees after seven percent had been earned on the preferred stock and ten percent on the common.

With the onset of World War I, Endicott was recruited to assist the war effort on the home front. He threw himself completely into the role, never once visiting his company office for the duration of the war. Endicott personally adjusted nearly 150 labor disputes to keep the American war machine rolling.

The effort seemed to sap the life out of him. He died in early 1920 at the age of sixty-six. Johnson assumed the mantle of presidency for America's leading shoe manufacturer. By the time Johnson stepped down in 1930, Endicott-Johnson had sold its one billionth shoe.

Foster Grant

In 1920, Jack Goodman received a large order for plastic dice embedded with rhinestones from Kresge stores. It was a huge account, and Goodman would do whatever he must to satisfy Kresge. That included taking a harrowing trolley ride twenty miles out to Leominster, Massachusetts to visit the Viscoloid Company, the leading plastics manufacturer of the day.

Viscoloid was too busy to fill Goodman's order. The account was too important to abandon his quest, and Goodman began to investigate the small plastics firms around Leominster that handled Viscoloid's overflow business. When he happened upon the dilapidated Foster Grant office it hardly seemed worth his time. But the thirty-seven-year-old man with the endearing Austrian accent he found inside soon changed his mind.

Samuel Foster turned out plastic dice of such superior quality that within a year he was making a third of all Goodman's plastic products, including combs and costume jewelry. In another two years, he was producing it all. The Foster Grant Company was a going concern at last.

Foster had been working ever since his family had arrived in New England in 1897, when he was fourteen. His first venture was making and selling fireworks, but the tiny enterprise literally exploded on him. He became a waiter and a maker of costume jewelry, until he went to business for Viscoloid supervising their plastic comb-making operations in 1907.

Foster stayed with Viscoloid for a dozen years, until leaving to start the Foster Manufacturing Company to produce tiny plastic flower jewelry. He took on a salesman-partner named William Grant. For whatever reason Grant lasted only three or four months. Returning Grant's investment left Foster so financially strapped that he couldn't afford to legally change the company name back from Foster Grant, and so it stayed.

Now with Goodman's business, Foster's fortunes swung. He found success with a four-by-six-inch plastic bird cage and plastic canary. He created a memo pad with attached plastic crayons capable of carrying imprinted advertising which were a huge hit.

No one knows when Samuel Foster first decided to make sunglasses; it was sometime between 1927 and 1929. He sketched a design on ordinary brown paper wrapping and moistened it in oil. He applied several pieces to plastic frames and temple bars fashioned on a jigsaw. The first pair of Foster Grants were made as a kiddie toy and sold for ten cents.

Tinted glasses had been used sporadically to that time, mostly as protection in industry. But as the movie industry grew in Hollywood, picture stars were photographed in fan magazines wearing sunglasses to shield their eyes from the California sun. The style quickly caught on with the public.

Foster Grant was a pioneer in plastic frames. In 1930, Foster brought a German machine to Leominster for injection molding of plastics. Foster Grant technicians made it the first commercially adaptable injection molding machine in the United States. By 1942, Foster Grant had perfected injection molding techniques.

Samuel Foster withdrew from the company at the age of 59. He took a financial settlement and headed to Los Angeles. Foster established a string of self-service gas stations and dabbled in real estate as Foster Grant became the most famous name in sunglasses.

ucci

In the 1970s, the Gucci shop in New York City earned the title, bestowed by *New York* magazine, as "The Rudest Store in New York." Gucci management was so "upset" by the customer abuse detailed within that the author was sent a five hundred dollar floral bouquet. After all, Guccio Gucci had cultivated snob appeal from the time he opened his first store in Florence, Italy in 1922.

Guccio was born in Florence in 1881, where his family managed a struggling straw hat factory. He had no intention of fighting his father's battles, and left for London at the turn of the century. Gucci found a job at the world famous Savoy Hotel, where he was waiter to the rich and famous for three years. On the job, Gucci paid studious attention to what the glamorous patrons wore and how they spent their money.

When World War I ended, Gucci was ready to implement his ideas. He learned the leather goods business with an Italian firm called Franzi, and then opened Gucci's. From the start, Gucci specialized in the highest quality leather luggage and handbags, many of his designs based on what he had seen in the Savoy. Gucci bags traveled on the arms of international trendsetters who had stopped in Florence to view the city's many art treasures.

Guccio Gucci created a linked GG symbol that resembled a jointed mouth bit for a horse and equine motifs became a Gucci trademark. The signature Gucci red and green stripe was borrowed from horse blankets. The Gucci trademark was internationally registered in 1953, launching an almost continuous barrage of lawsuits against Gucci knockoffs.

1953 was a landmark year for Gucci in other ways as well. Gucci opened its first New York store in a small nook in the Sherry Netherland Hotel, bringing the elegant Gucci moccasin and hand-stitched glove and other desirable luxury items to the United States. Americans would learn the name Gucci from movie stars like Elizabeth Taylor and Grace Kelly and Kim Novak, who were some of Gucci's best customers. But they would never get a chance to know Guccio Gucci; he passed away in 1953.

Haggar

Joseph Marion Hajjar was born into hardscrabble circumstances on a Lebanese farm in 1892. His father died in a fall from a horse when Joseph was just two, putting further hardship on the family to cull a living from the sparse soil. At thirteen, Joseph fled the impoverished village to join a sister in Mexico. He stayed three years, peddling on the streets until he left for the United States, paying two dollars border tax to cross into Laredo.

Penniless and speaking no English, Haggar, as he would now be known, got work on a railroad, then on a cotton farm. Eventually he migrated to the Little Lebanon region of St. Louis where he made his first real money brokering an oil lease. He further honed his business skills as a salesman for Ely & Walker, a dry goods wholesaler, where he closed deals in his native Arabic, acquired Spanish, and adopted English.

Having earned enough to marry and start a family, and supremely confident in his sales ability, Haggar went out on the road selling Oberman work pants on straight commission. By 1926 he was ready to open his own business, making menswear in Dallas. He sold only on a one-price policy, unique for the industry, which he hit upon while selling on the road.

Haggar's pants were unlabeled and just a cut above work pants. He sold enough to weather the Great Depression, and in 1939 he became the first manufacturer to nationally advertise branded slacks. At the time, the only men's clothing identifiable by name was Arrow shirts. Haggar was always ahead of the industry: first to offer two pairs of pants for a reduced price, first to sell prepackaged ready-to-wear slacks, first to manufacture double knit pants. Legend had it that the "Slacks King" could handle a piece of fabric and tell what mill it came from.

In 1976, on the occasion of his company's fiftieth anniversary, Joseph Haggar was presented with the Horatio Alger Award, in recognition of how far he had come from the rocky Lebanese desert. In the same year he received an honorary doctorate of law from Notre Dame University, an ironic tribute to a man who always crossed out the legalese on the back of contracts and scribbled in his own personal guarantee.

Hanes

Hanes is the only corporation in America ever to form from two independent, noncompeting businesses from the same family. That merger in 1962 brought the saga of the Hanes family, founded when Marcus Hanes settled in York, Pennsylvania from Germany in 1738, around full circle.

Marcus Hanes bought 1,060 acres in North Carolina and moved his family south. Here, brothers Pleasant Henderson Hanes and John Wesley Hanes grew up in the middle of the nineteenth century. Pleasant, five years older, was born in 1845 and served in Company E of the 16th North Carolina Cavalry during the Civil War. Hanes distinguished himself in duty and was named a special courier to Robert E. Lee, serving with the Confederate commander until Appomattox.

After the war, the brothers began selling plug tobacco from wagons they guided throughout North Carolina. In 1872, the brothers started a tobacco company in Winston. Pleasant and John shepherded the P. H. Hanes Tobacco Company through two factory fires until they had built the third largest tobacco business in America. A serious illness to John forced the brothers to sell the business to R. J. Reynolds in 1900 for $175,000. When John regained his health, the Hanes reinvested their profits into the textile industry—but as independent proprietors.

John Wesley concentrated on men's stockings and named his company Shamrock Mills; Pleasant manufactured a new type of knitwear, men's heavyweight, two-piece underwear. John's health broke again and he died in 1903. The company changed names in 1914 to the Hanes Hosiery Mills, and by 1920 women's hosiery had replaced men's socks as the firm's only product.

Pleasant Hanes continued in charge of his P. H. Hanes Knitting Company until his death in 1925 at the age of seventy-nine. The two firms continued to operate autonomously under the brothers' descendants until 1962, when the two Hanes companies consolidated—back under the family name once again.

Hart Schaffner & Marx

In 1887, Joseph Schaffner stopped in the shop of two of his close friends, Chicago clothiers Harry and Max Hart. He was seeking career advice. After seventeen years of bookkeeping in the credit business, Schaffner was contemplating a new opportunity in Minnesota, a total departure from his accounting work. Before making such a radical change, the Harts suggested, why don't you come into business with us?

Harry Hart, then twenty-one, and his brother Max, eighteen, had been selling men's clothing since 1872 when they pooled $2,700 their father had saved from their teenage days as delivery boys to start a men's store. The Harts figured that Chicago's estimated 100,000 homeless after the Great Fire of 1871 would need to be clothed. Within three years they were successful enough to open a second store, and began manufacturing suits for other retailers.

The Harts brought brothers-in-law Levi Abt and Marcus Marx into the business in 1879, and it was Abt who Schaffner would be replacing in the team's management. Schaffner, the lifelong book-keeper was, incongruously, a literary man at heart. With Hart Schaffner & Marx he supervised the firm's sales letters with such eloquence that when an anthology of *Selected English Letters* was published years later, one of the firm's sales letters was included alongside those of Jonathan Swift, Abraham Lincoln, and others.

Schaffner's literary bent led inevitably to the industry's first national clothing ads in 1897. The industry was not impressed, and it was years before other clothiers joined Hart Schaffner and Marx in print. Schaffner's illustrated ads were supported by moralistic books he penned on "Courage" and "Enthusiasm." Many booklets didn't even include the company in the copy.

Hart Schaffner & Marx assumed industry leadership in other areas as well. At a time when salesmen of the day lugged as many as twenty wardrobe trunks of samples into accounts, Hart Schaffner & Marx salesmen switched to displaying fabric swatches. They pioneered standard pricing, with no discounts for favored customers. A Hart Schaffner Marx suit was the first to be guaranteed to be 100% wool when it said 100% wool. In 1906, Hart Schaffner & Marx identified fourteen basic body types, which led to the creation of 250 specialty sizes in suits.

It seems the Harts had given Joseph Schaffner excellent career advice a generation before.

Kinney

For a man who had the burden of responsibility constantly thrust upon him in his personal life, it is ironic that George Romanta Kinney made his fortune by abdicating responsibility. Kinney was one of America's first franchisers—the managers of his stores made all day-to-day decisions while the "home office" was responsible only for purchasing.

Kinney was born to a Candor, New York merchant whose store failed shortly thereafter. His father died in 1875 when Kinney was nine. He raised money for the family working around town until the age of seventeen, when he left for the big city of Binghamton and a position with the Lester Shoe Company. In 1888, Kinney was promoted to manager of a store in Waverly, New York, providing enough of a stake to marry. But his wife died in childbirth in 1890, and the Lester Shoe Company went bankrupt.

Left alone to start over, Kinney bought the failing Lester's inventory for fifteen hundred dollars. He opened another store in Waverly with one employee, cobbler Milner Kemp. He sold shoes to the entire family at discount prices, at a time when few retailers sold mens, womens, boys, and girls shoes under one roof. Kinney hung his shoes on wallboards outside his shop and posted prices on the boards.

The innovations worked; Kinney was able to open a second store in Corning, New York within the year. By 1899, he was operating eight stores. Every new manager Kinney brought into the business was regarded as a partner. The partner invested in the store and ran the daily operations. Kinney retreated from the retail floor to the Woolworth Building in New York City, where he concentrated on buying shoes and shoe factories.

George Kinney's empire building was ended by his death in 1919 from complications stemming from a circulatory attack in 1907. At the time, the fifty-three-year-old Kinney had more than four dozen shoe stores in thirteen states.

Lee

All Henry David Lee wanted was to have his clothing orders filled on time. He was sixty-two years old and had built the dominant wholesale grocery business in the Midwest. But when he diversified his mercantile operation to include clothing, he discovered his textile suppliers were not as reliable as his growers. Lee solved the problem the best way he knew how; he built his own garment factory near his warehouse in Salina, Kansas in 1911.

Lee was born in Vermont in 1849 and started his business career distributing kerosene in Galion, Ohio. In 1888, he sold his business to John Rockefeller and left Ohio for Kansas. The next year he was back in business as the H. D. Lee Mercantile Company, distributing food instead of fuel. Over the next dozen years he added hardware, stationery, and notions—and the bothersome clothing—to his line.

Lee started in the garment trade with rugged overalls, jackets, and dungarees. A one-piece pullover called the Union-All, helpful in protecting regular clothing, was his first big seller. Developed in 1913, the Union-All was a pair of dungarees sewn to a jacket. It was adopted as an official fatigue by the U.S. Army in World War I, and by 1916 Lee had four garment plants in operation. The next year he pioneered national advertising for apparel in the *Saturday Evening Post*.

The Union-All marked the beginning of product innovation for Lee. Denim cowboy pants, which would become the famous Lee Riders, reached the market in 1924; two years later jeans with zippers appeared, and soon thereafter came tailored sizing. Henry Lee died, still president, in 1928. His company was well on the way to becoming America's largest manufacturer of work clothes.

Levi's

In 1877, two pairs of overalls arrived in the offices of Levi Strauss & Company in San Francisco. A letter was attached that read: "The secratt of them Pents is the Rivets that I put in those Pockets and I found the demand so large that I cannot make them fast enough. My nabors are getting yealouse of these success and unless I secure it by Patent Papers it will soon become a general thing. Everybody will make them up and thare will be no money in it.

"Therefore Gentleman, I wish to make you a proposition that you should take out the Latters Patent in my name as I am the inventor of it, the expense of it will be about $68, all complit . . . "

The letter was from Jacob Davis, a Latvian immigrant from Reno, Nevada.

Levi Strauss paid for Jacob Davis's patent for "Improvement in Fastening Pocket Openings." The patent would be among the most illegally imitated patents in United States history.

Levis Strauss was already successful when he learned about Jacob Davis, and had been for nearly thirty years. Strauss was born in 1829 in Bavaria, the youngest of six children. After his father died in 1846 he emigrated to New York to join his brothers Jonas and Louis in the dry goods trade.

In 1848, Strauss struck out on his own to sell dry goods in Kentucky. Peddling on the streets, Strauss often lugged hundred-pound loads to his customers. In 1849, Strauss sailed to San Francisco to join the Gold Rush. He went to work in his brother-in-law's store, in the midst of the greatest population explosion in American history.

At first Strauss served the miners, peddling goods in lawless boomtowns. The population grew so fast that every cargo ship that arrived in port was immediately under siege from eager merchants needing to replenish their shelves. Strauss made sturdy canvas work pants, often using sails and tents when material from his brothers in New York did not arrive on time.

The company grew steadily as Strauss established himself as

boss of the enterprise. He took over completely in 1861, and set up Levi Strauss & Co. By this time, Strauss was importing a French denim from which he made "waist high overalls." "Jeans" was a derogatory phrase referring to cheap work pants from Genoa, Italy. "Jeans" is from the French word for Genoa, "genes." Strauss dyed his denim blue to mask soil stains.

In 1865, Strauss built a new headquarters in downtown San Francisco. Wary of the numerous fires that flashed through town, he built his new offices out of brick and stone. Three months later an earthquake cracked its foundation.

Strauss was one of San Francisco's leading merchants when he bought Jacob Davis's patent. His name appeared on a list of men who were worth at least four million dollars in a local newspaper. He owned a large chunk of downtown San Francisco real estate.

Now his business exploded. Davis came to San Francisco to be head tailor, and Strauss expanded into factory production. He sold 21,600 pairs of riveted pants and coats the first year of production. So buyers could recognize the Levi Strauss brand, a special stitching was added to the pockets, shaped in a crossed double V in orange thread.

In the 1880s a new label made of leather was created. Levi's "Two Horse Brand" work clothes were even known in Paris. Strauss promised a "new pair free" if his riveted pants pockets ever ripped. In 1890 his patent was gone. Strauss kept his high quality work pants—known as 501s—in his catalog, but offered a cheaper version as well.

By this time, Strauss had turned much of the business over to his nephews. Partly due to the paucity of pioneer women in his younger days, Strauss never married. He traveled extensively and donated great sums for Jewish charities and education. He died in 1902 at age seventy-three when jeans were still a workman's pants.

Liz Claiborne

In retrospect, the concept seems so logical: design attractive clothes the average woman could wear and free working women from the standard office uniform of navy blue suits. But it took until 1976 to execute the idea. The result was one of the fastest growing companies in United States business history, reaching the *Fortune* Magazine list of 500 largest companies within ten years.

Liz Claiborne was a shy woman who always followed her own path. As a young girl, she lived in so many places following her banking father that she never finished high school. She wanted a career in fashion, but her father was against it, so she went to Paris and Brussels, her birthplace, to study painting. In 1949, at the age of twenty, Claiborne won a *Harper's Bazaar* design contest, and a year later she returned to the United States. Against her parents' wishes, she cut her long hair and got married. She took jobs as a sketch artist and New York model.

When she was in her mid-twenties, Arthur Ortenberg hired Claiborne as a designer. They shed their respective mates and married in 1957. Claiborne became chief designer at Jonathan Logan, where she spent years lobbying for a new line of clothes for the emerging class of highly paid working women of the late 1960s and early 1970s.

When their son reached age twenty-one in 1976, Claiborne and Ortenberg struck out on their own with $50,000. Two other partners brought in another $200,000. Claiborne designed well-made fashionable sportswear for the office, weaning women away from formless suits.

Within two years, Claiborne's designs were generating $23,000,000 in revenue. She had dreamed of a small company where she would make clothes for professional women. She was clearly onto something bigger. The four partners retreated to the Pocono Mountains for three days to chart their future. There were two votes to stay small—but they weren't from Claiborne and Ortenberg.

Ortenberg was the genius behind the organization. They created

"Claiboards" which showed department stores how to mix and match Claiborne fashions to maximize visual appeal. They hired no sales force, making buyers visit their offices to see new designs. Claiborne created six seasons rather than four, so there was a constant flow of material for the department stores, the exclusive outlet for Claiborne fashions.

By 1981 Ortenberg took the company public, with one of the most popular stock issues in history. Claiborne, as Chief Executive Officer, retained 4.3 percent of the stock in the two billion dollar company. Her designs clothed sixty percent of the twelve million women who went to work every day in the 1980s.

Ralph Lauren

Ralph Lifshitz was born in the Bronx in 1939, the son of an artist and house painter. His father changed the family name to "Lauren" in the 1950s, just before his son started a stint in the Army.

Lauren always had an interest in clothes. He spent most of his spare money on clothes and wanted to get into fashion designing after his discharge, but he had no portfolio, no sketches. "All I had," said Lauren later, "was taste."

He worked as a salesman and garment buyer until 1967, when he landed a design job with Beau Brummel Ties. Using unusual fabrics, Lauren created ties four inches and five inches wide, fifty percent wider than traditional ties. The tie was the only fashion statement a businessman could make, and Lauren's innovative ties were wildly successful. He persuaded Beau Brummel to allow him to start his own division, which Lauren called Polo because of its aristocratic image.

Lauren took Polo out on his own shortly afterwards. He built his entire empire on the shape of a tie. The tie made a larger knot, so he had to design shirts with large collars and suits that complemented the shirts. His clothes were distinctly American, with more shape than traditional menswear.

Lauren was widely criticized, not only for his clothes but for his lack of formal design training. He was accused of stealing styles and eras for his designs. Lauren was not affected by the carping. He was one of the first designers to leave a specialty and design across the entire spectrum of clothing. In 1971, he crossed over from men's clothes to women's clothes.

This line was popular as well, but Lauren's company was near collapse. Business was not Lauren's strong suit. He had been staked by Norman Hilton in 1968 for $50,000 in exchange for fifty percent of the business. He bought Hilton out for $633,000 in 1972, and strained the company treasury. Now he switched some lines from manufacturing to licensing to steady the ship.

The man who sells more than a billion dollars worth of clothes with a personal fortune in excess of four hundred million dollars personally favors faded jeans and tweed jackets: "I wanted to be a history teacher. I liked the gum-soled shoes and tweed jackets and the pipes. I never liked the business world because I wanted a life that was free of not being honest or straightforward."

Stetson

John Stetson stood transfixed on a St. Louis hillside as the rampaging Missouri River savaged his brickyard below. Finally, as the flood waters carried off his inventory, Stetson roared, "Let 'er go!

I'm not the first man to make a fortune and lose it." Stetson could embrace that philosophy more easily than most. He had, after all, only come out to the West to die.

John Batterson Stetson was born into a family of hatters in Orange, New Jersey in 1830. The youngest of the Stetson boys, John learned the family trade in his father's hat shop. But the education came at a terrible price. At the age of twenty-one, Stetson was diagnosed with tuberculosis, a malady common to early-day hatters. Doctors gave him only a few months to live.

Young Stetson decided to spend his final days outdoors and headed to the frontier. But by the time he reached St. Louis he had regained his health. He found work in a local brickyard, and two years later Stetson owned the business—just in time to watch it wiped out by the floods.

Stetson took off for the gold fields of Colorado, where he found his hatter's skills adapted well to the trail. Tents of the time were fashioned from joined animal skins. These crude shelters were routinely compromised by the elements, and quickly acquired an ungodly stench. Stetson was able to apply the ancient process of felting to produce a soft, waterproof tentcloth from the animal furs.

Turning to hats, Stetson crafted a roomy, wide-brimmed chapeau for himself that shaded the withering sun of the Plains and warded off pelting rain. One day a passing rider offered Stetson a five-dollar gold piece for his hat. That one sale represented a good portion of his earnings in the Gold Rush.

In 1865, he returned to Philadelphia with a hundred dollars, and set up a small one-room millinery. He busied himself repairing, trimming, and making the European-looking hats of the day. At most he was able to sell one or two hats at a time.

Impatient with his progress, Stetson created a daring hat based on his experiences in the American West. His "Boss of the Plains" was big, with a four-inch brim and a four-inch crown. It was natural-colored and sported a leather strap for a hatband. A "Boss of the Plains" sold for an extravagant five dollars. Finer material would run you ten dollars. And, at the top of the line, pure beaver or nutria could be had for thirty dollars.

Stetson sent a sample hat to dozens of merchants throughout the Southwest with a letter asking for a minimum order of a dozen

"Boss of the Plains" hats. It was a bold move. Stetson was risking his business and his line of credit on an entirely new style.

The plan worked. The new Stetson hat soon blanketed the West. John Stetson would eventually stitch together a network of 10,000 dealers and 150 wholesalers. His one-room millinery evolved into a modern factory—fireproofed with the finest in ventilation—covering an entire Philadelphia block.

In his later years, Stetson gobbled up thousands of acres of Florida real estate, including several orange groves, in which he took great pride. He founded Deland, Florida as his retirement home, and held a controlling interest in nearly all its industries and institutions.

He provided a million dollar endowment for Deland Academy, which was renamed Stetson University. He took an active role in the school's affairs, serving as president of the board of trustees. In 1906 John Stetson, who had been told he was going to die shortly fifty-five years earlier, died suddenly, in apparent good health, after a trustees meeting in Florida. A blood vessel had burst in his brain.

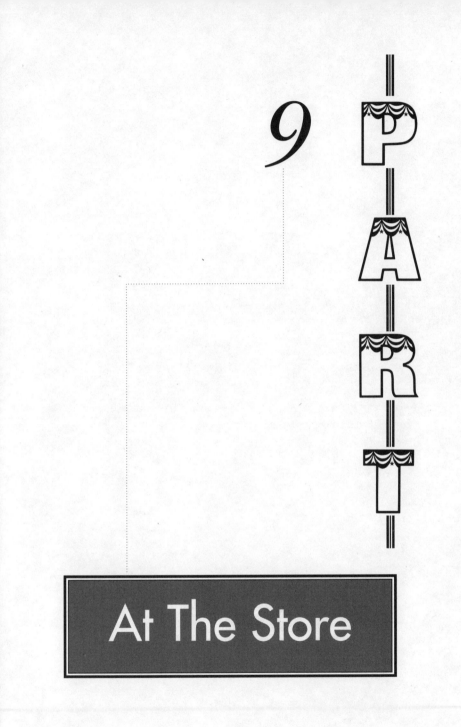

9

PART

At The Store

Bloomingdale's

Lyman Bloomingdale loved store windows. He rented his first store, with his brother Joseph, in 1872, far from fashionable Union Square in New York's depressed upper East Side. The building was only twenty feet wide by seventy feet deep, but it had two large, perfect plate glass windows.

Lyman set out to create exciting showcases in his windows, while Joseph looked after the books. Lyman believed that storefront windows were wasted if all they did was show merchandise. Bloomingdale's windows would be silent stages with eye-catching panoramas to lure curious customers inside.

Bloomingdale saw more in his location than attractive windows. He knew the city of New York had purchased a huge tract of land on the East Side and was developing a fresh, green haven to be called Central Park. New Yorkers would soon migrate to his location at the future park's southern tip, Bloomingdale figured.

The Bloomingdale family had a history of being on the cutting edge in New York. With his father, Lyman had operated Bloomingdale's Hoop Skirt and Ladies Notion Shop to keep New York women in step with high European fashion prior to the Civil War. Joseph was a successful traveling salesman, taking hoop skirts as far as California.

First day sales were only $3.68. But one month later the brothers knocked down the storeroom partition to provide more selling room. The Panic of 1873 caused a shift in merchandising philosophy to the best value at the lowest prices. Lyman Bloomingdale created the *19th Ward Gazette*, a free paper that supplemented his

241

regular advertisements. The paper provided light news and features in depressed times, binding the store to the community.

Meanwhile, New Yorkers migrated toward Central Park. Railroads developed, and soon Bloomingdale's marked the epicenter of Manhattan's web of mass transit routes. Lyman set out to let the world know that "All cars transfer to Bloomingdale's." He placed the phrase on placards in New York's trolleys, in his ads, and on his horse drawn delivery cars. A patron of the arts, he commissioned scenic European paintings on his exterior store walls.

By 1880, Bloomingdale's had grown into a five-story building— a department store with plenty of show windows. Lyman took out full page newspaper ads to draw people into the store. Inside, employees demonstrated new products. He had a young woman read from popular books of the day in the book department. He installed New York's first neon arc lights, fascinating shoppers.

The brothers built their grandest building in 1886, at Third Avenue and 59th Street. The new store was six stories high with 245 feet of street space for window shoppers. The first story was an impressive eighteen feet high, to better show off Lyman's displays. He used glass elevators he called "sky carriages" to transport customers throughout the magnificent store.

In 1892, Lyman installed his first escalator, a dream machine seemingly invented for him. It was not only a fantastic attention-getter, but gave people a slow, panoramic ride on their individual platforms gazing at his merchandise. Lyman invested in the escalator company.

Bloomingdale's continued catering to lower middle class patrons, but started importing fine European goods for society-conscious Americans. The brothers opened offices in Paris, Berlin, and Vienna to provide exclusive continental goods for Bloomingdale's.

Sales boomed. Rather than build another building, Lyman and Joseph bought adjacent buildings until they owned eighty percent of the block. Joseph retired from the business on New Year's Day 1896, while Lyman continued as sole proprietor until his death in 1905 at the age of sixty-four. Joseph had died a year earlier at age sixty-two. Lyman's son Sam carried on the five-million-dollar business built on its exciting store windows.

Eckerd's

Jack Eckerd was never one for waiting around. It was a trait that was to mold his business career and alter Americans' shopping habits.

As a nineteen-year-old in 1932, Eckerd set out to be a barnstorming pilot around Erie, Pennsylvania. He convinced his father to buy an airplane so he could fly Jack around to his small chain of drugstores. After two years, he flew to California for a one-year course in commercial aviation. But waiting around for a pilot opening was not for him, and Eckerd went east to the drugstore business.

He bought a quarter-interest in two Wilmington, Delaware drugstores, but World War II interrupted his blossoming retail career. Eckerd spent the war in the Air Transport Command delivering planes from Wilmington to Prestwick, Scotland. After the war he bought both stores outright.

In 1948, Eckerd bought two dilapidated drugstores from his father in Jamestown, New York. He didn't plan to just rebuild the tired stores. Eckerd had investigated self-service in California and was ready to try the no-waiting concept in his new stores. Customers were thought to want to rely on a druggist's help, but Eckerd anticipated the over-the-counter explosion with open access to goods.

When his small chain reached Erie, Eckerd was forced to call his self-service drugstore QuikCheck to avoid confusion with his father's stores. The new store was a phenomenal success but people still confused newspaper ads with the conventional Eckerd's stores. Jack Eckerd didn't want to change the name so he started considering a totally new market.

On a dreary March day in 1952 a direct mailing arrived in his Wilmington office from a Tampa druggist offering three stores for sale. The gray skies outside were excuse enough to fly to Florida and check out the properties. He raised $150,000 in cash, in part from his brother in exchange for fifty percent of the new stores and his Jamestown stores.

It took two years for the Florida stores to break into the black, and after six years only three stores were added. At that time, he was offered a chance to build five stores with Publix, the leading Florida grocery chain. This twinning of drugstores to supermarkets ignited Eckerd's growth. Eckerd built his chain to seventeen hundred stores from Florida to New Jersey.

Jack Eckerd spent the 1960s building his business. In the 1970s, dissatisfied with Florida government, he entered the state gubernatorial race. Despite never running for anything in his life Eckerd forced a runoff with the incumbent governor before losing. He lost a race for a United States Senate seat in 1974 and another bid for governor, but went to Washington and served as administrator of the General Services Administration under Gerald Ford. After his flirtation with politics, Eckerd retired, devoting his time to Christian charities and sailing.

Hallmark

"I'd like to be the kind of friend you are to me." Those words, from Edgar Guest, were the first to ever appear on a Hallmark card—in 1916. In the nineteenth century it was simply too expensive to pay a messenger to deliver sentiments on paper, and the thought of sending someone *else's* words was simply preposterous. Today more than one-half of all the personal mail delivered in the United States is greeting cards, about seven billion a year. And ten million cards sent each day bear the mark of the man who changed the holiday calendar in America: Joyce Hall.

Hall was born in David City, Nebraska, where his father abandoned the family when Joyce was nine. At the age of fifteen, he was working in a bookstore in Norfolk, Nebraska where his favorite merchandise was not the impressive new books but the intriguing picture postcards the store stocked from Europe. In January 1910, Hall moved to a room in the YMCA in Kansas City (there is even a postcard of the YMCA in Hall's autobiography).

The next year his brother Rollie joined him in opening a specialty store for postcards, gifts, and stationery. The boys were prospering until a fire in 1915 burned away their business. The promise shown by the young men was enough to land a $25,000 loan to rebuild the store and purchase a neighboring engraving firm. The first two Hall cards appeared in 1915. They were unfolded, a little smaller than a postcard, and decoratively handpainted.

Gradually the Halls built a business around gifts. During Christmastime in 1917, Joyce Hall ran out of red and green tissue paper and substituted decorative envelope lining paper. Gift wrap and greeting cards were empire-builders for Hall, but not all his innovations were hits. In 1924 he introduced "Greetaphones," flat cards with records containing an 8-line sentiment with a musical background which no steel needle could decipher when played.

Greeting cards became extravagances of the first order during the Depression in the 1930s, but Hall refused to lay off any employees. In 1936 he revolutionized the greeting card business with the introduction of lighted, eye-level display cases featuring rows and rows of cards. Prior to that, greeting cards were purchased by asking a clerk, who would select an appropriate card.

The British invented the Christmas card, but it was the rare greeting that was sent at any other time of year. In America, however, there seemed hardly any occasion that wasn't worthy of a greeting card. Hall stoked the passions for greeting cards with the first advertising in national magazines in 1928, and by 1944 all his radio commercials were trailed by the unforgettable, "When you care enough to send the very best." Hall had at first rejected the tag line—written by staffer Ed Goodman—as too long, but it soon came to symbolize his entire philosophy.

He started a Hallmark Gallery on New York's Upper Fifth Avenue as an elegant showcase for Hallmark products and sponsored high-quality television specials—he even aired an opera—as early as 1951. These critically acclaimed ventures were not financially successful, but the reputation Hall developed was priceless.

When he wanted to feature some of Winston Churchill's paintings on greeting cards, Churchill agreed when told it was for Hallmark. "A good firm," he said.

Hall retired in 1966, but still maintained a busy work schedule. He spearheaded the conversion of eighty-five ruined acres—twenty-five blocks—on the southern edge of Kansas City into the stunning Crown Center. Work was still underway on his last project when he died in 1982, but the new Hallmark headquarters when finished embodied the credo he always lived for, "Good taste is good business."

Kresge's

Sebastian Spering Kresge's first business enterprise was a single hive of bees he nursed into a colony of thirty-two hives as a young boy. He would keep bees as an adult hobby because, he said, "My bees always remind me that hard work, thrift, sobriety, and earnest struggle to live an upright Christian life are the rungs of the ladder of success."

The profits from his hives helped finance his schooling at the Eastman Business College in Poughkeepsie, New York. What he couldn't pay for he borrowed from his father with a bargain that he would give his father all his earnings, save board and clothing, until he was twenty-one.

At nineteen he worked one year as a country schoolteacher for twenty-two dollars a month, but was anxious to get underway in business and began clerking in a Scranton grocery store in 1889. With his obligation met at age twenty-one, Kresge began exploring the business field working in door-to-door selling, insurance, bookkeeping, and baking before settling into the sale of tinware for five years on straight commission.

One of his customers was F. W. Woolworth, who impressed Kresge with the size and efficiency of his cash-only business. Kresge attempted to join Woolworth's 5¢ & 10¢ business in 1896, but was not successful. He entered into other retailing partnerships with eight thousand dollars he had carefully saved, working in stores in Pennsylvania, Tennessee, and Michigan.

By 1899 he was on his own in Detroit. Kresge put a large number of items on open counters where they could be examined and appraised. The slogan over his door said it all: "Nothing over 10 cents." Immediately Kresge set about to build a chain of 5 & 10s.

He had an uncanny knack for site location, and saw each new store as a personal challenge. His stores were in heavily trafficked areas and appealed to bargain hunters. By 1916, he had 150 Kresge 5 &10 stores.

With inflation after World War I, the heyday of the 5 & 10 came to an end. As a result, Kresge started "Green Front Stores" in 1920 which featured goods from twenty-five cents to a dollar to distinguish them from his Red Front 5 &10s. Both concepts prospered.

Kresge retired as president in 1925, devoting much of his time to the Kresge foundation—which he endowed with $1,300,000 in cash and $65,000,000 in securities. Kresge was extremely generous with employees and associates, but never learned to spend money on himself. His personal frugality was legendary. His stinginess was cited as a complaint in two messy, highly publicized divorces.

He used a pair of shoes until they were completely worn out— and then lined them with paper. His inexpensive plain suits lasted until the last thread. One of his rare indulgences was an air-cooled Franklin motor car which, according to a close associate, "he ran until the wheels fell off." At age fifty-eight some friends persuaded him to take up golf, but he gave up the sport after three rounds because, he said, he could not afford to lose a golf ball.

After his retirement as president, he remained active in company affairs as chairman of the board, a post he retained until the age of ninety-eight when the company had grown to include 670 Kresge variety stores, 150 K Mart department stores, and 110 Jupiter discount stores. He died in 1966, within sight of his birthplace in Mountainhome, Pennsylvania where his Swiss ancestors settled in 1765, at the age of ninety-nine. He lived to within one year of his mother, whose picture he displayed in every Kresge store until she died in 1940 at the age of one hundred.

Kroger's

When he was thirteen, in the Panic of 1873, Bernard Kroger's German immigrant father's Cincinnati dry goods store failed. Young Kroger was forced from school into the working world, securing a position as a drugstore clerk. The wages were good, but his mother couldn't abide her son working on Sundays and made him quit.

Unable to find work in Cincinnati, Kroger traveled to a farm thirty miles northeast of town. He worked from 4:30 in the morning until nightfall before returning exhausted to his unheated loft on top of a shed. He soon contracted malaria, but couldn't afford to stop working and surrender his six dollars a month. Finally, after nine months and with his weight down to a hundred pounds, he gave up. Kroger walked the thirty miles back to Cincinnati to save the train fare.

Still ill, he applied the next day for work as a salesman for the great Northern and Pacific Tea Company. The owner was none too eager to take on the gaunt, shriveled figure standing before him. He didn't look like he would last the week. But Kroger talked his way into a trial. He left with a sample case of sugar, coffee, and tea.

Kroger was soon making a steady seven dollars a week in commission sales, more than he had ever earned. Times were good, but he realized that sales were slowly slipping. Kroger investigated and discovered the store owner was cutting back on his quality. Kroger learned the lesson that was to guide him through the rest of his business career: "You can't fool people on food."

Now experienced, Kroger had no difficulty in finding another sales position. He landed with the Imperial Tea Company, but the owners proved to be inept. Kroger was prepared to move on when he was offered managership of the store. He negotiated complete control and set out to implement his retailing theories: long hours, frugality, and quality for the price.

Eleven months later, Kroger had the store operating at a profit, but the owners would not meet his terms for continued employment. With no hesitation, Kroger and a friend opened their own little store. The Great Western Tea Company greeted its first customer on July 1, 1883. But owning your own business isn't always what it's cracked up to be.

Two week later Dan, his delivery horse, was killed and Kroger's wagonload of goods smashed in a railroad crossing accident. Then one of Kroger's brothers died and he had to assume funeral expenses. A month later the Ohio River overflowed and flooded the store. Yet, by year's end the store was established with not a debt outstanding.

Kroger bought out his partner for fifteen hundred dollars and by 1885 he was stocking four stores. He bought in bulk directly from producers which allowed him to cut prices. When the country experienced a general business downturn in 1893, he bought more stores. In 1902, when he owned forty stores, he changed the business name to The Kroger Company & Baking Company.

Kroger had become the first grocery store to bake its own bread in 1901. He was able to sell loaves of bread for two and a half cents a loaf and still make a profit. Other items Kroger wasn't looking to make a profit on; he introduced the practice of loss leaders to the industry. When Kroger became the first store to combine groceries and meat he entered a drawn out battle with butchers in the community.

In 1908, Kroger celebrated twenty-five years in business. His 136 stores, all painted bright red inside and out, were beginning to become known outside the Cincinnati area. Kroger's grocery business was booming, but he was unable to transfer his success to other businesses. A newspaper venture failed and a foray into railroading was equally unsatisfying. At one point a Kroger train collided with a Kroger delivery truck. When he learned of the accident the boss railed, "There is just one spot in the whole United States where one of my damn railroad cars could hit one of my damn trucks and you fellows succeeded in finding it."

Kroger met more success in banking when he founded the Provident Bank in Cincinnati. But nothing matched his grocery empire. Kroger established a great laboratory staffed with food experts and chemists to scrutinize every food item his stores sold. He had stores in more than a thousand communities in the midwest, thirteen bakeries, three packing plants, a candy factory, and plants for roasting coffee and packing tea.

In 1928 Kroger sold his shares in the company for twenty-eight million dollars. His life became one of golf in the morning and cards in the afternoon. When the market crashed he bought much of his stock back, but retired from business for good in 1932. His last six years were devoted to philanthropic interests. When Bernard Kroger died in 1938 the company he had founded operated 4,844 stores.

L. L. Bean

All he really wanted was to keep his feet dry on deer-hunting trips. The all-leather logger's boot popular at the time gave good support but was uncomfortable and became unbearably heavy when wet. Rubber boots kept his feet dry but were awkward in the field.

What he needed, Leon Leonwood Bean knew, was a good hunting shoe.

Bean would later write, "My life up to the age of forty years was most uneventful, with a few exceptions." One was his first hunting trip when he was thirteen. The exhilaration over felling his first deer cultivated a lifelong love affair with the outdoors.

Bean, born in western Maine in 1873 and orphaned at age twelve, made his way by working on the farms of friends and relatives. As a young man he survived by trapping, selling soap door-to-door, and doing anything that came along that didn't take too much time away from hunting.

In 1912 Bean attached some rugged lightweight leather uppers to rubber overshoe bottoms. He field-tested the new boot himself and was delighted. He made some boots for friends. They were pleased as well. Anybody who hunts should have these, he decided.

L. L. Bean obtained a mailing list of Maine hunting license holders and prepared a three-page brochure that proudly trumpeted: "You cannot expect success hunting deer or moose if your feet are not properly dressed. The Maine Hunting Shoe is designed by a hunter who has tramped the Maine woods for the past eighteen years. We guarantee them to give perfect satisfaction in every way." When the rubber bottoms separated from the leather tops on ninety of the first hundred pairs of boots, Bean kept his promise and refunded everyone's money.

He borrowed money, perfected the bottoms, and resumed selling his boot with unshaken confidence. The public could not resist the common sense or the genuine enthusiasm of his appeal. By 1917, he had sold enough boots to move to another location in the heart of Freeport, Maine.

In 1917, he added hunting apparel items to his line. Bean personally used each item and chose only those he thought his customers would appreciate. In 1927 he added fishing and camping equipment to his catalog with the good news: "It is no longer necessary for you to experiment with dozens of flies to determine the few that will catch fish. We have done that experimenting for you."

By the 1920s, the Maine Hunting Shoe had gone to the North Pole with Admiral MacMillan, and L. L. Bean was employing twenty-five people. Word of mouth and customer satisfaction were paramount to his success. He was genuinely shocked if one of his products failed. He would barge around the factory bellowing for an explanation. He would then write the customer, return his money, enclose a gift and maybe invite him up to Maine for some fishing.

Bean was obsessed with building his mailing lists and advertised extensively in the outdoor magazines to promote his "free catalog." The book he mailed was a cluttered, fun-to-read compendium of practical, high-quality outdoor merchandise. Despite the Depression, business increased four hundred percent. Sales passed one million dollars a year in 1937; "L. L. Bean. Freeport, Maine" was all that was scratched on many envelopes he received.

In 1942, Bean wrote a short book called "Hunting, Fishing and Camping" to "give definite information in the fewest words possible on how to hunt, fish and camp." It sold two hundred thousand copies.

The L. L. Bean factory was always a lively place to work. In 1945, Bean set up a special retail salesroom in the middle of the factory with a night bell for the convenience of hunters and fishermen who might need a license or a packet of flies at 4 A.M. In 1951 the single L. L. Bean retail store opened twenty-four hours a day, 365 days a year. "We have thrown away the keys to the place," boomed Bean.

He died in 1967 at the age of ninety-four. L. L. Bean summed up his success as "the fact that I tried on the trail practically every article I handle. If I tell you a knife is good for cleaning trout, it is because I found it so. If I tell you a wading boot is worth having, very likely you might have seen me testing it at Merrymeeting Bay."

His customers included Babe Ruth, Ted Williams, Franklin Roosevelt, John Wayne, and Amy Vanderbilt. L. L. Bean was a cult. Across the country people named dogs, and even babies, "Leonwood" in honor of Bean's little-known middle name.

Levitz

Pottstown, Pennsylvania seemed an unlikely spot for a revolution. Here, for more than a quarter-century, Ralph and Leon Levitz operated two furniture stores that looked pretty much like their father's store which had opened in nearby Lebanon in 1910. In fact it looked pretty much like every one of the other twenty-five thousand furniture stores across the country.

The Levitz family netted about $60,000 in a good year and had built a net worth of maybe $500,000. Each year they advertised a year-end clearance sale from their warehouse and customers came in droves. The rest of the year they made the occasional buck waiting for the year-end bonanza. What would happen with warehouse sales all year round?

The first Levitz warehouse store opened in Allentown in 1963. Immediately inside the door, the customer was dwarfed by cartons stacked twenty feet high and spread over a warehouse the size of a football field. On the other side of the warehouse was a showroom with 250 model-room vignettes.

Selling brand name furniture without delivery charges, no decorating services, and a limited choice of fabrics, the Levitzs were able to slash prices by twenty-five percent. Also, the American population was becoming increasingly mobile and didn't want to be tied to expensive furniture. The first wave of post-World War II retirees were buying second homes and not looking to plow a fortune into furnishings. The cash register never stopped ringing.

Ralph Levitz, a quiet, genial fifity-eight-year-old conventional furniture retailer, had stood the staid, sleepy furniture industry on its ear. Levitz wasted no time in spreading his "concept" of warehouse selling. He targeted fifty-five major markets, opening outlets near highway interchanges where land and rental costs were below prime downtown locations and near railroad sidings to keep delivery costs down.

In ten years, Levitz sales ballooned to $175,000,000 a year. The Levitz stock became the darling of Wall Street, exploding from $4 a share to $150. The family net worth jumped past three hundred million dollars. It was all a bit much for small town furniture retailers. In 1974, a professional manager was recruited as president and chief executive officer to shepherd Levitz through its era of protracted expansion.

Macy's

Rowland Hussey Macy was born of Quaker stock on Nantucket Island, Massachusetts, and like many young men was seized by the sea. He sailed at the age of fifteen on the *Emily Morgan*, bound for Cape Horn and beyond. He spent four years sailing through the South Seas before returning to Massachusetts. Although he was often called Captain Macy in later years he never again set to sea, save as a passenger.

Macy had no clear idea what to do after his sea adventures, and for several years his trail is lost to history. He surfaced in the dry goods trade in Boston in 1844—his first of several marginally successful retail operations. In 1849, Macy headed for San Francisco in the Gold Rush, leaving behind his wife and family.

His success in the gold fields is unknown. By 1850 he was doing business in Marysville as Macy & Company, but the merchant partnership was soon put up for public auction. We next find Macy back in Haverhill, Massachusetts operating a store offering a full line of dry goods in 1853. He was experimenting with many of the principles that would later become Macy staples: dealing only in cash, a single price policy, and extensive advertising. But this venture failed also.

Macy tried brokering for a short while and then bolted to Superior City, Wisconsin in 1857 to engage in land speculation just as the boom shipping town was going bust. At the age of thirty-five, struggling in the nation's heartland, it was hard to see how Rowland Macy had laid the foundation for creating the world's most famous department store.

Macy came to New York in 1858 and opened a small fancy goods store. He chose a corner uptown from the main shopping district where several merchants before him had failed. As an adventurer from Boston, veteran New York merchants suspected Macy would meet the same fate.

His tiny twenty foot by sixty foot store had counters running down both sides and through the middle, leaving but two narrow aisles. Was the site selection foresight or simply the result of lack of funds? For years the location was no great advantage, but slowly the New York trade moved away from the southern end of Manhattan towards Macy.

Three weeks after opening Macy was burglarized of over a thousand dollars worth of goods. Several months later a window fire cost him two thousand dollars in losses. They were setbacks a merchant grossing five dollars a day at the start could ill afford. For two years Macy's was only one of scores of similar stores struggling to survive. He began to offer a department of "French and German fancy goods": pocketbooks, handbags, frames, games and dolls.

Gradually, Macy's store was becoming a department store, although there was no such appellation at the time. He had twenty-two distinct lines of goods, and struggled with a suitable name for his business. He tried such cumbersome titles as "Macy's Grand Central Fancy Goods Establishment."

By whatever name Macy prospered. He advertised relentlessly and with great innovation. He was not afraid to use white space in the gray, copy-heavy papers of the time. He repeated words and used special eye-grabbing patterns with his headlines. Macy wrote his own copy in a personal anecdotal style rather than the formal tomes of his competition.

Macy continued his policies, first nurtured in Massachusetts, of dealing only in cash, offering his goods at the lowest prices possible, and setting a single price for all. These tenets would become standard practices by the department stores that would follow Macy's.

Macy pioneered many promotional selling tactics. He began using a five-point red star to identify his goods as early as 1862. He used clearance sales, free delivery, and solicited mail orders. Macy introduced fractional and odd pricing to suggest bargains. His ads proclaimed that "Macy's will not be undersold."

The small original store expanded piecemeal until Macy had the ground space of eleven stores, employing over four hundred people. Receipts had grown into the thousands each day. Macy, however, began to suffer the ill effect of constant attention to his business. In the 1870s, he contracted Bright's disease of the kidneys.

He sailed to Europe for rest and medical treatment in 1877.

Suspecting the gravity of his situation, Macy had arranged his affairs so his partners could continue the business in the event of his death, which in fact came in Paris at the age of fifty-five.

Marshall Field

"The customer is always right!" History does not record exactly when—or even if—Marshall Field, the nineteenth century's wealthiest merchant, ordered that declaration, but it exemplified his retailing philosophy and came to represent the American retailing credo. In an era of "caveat emptor," Field's stores emphasized full credit refunds for any reason whatsoever.

Marshall Field did not carry the stamp on greatness upon him in his early years. After Field achieved unprecedented success in Chicago, his first employer remarked about Field's four years as a Pittsfield, Massachusetts clerk, "Well, I'd never thought it of him. He was about the greenest looking lad I ever saw when he came to work for me."

With a thousand dollars saved from his Pittsfield job, Field, a slender, handsome man of average height, went to join his brother in Chicago in 1856. His brother got him a clerk position in the largest wholesale dry goods house in Chicago. Field's salary was four hundred dollars a year. He slept on the premises and saved two hundred dollars.

Field progressed rapidly and became a partner in 1860 at the age of twenty-five. Prices rose with the Civil War brewing, and when the war ended Field bought into the store of Potter Palmer, who introduced fashion to the rough frontier town of fifty thousand that was Chicago in 1865.

Palmer soon concluded that his Lake Street location did not hold as much promise as a State Street address. State Street was little more than a muddy ribbon flowing through rows of dilapidated shacks, but Potter quietly acquired all the property on State Street. He built a street a hundred feet in width, erected a six-story building, and opened his doors. State Street was on its way to becoming one of the great shopping streets in the world. Field and his partner Levi Leiter leased the new building.

In 1871, Field was turning over $8,000,000 of inventory each year when the Great Chicago Fire destroyed the city. Field's losses were over $3,500,000, and only $2,500,000 was insured. The firm was caught in the financial panic of 1873, and in 1877 the store again burned to the ground. Despite the setbacks of the 1870s, the company not only survived but prospered.

In 1881, Field bought out Leiter for $2,000,000. Over the next twenty-five years sales tripled from twenty-five million dollars to seventy-three million. Field stressed quality, and would have nothing to do with shoddy merchandise. He believed in providing his customers with the most attractive facilities possible in which to shop.

Outside of retailing, the merchant dabbled in railroads, real estate, banking, and steel. He financed the Chicago Museum of Natural History with over ten million dollars. When Marshall Field died in 1906 his estate was estimated at $150,000,000. He was the largest taxpayer in the United States.

Montgomery Ward

The Montgomery Ward catalog has been chosen on many lists as one of the hundred most influential American books ever published. One such nominating committee, the Grolier Club, stated: "The mail order catalogue has been perhaps the greatest single influence in increasing the standard of American living. It brought the benefit of wholesale prices to city and hamlet, to the crossroads and prairie."

It wasn't so obvious at the time.

Aaron Montgomery Ward was born in Chatham, New Jersey in 1844. His family went west to Niles, Michigan in 1853, where his father took up the cobbler's trade. Aaron left school at fourteen to work in brickyards and a barrel factory, where he learned his most valuable lesson: "I learned I was not physically or mentally suited for brick or barrel making."

He clerked at a shoe store and then a country store earning six dollars a month—plus board. Ward was ready to go to the big city. In the 1850s Chicago was home to 30,000 people and was known, none too affectionately, as "The Mudhole of the Prairies." The streets were barely above the level of Lake Michigan and were covered with bottomless goo.

But by the late 1860s, Chicago was teeming with post-Civil War energy. Fifteen railroad lines moved 150 trains a day out of the busy terminals. Like thousands of other young men, Ward arrived in Chicago in 1866 and began work in various dry goods firms, including one operated by Marshall Field. He became a salesman, his income rising to the princely sum of twelve dollars a week.

As he made his tedious rounds through the mud in his horse and buggy, he took particular notice of the country stores on his route. They were congenial places with pot belly stoves, and they made fine meeting places for local farmers—but they were far from friendly when the farmers had to actually buy something. Selection was small, prices were high. The storekeeper was at the mercy of the big city wholesalers.

Ward considered how he could help the disadvantaged farmer. He decided on a mail order store. He would set up in the big city where he could easily reach suppliers and buy in quantity to get the best prices. A catalog listing his prices would be sent to farmers who would receive their order by mail, cash on delivery. It was not a new idea, but the few direct mail firms at the time sold only one or two items. Ward was going to bring the whole store to the farmer.

Ward worked and saved. He talked about his idea with friends and associates. They all agreed he would go broke trying to sell goods sight-unseen to back country folk. He was not dissuaded.

By 1871 he finally saved enough money to buy a small amount of goods at wholesale prices. On October 8, 1871 the Great Chicago Fire engulfed the city for thirty hours. Every building within a four-square mile area was destroyed. So was Ward's inventory.

Back to work. By August 1872 he scraped up some money and convinced a few people to join him, raising sixteen hundred dollars in working capital. He printed up a one-page price list and hand-addressed the first circulars to the Grangers, a cooperative farm supply organization. One of his earliest price lists contained 163 items under the banner "Supplied By The Cheapest Cash House In America." Most of the items cost a dollar, including clothing, a six-view stereoscope, and a backgammon set.

For most of 1873, Ward's mailbox was bare. His partners wanted out and Ward, who still had his sales job, managed to buy them out of their small investments. The Panic of 1873 was sinking established traditional retailers, let alone his radical enterprise.

His business was ridiculed by the *Chicago Tribune* as a disreputable firm "hidden from public gaze with no merchandise displayed and reachable only through the post office." Under threat of a lawsuit, the *Tribune* printed a retraction. The retraction was added to the next flyer and sales increased.

About this time, ready-made clothing began appearing. It was always believed that no two people had the same measurements and tailors were needed to make quality clothes. But the crunch for uniforms in the Civil War demonstrated that certain combinations of measurements could be standardized. Ward told his far-away customers—"Give your age and describe your general build and we will, nine times out of ten, give you a fit."

Ward, a short, stout man, wrote all the early copy. He always included a message in his catalogs, often educating the reader about buying and selling, "It is best to make your order around five dollars. Shipping charges on small orders will eat up your savings. Consider joining a buying club with your neighbors."

Business began to grow rapidly as consumers came to trust Ward's unseen store. He bound his first catalog in 1874, and the book exploded to 72 pages in 1875. Ward began to worry he might become too big, and took an ad in *Farmers Voice* just to reassure his customers he had not lost touch with their needs.

In 1893, Ward sold controlling interest to George R. Thorne, who had come on as a partner late in 1873. Ward remained president, but after a while he even stopped attending board meetings. The last twenty years of his life were spent preserving the Chicago waterfront as a park for the people. He spent over two hundred thousand dollars of his own monies to defending the public's right to open space.

His longtime efforts to prevent the erection of buildings along Lake Michigan won him the title of "The Watch Dog of the Lake Front." At one time there were forty-six building projects planned in the park and he fought them all successfully, losing many influential friends along the way. Finally, just before his death in 1913, he won his final legal battle to forever keep the waterfront an open area. The *Tribune*, no friend of Montgomery Ward, wrote, "We know now that Mr. Ward was right, was farsighted, was public spirited. That he was unjustly criticized as a selfish obstructionist or as a fanatic. Before he died, it is pleasant to think, Mr. Ward knew that the community had swung round to his side and was grateful for the service he had performed in spite of misunderstanding and injustice."

Penney's

James Cash Penney named his first store "Golden Rule." He was going to combine ethics and business in his store on the frontier. The ethics he had learned growing up as a minister's son in Hamilton, Missouri. The business instincts seemed to come naturally.

His career started in 1883 at the age of eight when his father

told him he would have to buy his own clothing. James had saved
$2.50 from errands and bought a pig. He fattened the pig for sev-
eral months, sold it at a profit, and reinvested in more pigs. Soon
he had a dozen pigs—and some unhappy neighbors. His father
forced him to give up his young business.

As a young man, Penney worked as a clerk. His first job paid
$2.27 a month. He journeyed to Colorado for health reasons, and
invested his small savings in a butcher shop. His meatcutter told
him his most important duty would be supplying the chef at the
local hotel with a bottle of bourbon each week. Penney did it once
and regretted it immediately. He ended the liquor bribes and lost
his biggest account and the business.

In 1902, Penney went to the mining town of Kemmerer, population one thousand, in the southwestern hills of Wyoming. With
five hundred dollars of his own money and fifteen hundred dollars
of borrowed capital, he joined a one third partnership in a store
Penney would run.

The Golden Rule was a shack on a muddy sidestreet in downtown Kemmerer. On one side was a laundry, on the other a board-
ing house. Penney lived upstairs with his family. The venture was
not without risk. At the time, part of a miner's wage was scrip
redeemable only at the mining company store's inflated prices.
Outside competition was decidedly not welcome.

Penney was determined to sell goods at prices as low as possible with a one-price policy for all. He would cater to the needs of
rural America by selling basic types of merchandise his customers
would need. His concepts were well-received. First day cash
receipts totalled $466.59.

Penney did so well he was able to buy his partners out for thirty
thousand dollars in 1907. Right from the start he had dreamed of
chain stores. He developed a partnership idea where the new store
owner would own a third of the new Golden Rule, provided he had
a man trained to run the store. These men trained others who
would go and start their own stores in new Western towns. The policy led to rapid and successful expansion. By the 1930s, there was
a Penney's store in every western town with a population greater
than five thousand.

In 1913, Golden Rule became J. C. Penney. The name was so
trusted that lumberjacks were known to leave six months pay for

safekeeping with a Penney's manager whom they had never seen but whom they trusted merely because he was a Penney's man.

In 1917, James Penney retired as President to devote himself to philanthropic interests. He remained as chairman of the board, a strictly honorary position. The Stock Market Crash drained his forty million dollars fortune. Broke, discouraged and ill Penney entered a Battle Creek, Michigan sanitarium where he prepared himself to die, considering himself a failure.

But he recovered and returned home with a renewed interest in the Penney Company. He traveled around the country attending company conventions and rarely missed an important store opening. Everywhere he went people were thrilled to see *the* J. C. Penney in their store. He raised prize cattle, his life having come full circle. Penney lived to be ninety-five, just short of his oft-stated goal of a hundred. He was the last of the great merchant princes.

Sears & Roebuck

First some facts. In its heyday Sears & Roebuck had the most stores, the most customers, the biggest building. The company was the biggest publisher in America. They shipped enough catalogs to fill a train of boxcars thirty miles long. One out of approximately every two hundred American workers worked for Sears. Sears alone accounted for one percent of the American Gross National Product.

And it all began with a shipment of refused pocket watches.

Richard Sears was fifteen when he became the family breadwinner in 1879. He worked in the offices of the Minneapolis-St. Louis Railroad, but pestered his bosses for a field job. They sent him to North Redwood, Minnesota as a freight agent.

Checking shipments in the station every day, Sears quickly learned about the mail order business. In 1886 a town jeweler refused a shipment of "yellow watches." The Chicago commission house handling the watches wired Sears that as the station agent he could have the watches for twelve dollars each rather then incur the return shipping costs.

Sears knew the popular gold pocket watches were fetching twenty-five dollars in retail stores. But he wasn't interested in retailing. He took the watches and sold them to local station agents down the line for fourteen dollars each. Anything they made over that they could keep.

Sears was hooked. As a bonded freight agent, he did not have to pay to take delivery. He could settle his account when other agents paid him. It was a venture without risk, only profit. Sears began ordering more watches C.O.D. In six months, he amassed more than five thousand dollars, a substantial fortune in 1886.

He moved to Minneapolis, the biggest city he knew, and founded the R. W. Sears Watch Company. He began advertising watches in the paper, unheard of at the time, and found he had a natural flair for the work. So many orders poured in he needed to move to Chicago to facilitate shipping in 1887.

In April 1887, an advertisement appeared in the *Chicago Daily News:* "WANTED—Watchmaker with reference who can furnish tools. State age, experience, and salary requirement." A tall, lean man from Hammond, Indiana answered the ad. He presented Sears an example of his best work. Sears studied it closely for a moment and admitted, "I don't know anything about watchmaking, but I presume this is good, otherwise you wouldn't have submitted it to me." Alvah Curtis Roebuck was hired.

Sears continued to build his business by undercutting the competition in price, often buying discontinued lines from suppliers. With low prices come suspicions of poor quality. Sears quelled such doubts with the strongest guarantees in the business.

Richard Sears was an aggressive, dynamic salesman who thrived in business competition. But a large part of him also longed for the bucolic country life. In 1888, Sears sold his watch company for seventy-two thousand dollars, retaining a half-interest in the firm's Toronto branch. Roebuck owned twenty-five percent

of the Canada business. Sears invested sixty thousand dollars of his
money in Iowa farm mortgages.

By 1889, Sears was again selling watches in Minnesota, doing
business as the Warren Company, his middle name. Again he lasted
only a year before retiring. This time he sold his Toronto business
and his Minnesota concern to Roebuck.

A week later he was back. He asked Roebuck for half the company and soon their first watch catalog, featuring fifty-two pages,
was published. Sears added products to the book as they caught his
fancy. By 1893 he had added bicycles and organs and other general
merchandise and the catalog grew to 322 pages. It was the first
familiar all-purpose catalog from Sears & Roebuck, "The Cheapest
Supply House on Earth."

The business was always buoyed by its pledge: We Guarantee
Satisfaction and Safe Delivery on Everything You Order. The story
circulated through the Midwest of a customer who had come to
Richard Sears with a crusty, bruised watch he had dropped on a
rock in the mud. Sears handed him a new watch. When the customer protested that the damage was his own fault, Sears stopped
him, "We guarantee our watches not to fall out of people's pockets
and bounce in the mud."

Sears wrote to the farmers in their own language—simple,
earthy and direct. He called his catalog "the farmer's friend," and
built confidence in rural America that they could comfortably
write to the big city. Sears called his business plan "Iowaization."

In 1893, Sears & Roebuck again outgrew Minneapolis and
returned to Chicago. Despite the general economic panic, Sears
stepped up his advertising, driving the company into debt but
boosting sales. If the orders slowed the company would fail, and
Sears kept expanding.

It was the proper strategy for longterm growth, but the short-
term risk was too much for Alvah Roebuck, who was at heart a
tinkerer, not a high-stakes gambler. In 1895 he asked Sears for
twenty-five thousand dollars for his share of the company and got
out. In short order, Sears located two new partners. Roebuck
returned as the firm's head of watches and jewelry, seemingly not
perturbed at the new arrangement.

Richard Sears was something of a loose cannon. His outra-
geous advertising claims were legendary. Once he started a bank-

ing department where customers could drop off savings for five percent interest, in complete violation of state banking laws. A sound businessman was needed to balance the irrepressible Sears. Alvah Roebuck gave up, but Julius Rosenwald, his next partner, steadied the enterprise.

Sears & Roebuck continued to expand as the economy strengthened. In one issue of *Comfort* magazine Sears placed seventy different ads, each bursting with copy from border to border. Sears traveled extensively in Europe seeking medical help for his ailing wife, but kept a steady stream of ideas flowing to Chicago.

The Panic of 1907 exacerbated the differences between the expansionist Sears and Rosenwald. His chief satisfaction was derived not in making money but in making the company grow. In 1908, Sears resigned as president. He was named chairman of the board but never attended a board meeting. He spent his time on his great farm outside Waukesha, Wisconsin until his death in 1914 at the age of fifty.

After Alvah Roebuck left the company in the early 1900s, he made a modest fortune developing equipment in the infant motion picture industry. He was wiped out by the Depression, and returned to Chicago at age sixty-nine to seek work with the company that bore his name.

He stopped by a local store and the manager asked if he could publicize the visit of one of the founders. People poured in to see the Roebuck of Sears & Roebuck. He went on salary, touring for several years and writing a personal history of the company's early days. He died in 1948 at the age of eighty-four, once again a shareholder in Sears, Roebuck & Company by virtue of the firm's profit-sharing plan.

Tiffany's

In 1837, at the height of America's first great Depression, Charles Tiffany and John Young opened a fancy goods store in lower Manhattan with a thousand dollars borrowed from Tiffany's father. Tiffany had first operated a store ten years earlier when he ran a country store for his father, a wealthy mill owner. Now he put his retailing ideas to work in a simple wood-and-brick structure opposite City Hall.

The first week's profits totalled thirty-three cents. But Tiffany & Young had correctly gauged the popularity of imported Chinese goods, and their business flourished. The fancy goods business expanded through 1838. On New Year's Day 1839, robbers invaded the emporium and carted away everything transportable, over four thousand dollars of goods. Fortunately the partners had taken all the cash home with them for the holiday, enough to restock. Quickly they were growing again, adding costume jewelry for sale for the first time. Tiffany would later recall the popular baubles as cheap, garish, in poor taste, and crudely made. But real gems of any sort were rare in the United States at the time.

Tiffany's instituted a firm price policy. The price on the tag was the price to be paid—no haggling as was the custom of the day. It was a policy Tiffany's would later adhere to even with hundred thousand dollar necklaces.

In 1845, Tiffany & Young discontinued paste jewelry and began featuring gold jewelry. In 1847, Swiss jeweled watches were added to the line, and a year later Tiffany started a goldsmithing shop, making the first company-designed jewelry. He brought out the first Tiffany Blue Book catalog, adopting the famous "Tiffany blue" packaging.

Charles Tiffany was a master of publicity, teaming with neighbor P. T. Barnum on several occasions. Tiffany's crafted a tiny silver horse and carriage for the wedding of Barnum's celebrated midgets, General Tom Thumb and his bride Lavinia.

The New York press dubbed Tiffany the "King of Diamonds"

when he displayed the French crown jewels, although the gems were actually purchased by his partner Young. From that day to this, Tiffany's has been regarded as America's greatest jeweler. In 1853, Charles Tiffany bought full control of the business and moved the Tiffany & Co. store uptown.

Prior to the Civil War, the United States had no standing army. Tiffany prepared for the hostilities by submitting the first list of equipment used by the French army to the quartermaster general. Thereafter his firm sold gold epaulets, cap ornaments, navy lace, and other military accouterments. Mrs. Lincoln, who was coldly received by Washington society, consoled herself with several shopping sprees at Tiffany's. When the war ended, Tiffany did a brisk business in commemorative swords for returning heroes.

After the Civil War Charles Tiffany was ready to outfit America's Gilded Age. "We'll give the customer what we want," proselytized the country's leader in good taste. In 1867, Tiffany's won the first international medal awarded to a United States silvermaker at the Paris Exposition Universelle. Tiffany's would continue to win prizes—and valuable publicity—everywhere its jewelry was exhibited.

In 1870, Tiffany built a new iron store on Union Square. *The New York Times* hailed the store as "a Jewel Palace . . . the largest of its kind in the world. A school of taste . . . a teacher of art progress." Tiffany's now became a museum that incidentally sold its exhibits. A trip to Tiffany's was a must on every rich traveler's New York itinerary.

The gem that attracted more visitors than any other was the Tiffany Diamond. Found in the new Kimberly mines in South Africa in 1877, it was once purchased for eighteen thousand dollars. Tiffany thought it might just be just one of many yellow diamonds found, and cut it and held it for years without publicity. But the Tiffany Diamond remains the largest flawless and perfectly colored canary diamond ever mined. It is worth over two million dollars.

Charles Tiffany's biggest problem in the last quarter of the nineteenth century was finding diamonds, not selling them. Newly discovered mines in South Africa helped, but by far the most romantic source was the royal houses of Europe—who sold their collections when they became strapped for cash. Tiffany routinely sold six million dollars of diamonds a year. At times he could have forty million dollars in gems in his vaults.

In the 1880s and 1890s, a new millionaire could prove his status to his associates merely by sending his wife to a ball weighed down with enough jewels to cripple a good Sherpa. Tiffany catered to the new money as well as the old.

The store kept seven employees just to get information and photographs on the wealthy in every American city. If someone walked into Tiffany's and his photo and financial status were on file, the new customer could take his jewels without payment. "When we give credit to anyone who had supposed himself unknown to us, we are sure to retain him forever," said Tiffany.

Charles Tiffany was inexorably linked with the rich and famous of America, although he lived comparably simply. He enjoyed nothing more than a hearty walk. When he discovered a new pedometer, he added it to his Blue Book. He died in 1902, at the age of ninety, leaving an estate of thirty-five million dollars. He was planning yet another uptown move for Tiffany's.

Wanamaker's

John Wanamaker had sacrificed his job in a Philadelphia clothing store to weakening health, and began a supposedly more benign employment as permanent secretary for the YMCA, the first such paid position in the country. But he soon found himself amid the toughs of south Philadelphia trying to establish a new Sunday School. Wanamaker's untiring efforts would eventually make Bethany Mission, which he opened in 1858, the largest Sunday school in the world.

His work in the religious movement also yielded two unexpected bonuses: a wife and his first business partner. In 1860, the twenty-two-year-old Wanamaker took Mary Brown as his wife and teamed with her brother Nathan to start a clothing store. Wanamaker had learned the retailing business thoroughly at Tower Hall, the most prominent clothing establishment in Philadelphia.

Oak Hall, as the partners named their new store, floundered in the beginning, but a rush of orders for military uniforms at the outbreak of the Civil War started the store on the road to success. The influx of cash enabled Wanamaker to test his flamboyant advertising methods. He distributed handbills and calendars at county fairs, launched huge balloons from the roof with prize offers of a free suit inside, and plastered the Oak Hall name around town wherever he could.

But where Wanamaker truly made his mark was in newspaper advertising. Hardly a paper hit the Philadelphia streets without a Wanamaker ad in it; he eventually pioneered half-page and full-page mercantile advertisements. He wrote most of the copy himself, especially favoring rhyming couplets. Even though this rendered many of the ads nonsensical, it made Oak Hall one of Philadelphia's most popular stores by the end of the war.

Nathan Brown died in 1868, and Wanamaker was sufficiently well off to buy his partner's interest. Wanamaker immediately set out to build a second store, a "New Kind of Store," as he envisioned it. At a time when retailing was confined to specialty shops, Wanamaker wanted to put the widest possible variety of goods under one roof, with each department more richly stocked than the leading specialty store with which it competed.

When a huge abandoned Pennsylvania Railroad shed became available, Wanamaker bought it and converted it into the most varied retail store in the world. Counters of goods radiated from the center of his Grand Depot in concentric circles, with items Wanamaker had stocked from trips across Europe. His "New Kind of Store" opened in 1877 with 650 employees. By 1882, the store was such as success that the payroll swelled to three thousand.

With his two stores booming, Wanamaker had become one of Philadelphia's leading citizens. He left everyday affairs to his younger brothers and sons and entered politics. He served as chairman of the Republican national finance committee in 1888, raising the largest campaign war chest ever seen. As a reward, he was named to President Benjamin Harrison's cabinet as Postmaster General.

After his stint in Washington, Wanamaker made unsuccessful runs for the Senate and the governorship of Pennsylvania. All the while, Wanamaker never slackened in his work for Bethany Mission. While in Washington, he returned to Philadelphia every Sunday to teach his class. But as rewarding as the spiritual side of his life was, it couldn't fill a man as inexhaustible as Wanamaker.

In 1896, he acquired the lease on the world-famous A. T. Stewart emporium in New York City, when the store of his idol slipped into bankruptcy after the founder's death. To meet increasing competition in New York, Wanamaker built the largest department store in the city in 1907. The store was an immediate success, and Wanamaker returned to Philadelphia in 1910.

Now seventy-two, the "father of the modern department store" was not quite finished. Across the street from Philadelphia's City Hall, Wanamaker built the largest building ever devoted to selling goods. It covered an entire city block, reached twelve stories into the sky, and contained forty-five acres of floor space. It was as ornate as it was grand. The organ in the gallery was so large it required thirteen freight cars to transport it from the St. Louis Exposition. And it was only one of three organs in the store.

Profits in the Wanamaker stores skyrocketed during World War I, in part due to sharply inflated prices. After the war, Wanamaker gambled that prices had reached their zenith and, seeing a chance to perform a public service as well, he reduced all merchandise in both his New York and Philadelphia stores by twenty percent. The sale lasted two months. Extra help was hired to handle the volume. His timing was prescient; prices indeed had peaked and began dropping rapidly.

The great sale of 1920 was Wanamaker's farewell gesture. He turned over both stores to his son and focused on his religious work. In 1922, heart failure caught up with him, and John Wanamaker died at age eighty-four. His list of innovations from sixty years of retailing stretched beyond any other.

Woolworth's

As a young boy growing up in Jefferson County, New York, Frank Winfield Woolworth knew he was going to be a merchant. He thought store, he dreamed store, he played store. Often in the evening he and his brother would arrange make-believe merchandise on the dining room table and take turns selling to each other.

Yet the man who was to build the largest chain of stores in the world was turned down time and again in his quest to land his first retailing position. In 1871, at the age of nineteen, Woolworth drove around Watertown, New York in an old sled looking for a sales job. Finally he was offered an opportunity at the Dry Goods firm of Augsbury-Moore. Of course he wasn't going to be paid, but he wouldn't be charged anything for being around and learning, either.

After two and a half years, Woolworth worked hard enough to command a salary of six dollars a week. He left for an offer of ten dollars a week, but was soon cut to eight dollars for not moving enough goods. His health broke soon afterward, and Woolworth returned to the family farm to recuperate.

In 1877 his former employer Moore asked Woolworth to run his store for ten dollars a week. In the spring of 1878, Woolworth arranged a number of slow-moving items on an old sewing table and priced them for five cents each. All the goods, heretofore unattractive to customers, sold on the first day. It was the beginning of Woolworth's career selling an assortment of goods at one low price.

He convinced Moore to stake him with three hundred dollars to open a 5-cent store in Utica, New York in February 1879. At first the goods sold briskly, but sales dropped to $2.50 a day and the store closed. Moore and Woolworth did not give up on the idea, and launched another store in Lancaster, Pennsylvania on June 21 of the same year.

The Lancaster store was a modest fourteen by thirty-five feet. The opening inventory was worth $410, comprised totally of nickel items. First day sales totalled $127.65, nearly thirty percent of his inventory. Woolworth later added ten-cent items, and the Lancaster store became the first of over twenty-three hundred Woolworth 5 & 10s across the world.

In the 1880s, few manufacturers would consider dealing with retailers. Woolworth realized the only way to give his customers the best deals was to buy directly from the suppliers. Only through persistence and imagination was he able to break through these traditional retailing barriers. By buying in large quantities, he was able to offer high quality merchandise for five cents and ten cents.

Woolworth expanded the idea rapidly. He brought his brother, his old store-playing partner, into the 5 & 10 business. His brother, Moore, and other close friends and associates all started chains of 5 & 10 stores, six chains in all. In 1912, the F.W. Woolworth Company organized to take over all the 5 & 10 stores, numbering 596. The men had never been competitors, and often bought and consulted together. The consolidation was a logical progression.

In 1913, Woolworth built the world's tallest building—the 792-foot Woolworth Tower. Other buildings were to grow taller, but none so captured the imagination of the public, erected as it was in an age when the public was entranced with the romance of American business. Woolworth paid for the entire cost of $13,500,000 out of his own pocket—a gargantuan monument constructed literally from nickels and dimes.

Woolworth remained active in the business until his death in 1919, accumulating a fortune of $65,000,000—never having sold an item for more than a dime.

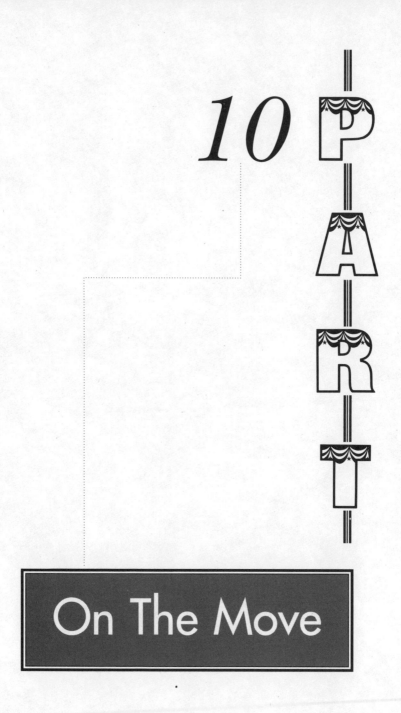

10 PART

On The Move

Avis

As an Air Force combat flying officer during World War II, Warren Avis traveled many hard miles in Europe and America. Unfortunately, much of it was after landing—making his way between the airport and his destination. Decent ground transportation was so scarce Avis sometimes carried motorcycles in the bomb bays of his planes so he would be able to get around when he landed.

The solution was simple enough: a car-rental system needed to be set up at airports. It was not a new revelation, but anyone who had thought of it considered it impossible. A national car-rental network would be required; huge fleets of cars would be necessary; elaborate controls would be mandatory. Even industry giant Hertz was reluctant to tackle the logistical nightmare presented by the airport market.

It was left to Avis—who mustered out of the Air Force in 1946—to be the first to rent cars at airports. Avis, who started dealing bikes and used cars as a teenager, was an auto dealer in Detroit and began there. He signed an exclusive contract to open the Avis Airlines Rent-A-Car System at Detroit's Willow Run Airport. Simultaneously, he opened a rental location at Miami Airport, a favorite destination for both vacationers and business travelers.

There was much to overcome. Many people didn't know how to rent a car in those days; Avis set up counters near the baggage pickup areas where he had twenty minutes or so to educate travelers on the Avis rental system. There were scores of details to work out: where to park the cars, how to advertise the service inside airports, what kind of insurance should be offered, how to train and staff counter workers.

Once Avis figured everything out in Miami and Detroit, other Avis-owned airport operations sprouted in New York, Chicago, Dallas, and Washington. By 1948, Los Angeles and Houston had come on board. As the system expanded, Avis began to align himself with the airlines. He wangled Avis pamphlets into the airplane seat pockets—the first non-airline information allowed in seat pockets. He advertised jointly with American Airlines, welding Avis's rental cars with the airline in the public's mind.

For three years Hertz, the industry giant, sat on the sidelines and watched. They were still convinced Avis would fail. Instead, Avis prospered mightily—so much so he entered the Hertz stronghold of downtown hotels and offices in 1948. When Hertz finally moved into airports they were always playing catch-up.

At the time, Hertz was owned by General Motors. A Ford dealer, Avis had no problem striking a deal with Ford Motors. He began the unheard-of practice for car renters of buying new Ford autos every year. Avis pointed out that his renters would, in essence, be test-driving new Ford models. Ford let the cars go cheaply and Avis got a reputation for quality from a fleet of reliable autos.

It was an exciting time. But Avis was a builder, not a manager. In 1954, with 185 Avis locations in the United States and another dozen in foreign countries, Avis sold his Avis System for a reported eight million dollars. Over the years that followed, Avis was in and out of over thirty businesses. He did well in real estate, not so well in oil. Condominium conversions were a success, flowers-by-wire less so. He authored books and built Avis Ford into the largest Ford dealership in Michigan.

In his business adventures, Avis always sought to make a contribution to society. For most of his years he did this through his companies. In 1988, however—saying, "We have to stop being a conflict society"—Avis established a two million dollar encounter group program in Ann Arbor to explore peaceful coexistence. To many, world peace is a pipe dream. Exactly what they said about rental cars in airports.

Boeing

Today there are more Boeings in the air than any other airplane. Boeing is America's number one exporter with a fifty-five percent share of the most expensive product in the world not awarded by the bidding process. For a while in the beginning it looked like that product would be bedroom bureaus and chests, not airplanes.

It all began as a hobby for William Boeing. The son of a Great Lakes timber and iron baron, William was raised in Michigan and educated in Switzerland. He matriculated at Yale, but before his class graduated, William was in Washington state buying timber lands for the family business.

He settled in Hoquiam, Washington in 1903 at the age of twenty-two. The lumber business continued to be good to Boeing. In 1912, William Boeing was introduced to Conrad Westervelt at the University Club in Seattle. The two men hit it off immediately. Both liked fast boats and a lively hand of bridge. Both had studied engineering. And although neither had ever been in a plane, both evinced an interest in early aviation.

Boeing and Westervelt began building seaplanes as a lark. On June 15, 1916 Boeing took off from Lake Union in a clumsy-looking flying machine christened *Bluebill*. It was their first successful flight. Shortly afterwards, the Pacific Aero Products Company was incorporated with Boeing as president. The business would sell planes if possible, but the two men were also prepared to operate flying schools, stage exhibitions, and carry passengers and freight.

World War I loomed on the horizon for America. The United States Navy became interested in developing successful seaplanes. The *Bluebill* would not be one of them. It flunked its Navy tests. Years later Boeing would sell the plane to New Zealand where it set altitude records, but for now the Navy urged Boeing to hurry production on a new model. He hired an aeronautical engineer.

The United States declared war on April 8, 1917. The Navy scheduled tests for Boeing's new "C-model" planes in July. He packed two planes on trains bound for the Naval testing site in Pensacola, Florida.

The weather for the trials was abominable. Waves crested at over four feet, winds whipped the beaches at more than thirty-five miles per hour. But the Navy fliers praised the Boeing "C" planes as the best they had ever flown. The Navy ordered fifty planes from the newly named Boeing Airline Company. William Boeing personally invested thirty thousand dollars to meet production goals.

The war ended, and with it so did business. Boeing issued more stock to raise money, most of which he bought himself. Many aircraft companies simply went out of business. Boeing survived with the manufacture of non-aircraft items, mainly bedroom furniture and phonograph cases. Even with the new products, it did not appear Boeing would survive.

In November 1919, Boeing landed a remodeling contract for a British plane. Over the next several years, the company subsisted by building other engineer's designs and by its remodeling contracts. Boeing supplied planes to Edward Hubbard, whose Hubbard Air Transport was the world's first airline. Finally convinced of the viability of his business, Boeing surrendered the presidency and became chairman of the board in 1924.

In 1925, Boeing gambled on a new aircraft designed for the United States Postal Service. He sold only one Model 40. But in 1927 when postal bids were accepted for the western routes of the transcontinental mail system, Boeing was ready. The new Model 40A was so light and could carry so much more of a greater payload than its competition that Boeing's bid was only fifty percent of what the Post Office was prepared to pay. It was so low that William Boeing had to personally underwrite a $500,000 bond to guarantee the job.

Even in the mail business where each additional letter was added revenue, William Boeing insisted on including a passenger seat in the Model 40A. "From the start of the mail operation, I looked ahead to the time when we could 'wash out' the mail and not care about it. I expected passengers to become of primary importance," he would say later.

The new division, Boeing Air Transport, was a success from the beginning with its versatile and popular Model 40A. Boeing secured more and more mail routes, eventually forming the original United Airlines. But the new Franklin Roosevelt administration became convinced that the original mail routes were awarded unfairly. After Federal investigations and hearings, Roosevelt suspended all air mail contracts on February 9, 1934. the Army took over delivery of the mail.

It was a disaster from the outset. Planes crashed and men died. There was over $300,000 in damage in the first few months. The cost of transporting a pound of mail went from $0.54 to $2.21 a mile. The public outrage forced Roosevelt to reinstate mail bids, but only to new or reorganized airlines. Companies like Boeing could either serve as carriers or manufacturers, but not both.

William Boeing chose neither. He had always intended to retire at fifty and was already three years into his intended "retirement." He was tired of the political headaches indigenous to the aircraft industry. He sold all his stock in Boeing.

William Boeing retired to a life of leisure as his company established itself as the world's leading manufacturer of airplanes. He died on his yacht in Seattle in 1956, months before the introduction of the first commercial jet plane, the Boeing 707.

Buick

In 1928 Bruce Catton, a young newspaper reporter who would later gain fame as a Civil War historian, was talking to "a thin, bent little man" working behind the information desk at the Detroit School of Trades. The forgotten seventy-four-year-old man had a story to tell. The man who built the cars that would be the cornerstone for the world's largest industrial corporation couldn't afford to keep a telephone in his home, let alone buy one of the automobiles that bore his name.

David Dunbar Buick was born in Scotland in 1854, but came to

Detroit with his parents when he was only two. His father died three years later and his mother worked in a candy store to support the family. At age fifteen, Buick went to work for the Alexander Manufacturing Company, a Detroit fabricator of plumbing fixtures.

In 1882 Buick and an old schoolmate, William Sherwood, took over the business when it failed. Over the next several years Buick & Sherwood, with David Buick as president, became successful. Buick himself is credited with many inventions, including improvements to bathtubs, water closets, flushing devices, and a lawn sprinkler. His most notable achievement was a method for bonding enamel to cast iron, making possible the colorful bathroom and kitchen fixtures of today.

With this promising start, Buick could probably have become wealthy in the plumbing business. But David Buick was more interested in making things than making money. Like many tinkerers of the late nineteenth century, he became fascinated with the new gasoline internal combustion engines.

His growing obsession with engine experimenting created a rift in an already tenuous business partnership. Sherwood finally delivered the ultimatum, "Dave, either get down to work or get out." So in 1899, at age forty-five, Buick sold the company for $100,000. He used his share to form the Buick Auto-Vim and Power Company to manufacture gasoline engines.

Initially he set out to build marine and stationary engines. The origins of the first Buick automobile are unknown. It was either built by Buick or Walter Lorenzo Marr, a gifted machinist hired by Buick. At any rate Buick, strapped for cash, sold the first car to Marr in August 1901 for $225.

The next year the company became the Buick Manufacturing Company and developed the "valve-in-head" engine which would become the standard in the industry for its power and efficiency. In 1903 the Buick Motor Company was organized, but under terms that would haunt David Buick forever.

The firm was capitalized with $100,000 in stock—$99,700 for Benjamin Briscoe and $300 for David Buick. Buick was president and he could gain control of all the stock if he repaid Briscoe $3,500 he owed him within four months. If he couldn't repay the loan, Buick would forfeit all interest in the company. All Briscoe wanted out of the new company was his money back.

Prior to the deadline Buick sold the company to Flint Wagon Works, who were seeking a way into auto manufacturing, to meet his obligation with Briscoe. But Buick became entangled in a worse bargain with the new owners. The Buick Motor Company moved north to Flint, with David Buick becoming secretary of the new car works. He was allotted fifteen hundred shares, but would not receive the stock until his dividends paid off his personal debts.

Buick cars were in production in 1904 when carriagemaker William Durant took over. Buick's role in the business declined rapidly, until he finally lost the manager's title to Durant in early 1906. At the end of 1908 Buick sold his stock to Durant for $100,000, stock that would soon be worth $115,000,000.

Thereafter Buick was plagued by bad business deals. A questionable oil venture in California and speculative land deals in Florida went bust. He reentered the auto business after the age of sixty-five to try and make his patented carburetors. He designed a car in 1923, but produced only a single prototype.

When Catton found him in 1928, Buick was impoverished and subsisting on menial jobs. Still, in the interview he professed no bitterness nor regrets over his career. Buick died a year later from pneumonia he contracted after an operation on a cancerous bowel obstruction.

In 1937, after years of being the forgotten man in Buick history, General Motors adopted the genuine ancestral crest used by the ancient Buick family for its cars. To date, the Buick name has been stamped on over twenty-five million cars.

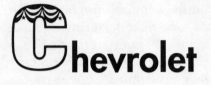hevrolet

Louis Chevrolet never found a way to make money from his talents, skills, and experiences. That his name lives on as one of the most famous names in the automobile industry is attributed more to its romantic sound than the man himself.

The name "Chevrolet" is thought to be a French corruption of "goat's milk." Louis Chevrolet was born on Christmas day 1878 in Swiss Jura, the center of the French dairy industry region. The son of a watchmaker, Chevrolet showed a similar mechanical aptitude at an early age. He showed no inclination for school, however, and his parents were happy to encourage his wage-earning pursuits.

Chevrolet began a career in bicycle repair, and soon the muscular six-foot youth was racing bikes. In his first three years he won twenty-eight competitive events. He built bikes until he discovered cars. Chevrolet became an auto mechanic in the pioneering French auto industry. He jumped from job to job, gaining valuable experience, before coming to Montreal in 1900.

Chevrolet worked as a chauffeur in Canada for six months before coming to New York, his ultimate destination. Driving hard-steering, rough-riding racing cars required a great deal of muscle at the turn of the century. The hulking Frenchman was ideally suited to this pursuit. Slowly he established his reputation as a mechanic and a racer, winning his first road race on a cinder track in Morris Park, New York on May 20, 1905.

Chevrolet brought his younger brothers Arthur and Gaston to America, and left for Flint, Michigan to drive for W.C. Durant, founder of General Motors. Chevrolet drove a Buick in the first Indianapolis 500 in 1911, but a broken camshaft put him out of the race early. Meanwhile Durant split from GM and privately hired Chevrolet to make the car of his dreams. Chevrolet was a consulting engineer, not an officer, in the Chevrolet Motor Car Company.

When the Chevrolet Classic Six reached production in 1912, there were 275 other automakers in the United States. The first

Chevrolet was envisioned as a rich man's car, not the best-selling American car it would become. The Classic Six was big, powerful, and pricey. It carried a sticker of $2,150, out of the reach of all but the wealthy.

Durant realized he needed to compete with cheaper cars he could sell at high volume. Chevrolet believed his name only belonged on a big, impressive automobile, and resigned in October, 1913. He sold his stock, securities which would have made him a millionaire many times over, when he left.

Durant would never miss him. The rough-hewn, uneducated Chevrolet did not fit in with the polished wheeler-dealers in the early auto industry boardrooms. Durant hated the man, but loved the name. He was soon putting the Chevrolet name on many of his brands of cars. Meanwhile, General Motors reorganized with Chevrolet becoming its leading division.

Without even his name, Chevrolet formed the Frontenac Motor Corporation. By 1917 he had a new and very advanced racing machine, complete with an aluminum engine block, but no production system. Seeking a regular paycheck he signed on as vice-president and chief engineer for a new company called the American Motors Corporation. He helped develop their American Beauty, but when development got under way his services were deemed expendable.

The Monroe Company next hired Chevrolet to build a race car. He updated his Frontenac racer and with his brother Gaston at the controls, won the 1920 Indianapolis 500. Tragically, Gaston would die before the year was out in a fiery crash on a boardwalk raceway in Beverly Hills, California.

With the prestige garnered from his Indianapolis victory, Chevrolet obtained backers to incorporate Frontenac Motors, but the company went bankrupt with his cars still on the design table. Another car company failed in 1924, and Chevrolet turned to boat racing, winning the Miami Regatta in 1925. But the victory did not translate into widespread success.

In 1929, Louis and Arthur Chevrolet left the auto business altogether to form the Chevrolet Brothers Aircraft Company with a new engine of their design, but lost the business to Glenn L. Martin. Finally in 1934, out of charity and a moral obligation towards the man who gave their best-selling car its name, General

Motors put Louis Chevrolet on their payroll.

Illness forced Chevrolet to retire in 1938. He and his wife lived in a small Florida apartment, but the humid climate accelerated his decline in health and he returned to Detroit for a leg operation in early 1941. Complications forced a complete amputation, from which Chevrolet never recovered. He died on June 6, 1941 at the age of sixty-three. He was buried in Indianapolis, scene of his greatest racing triumph.

Chrysler

Walter Percy Chrysler always considered himself a "transportation man." He called his autobiography the *Life of an American Workman.* Chrysler grew up on a farm near Ellis, Kansas, the son of an engineer who piloted an old wood burning locomotive for the Kansas Pacific Railroad.

In 1892, at the age of seventeen, Chrysler began working in Ellis railway shops for seven cents an hour. Short of temper and highly competitive, Chrysler worked hard and played hard through roundhouses across the United States. As a journeyman machinist, Chrysler moved upward through such posts as general foreman, master mechanic, and superintendent.

In 1908 Chrysler took a job as plant manager for American Locomotive in Pittsburgh, where his skills soon attracted the attention of the young auto industry. It was a mutual attraction. While on a trip to Chicago, Chrysler became infatuated with a new ivory-colored Locomobile with red leather seats and trim. The new car cost five thousand dollars, a steep price for a man with seven hundred dollars in cash and a $350-a-month job. Chrysler convinced a banker friend to lend him the money to buy the car.

But Chrysler's dream car was not to drive. He shipped it home to his barn where he took apart the car and examined it in minute detail. His first drive didn't come for three months. But Walter Chrysler now knew as much about the workings of an automobile as any man.

In 1911, Chrysler accepted his first automobile job as plant manager with the Buick Motor Company. He took a pay cut from twelve thousand dollars to six thousand dollars to launch his automotive career. As works manager Chrysler quickly raised production from 45 to 560 cars a day by eliminating useless steps in the manufacturing process. Within five years, Chrysler had risen to the presidency of Buick and was vice-president of General Motors. He was making $500,000 a year of which he took $380,000 each year in General Motors stock.

After more than three stormy years spent among similar strong-minded auto men, Chrysler left the industrial giant in 1920, ostensibly to retire at age forty-five. He returned after six months, quickly gaining a reputation as "the doctor of sick motor car companies."

He first worked his magic on Willys-Overland, a maker of harvesters and airplanes as well as cars, by reducing indebtedness and liabilities by millions of dollars. Next Chrysler took over the ailing Maxwell-Chalmers Car Company, while beginning experiments on his own car.

The first Chryslers appeared in 1924. The Chrysler B-Series automobiles featured six body styles. His first year, Chrysler sold $50,000,000 worth of automobiles. The company already ranked thirty-second among car manufacturers. By 1927 Chrysler was number five.

In 1928, Chrysler introduced the Plymouth and engineered the purchase of the Dodge Corporation, which had been sold to an investment banking group after the Dodge Brothers' death. In an exchange of $170,000,000 of stock, Chrysler changed the "Big Two" to the "Big Three." Years later he would remark, "The greatest thing I ever did was buy the Dodge."

None of Chrysler's four children followed him into the automobile business. In 1929, he began work on the Chrysler Building in New York City. Company headquarters would never leave

Michigan. It was strictly a real estate investment "to give the children something to do." When completed in 1934, the seventy-seven-story Chrysler Building was second in size only to the Empire State Building.

Chrysler gave up the presidency of the corporation in 1935. He remained chief executive officer but as he put it, "I'm just watching it now." In 1938 he began suffering from a circulatory ailment, and lived the final two years of his life as an invalid. In his office in the Chrysler Building, a tool chest containing mechanic's tools Walter Chrysler fashioned himself remained proudly on display.

Dodge

John Dodge and his brother Horace were inseparable. The brothers survived high school in Niles, Michigan and hastily began careers as machinists. They worked as a team; hire one, hire both. John, four years older and more outgoing, would typically do the talking for the brothers, with Horace remaining a shadowy presence.

They worked in Battle Creek and Port Huron and finally migrated to Detroit in 1886, where the Dodges worked for the Murphy Boiler Works. In 1894, at the age of thirty, John was stricken with tuberculosis. Although he made a complete recovery, the brawny John Dodge was no longer interested in the strenuous physical labor he had heretofore thrived on.

The brothers landed at the Dominion Typograph Shop, described as "manufacturer of typesetting machines and bicycles." In 1897, Horace Dodge patented a dirt-resistant ball bearing and the brothers started their own bicycle business, Evans & Dodge Bicycle Company.

Two years later, the company was absorbed by National Cycle and Automobile Company, a Canadian firm. Horace was retained as a machinist in Windsor, Ontario while John was sent to manage a plant in Hamilton, two hundred miles away. It was to be the only time the Dodge brothers would ever be apart.

After a year the business was sold again, and the Dodges received $7,500 and royalties for the ball bearing. With this capital John and Horace returned to Detroit in 1901 and opened a machine shop. Unlike many machine shops of the day, the Dodge Brothers did not operate out of a flimsy shack or backyard shed. They rented space in the attractive Boydell Building in downtown Detroit, giving the concern an aura of substance and vitality.

But finances were tight. When John's wife died later in the year, he had to borrow money for her burial. One of the first orders to come to the Boydell Building was for some automobile engines from Ransom Olds, who was just starting to make cars. The quality of the Dodge engines was so superior that by 1903 Dodge Brothers was supplying all the transmissions for the popular Oldsmobiles. That relationship alone insured they would be one of the largest suppliers in the infant auto industry.

In 1903 John and Horace signed an agreement to deliver 650 "automobile running gears" to a new, undercapitalized, and highly speculative venture—the Ford Motor Company. It was a strange business marriage. The Dodge Brothers were risking a highly prosperous business, since they had to turn away every other client for this new car. There was no warm affection between Henry Ford and the brothers. In fact Ford, who was highly superstitious and said to look for a white horse every time he saw a redhead, must have suffered great consternation every time he dealt with the redheaded Dodges.

From the beginning, it was apparent the Dodges were not going to receive payment on terms. As builders of the new Model A, the Dodge brothers accepted ownership in the company to deliver the cars. All 650 Model A cars sold quickly when they reached the market, and John and Horace were not only suppliers but part owners in a successful automobile business.

By 1906 Ford maneuvered partners out of the business and announced plans to manufacture engines himself. The Dodge brothers still owned ten percent of the Ford Motor Company, but were now only supplying axles and transmissions. It was obvious to John and Horace that it was only a matter of time before they would no longer be a Ford supplier and they began making plans for their own car.

By 1913 John and Horace were ready. They canceled their relationship with Ford and announced their intention to build a touring car under their own name. The Dodge reputation set the auto industry abuzz. Twenty-two thousand people applied for a new Dodge dealership. The *Michigan Manufacturer and Financial Record* predicted, "When the Dodge Brothers new car comes out there is no question it will be the best thing on the market for the money. The Dodge brothers are the two best mechanics in Michigan."

They set about to build the best car they knew how. Horace worked on the engine. John dropped tires off the roof of the four-story factory to see how they survived. He personally drove cars into a brick wall at twenty miles per hour.

On November 14, 1914 the first Dodge, called "Old Betsey," was ready. In 1914 there were 120 new makers of automobiles in addition to the Dodge Brothers Motor Company. Five years later, the brothers were the number three car-maker in America, behind only Ford and the new conglomerate, General Motors.

The plant was completely retooled, tripling capacity at a cost of over one million dollars—all Dodge money. Their entire lives the brothers never had a line of credit at a bank. Seeking to cut off the capital to a formidable competitor, Henry Ford suspended dividends on Ford stock. The Dodges sued to force the dividends to be paid and a defeated Ford bought the last of their stock in 1919 for $25,000,000.

With their ownership in Ford and as makers of dependable cars themselves, only Henry Ford amassed a greater personal fortune from Detroit's auto industry than John and Horace Dodge. Horace loved to spend his money on yachts; John lavished his riches on mansions.

In 1920, the brothers traveled to New York for a dealer's convention. Horace fell gravely ill from an undiagnosed malady. Keeping a round-the-clock vigil in the doorway between their rooms, John also fell ill and deteriorated rapidly, dying two days later at the age of fifty-six. Horace recovered but never completely regained his robust health; he passed away before the year was out.

Rumors spread that the Dodge brothers had been poisoned in New York but doctors clung to a diagnosis of influenza. The minor scandal died away and their heirs quickly sold the company, leaving only the Dodge name as the brothers' legacy to the auto industry.

errari

World War I found the man whose name was destined to become the most glamorous in the automotive world shoeing mules for the Italian army. It was not long before Enzo Ferrari discovered more suitable transportation.

Enzo Ferrari was born in Modena in northern Italy in 1898. After his military obligations were fulfilled, Ferrari hired on as a test driver for Costruzioni Meccaniche Nazionale, fulfilling a dream held since seeing his first automobile race at the age of ten. Ferrari switched to Alfa Romeo in 1920, becoming a member of Italy's national racing team. In addition to his duties as a driver, Ferrari was in charge of a group of designers, engineers, and mechanics building a new Alfa Romeo racer.

In 1923 Ferrari took the checkered flag at a minor road race in Savio, and was awarded a prancing-horse crest by the Countess Paolina Baracca. From that point Ferrari adorned all his racers with the crest, using a canary yellow background symbolic of his native Modena. His racing career flourished in the 1920s. In 1924 he was knighted for upsetting a powerful German team, and in 1928 Benito Mussolini bestowed upon Ferrari the title *commendatore*, by which he was often referred until his death.

Ferrari retired from racing in 1929 at the age of thirty-one, and returned to Modena where he oversaw freelance mechanical work for his wealthy friends enamored with amateur road racing. In 1932, Alfa Romeo appointed Scuderia Ferrari as its official racing team, and the next year Ferrari won twenty-seven of the thirty-nine races it entered. For the rest of the decade before World War II , Ferrari drifted in and out of racing while dabbling with his own sports cars on the side.

He continued to design racing cars during World War II, but his manufacturing activities were limited to machinery for the Italian war effort. In 1946 the first racer to sport the Ferrari marque, an open two-seater powered by a V-12 engine, was introduced. Before he died more than forty years later in 1988, Ferrari would produce fewer than 50,000 automobiles.

Ferrari sold cars only to pay for his racing program. On the race track he would win more than five thousand times. The cars that fueled this success were greeted with the most enthusiastic praise possible. A Superfast model, selling for eighteen thousand dollars in 1957, was called by *Road and Track*, "one of the most beautiful cars in the world, with a performance which is so fantastic as to be almost beyond comprehension."

Most of these cars were produced only in the hundreds; some models number fewer than a dozen. In 1987, a 1963 Ferrari sold for eleven million dollars. The value of Ferrari's cars to collectors virtually forced them off the road. This phenomenon was cited in *Sports Illustrated*: "Even the true Ferrari lover who can resist the temptation to peddle his car for a big profit dares not drive the car on the street . . . An automobile famous for its performance, its power, its racing victories has become too valuable to drive."

irestone

In 1895 Henry Ford, a machinist fiddling with new gasoline engines, walked into the Columbus Buggy Company store in Detroit. Harvey Firestone sold him a set of rubber carriage tires. The two men wouldn't meet again for ten years, but when they did it changed the automotive industry.

The son of an Ohio farmer, the twenty-two-year-old Firestone joined his uncle's buggy company as a salesman in 1890. Firestone quickly demonstrated a flair for sales; by 1892 he was in charge of the entire Michigan district. The sale to Ford proved to be one of his last, as the buggy business went bankrupt in 1896. By that time, however, Firestone had seen the future: rubber tires would surely replace bone-rattling iron-banded wheels.

A friend staked him to a retail tire venture in Chicago and it prospered mightily. He sold out for forty-five thousand dollars in 1900 and left for Akron, already the rubber capital of the world. Firestone took with him not an improved rubber tire, but a patent for attaching tires to rims. He organized the Firestone Tire and Rubber Company, contributing his patent and ten thousand dollars to acquire fifty percent of the company which, was capitalized at fifty thousand dollars.

For the first few years other companies provided Firestone with tires, but when he began manufacturing his own solid tires the firm became established. He developed a pneumatic tire, which caught the fancy of Henry Ford, who placed an order for two thousand sets to carry his new runabouts. It was the largest single order for tires ever placed by an auto manufacturer at that time.

The Ford Motor Company sold so many cars that one in every fourteen Americans soon owned a car (the figure in Europe was on the order of one in 150). Most of those cars traveled on Firestone tires. Flush with Ford money, Firestone developed into the world's most innovative rubber company, producing the first dismountable rim for easy tire changes, the first balloon tire, and the first low-pressure truck tire.

Firestone was the foremost advocate of truck transportation in America, campaigning for improved highways and the elimination of railroad grade crossings. He promoted his tires aggressively in racing competitions to prove their safety and durability.

World War I eviscerated the world rubber market, and the postwar depression threw Firestone into a debt approaching forty-three million dollars. He slashed prices to reduce inventories, and was able to completely pay off his obligations by 1924. But when Britain put restrictions on rubber production in her possessions, Firestone had suffered enough of the vagaries of the world rubber market.

He arranged to lease up to one million acres of Liberian land in Africa in return for a five-million-dollar personal loan and an agreement to improve the Monrovian harbor. By 1936, sixty thousand acres had been planted, and during World War II the plantation turned out to be a valuable source of rubber for the Allies. Firestone also acquired textile mills, steel and rim-making plants, and cotton plantations.

Having taken some steps to shore up the supply side of his operation, Firestone turned to the retail side. His tires were sold through a network of over thirty thousand dealers but were facing stiff competition from the great mail-order houses—Montgomery Ward and Sears—who were beginning to sell tires in retail outlets. Firestone pioneered one-stop service stations offering gas, oil, brakes, and of course, his tires.

Firestone and Henry Ford forged a relationship outside their business dealings. Together with Thomas Edison they frequently disappeared into the wilderness on camping trips. America's most celebrated campers also enjoyed reunions at their winter homes in Florida.

It was while vacationing on his Florida estate in 1938 that Firestone died at the age of sixty-nine. He spent his last hours before passing away in his sleep doing what he enjoyed best: riding in a sulky behind his favorite horse on his hand-built bridle path. He had never quite accepted that horseless carriage.

Ford

Henry Ford grew up on his father's farm along the River Rogue outside Detroit. William Ford had fled the potato famine in Ireland in 1847, and Henry, his first son came along in 1863. Henry toiled at his chores, but it wasn't long before he realized he was more interested in the tools he was working with than the soil he was working.

Ford finished school at sixteen and left for the city. His first job at Michigan Car Works lasted only six days, but he soon hired on as a machinist's apprentice. At night he repaired watches for a jeweler. When his apprenticeship ended, Ford returned to Dearborn and set up a sawmill on eighty acres of land borrowed from his father.

Ford married in 1888, and set about farming and repairing steam engines. Three years later he returned to Detroit and began work with the Edison Illuminating Company, furnishing electricity to the city. He was soon chief engineer.

In 1893 Ford visited the Chicago World's Fair and familiarized himself with the wondrous exhibits of internal combustion gas engines and horseless carriages. When he returned, Ford resumed his mechanical tinkering—only this time with gas engines instead of steam.

Newspapers started carrying tales of strange "horseless wagons" in the French countryside. In 1895 three of the "horseless wagons" arrived in New York and Ford traveled east to see them. Later that year the *Chicago Times-Herald* announced a five-thousand-dollar race for the new contraptions. Only four cars were ready on the big day, and only two got away from the starting line—a Duryea and a Benz. The Benz won. Ford left the race in awe—and with some new intake valves for his experiments.

By the spring of 1896 Ford had built his own horseless carriage. William H. Murphy, a prominent Detroit businessman, heard of Henry Ford's motor car and saw it as a chance to get into the exciting new business of racing cars. They formed the Detroit

Automobile Company, with Henry Ford abandoning his lucrative job at Edison Illuminating to work full-time as chief engineer.

Sixty-eight thousand dollars later there were no cars in production. Ford left and went to work on his own racer. In 1901, Ford challenged Alexander Winton and his world champion "Bullet" at Grosse Pointe race track outside Detroit. Three cars lined up for the ten-mile race, but only Ford and Winton left the line. Winton led Ford for eight miles, but sputtered badly as the Ford racer puttered past. Newspapers the next day anointed Ford as "top rank of American chauffeurs."

Racing was the way to sell cars in the early 1900s. Motor cars were the exclusive province of sportsmen and the very wealthy. In November of 1901, the Henry Ford Company was organized to manufacture automobiles, but the venture was short-lived. Four months later Ford was making racers on his own again. He developed the "999" and hired bicycle champion Barney Oldfield to drive. This time the Ford car led wire-to-wire in the ten-mile Manufacturers Challenge Cup Race at Grosse Pointe, winning by more than a mile.

In 1903 Ford and eleven others pooled twenty-eight thousand dollars to start the Ford Motor Company. Their early Model A sold for $950, as its makers touted the new car as "Boss of the Road." Its two cylinders powered it to thirty miles per hour. At the end of the first year, Ford had sold over seventeen hundred Model A motor cars. Some stockholders cashed in on the quick profits, and Ford became majority owner.

Other models were designed and some appeared on the streets. In October 1908, the Model T was introduced with the boast, "We can devote all our time and money to taking care of the orders for the car that people have actually been waiting for—a family car at an honest price." The Model T featured a new and "get-at-able" engine for owners who mostly repaired their own cars.

Ford's secret was simple design, the latest machinery, and standardized parts. Most importantly he made the entire automobile in his own factories. He introduced the assembly line in 1914 with cars rolling by on a floor conveyor. By 1915 Ford had put a million Model T cars on the road and was building a new one from scratch every ninety minutes.

Every advance in manufacturing brought the price lower. Ford constructed a mammoth industrial complex on thousands of acres along the River Rogue the likes of which had never before been seen. By 1925 Ford had built fourteen million Model T cars and was producing ten thousand new cars a day. But Ford realized that increased competition would soon mean the end of the legendary Model T.

He completely shut down the River Rogue plant and the world waited for his next move. His retooled factory geared up for a new Model A with gear shift, four-wheel brakes, and foot throttle. Attendance records were shattered everywhere the car was introduced. There were five million Model A cars in service by 1932.

Outside the auto business, Ford assembled a massive collection of everyday objects as "the history of our people as written into things their hands made and used." He often sent buyers out to purchase entire estates for his Henry Ford Museum and Greenfield Village. Ford died at his Dearborn home in 1947 at the age of eighty-three, a true king of industry.

Getty

In 1957, *Fortune* published a list of the richest American men. Atop the list, to the amazement of everybody, was not a Rockefeller, not a Ford, not a Mellon, but an unknown oilman named Jean Paul Getty. The billionaire as celebrity was born.

For the first sixty-four years of his life, Getty built a fortune of one billion dollars in relative obscurity. His father, a lawyer who had made a fortune in the Oklahoma oil rush in the early 1900s, staked Jean Paul to explore low cost leases in the midwest. Getty set up in a seedy six-dollars-a-week room in Tulsa and bounced around Oklahoma in a Model T Ford checking on prospective leases. In 1915 he capped his first well. The following May, the Getty Oil Company was incorporated as a father-son venture. At the age of twenty-three, Getty was a millionaire.

The first thing he did was quit. He bought a Cadillac V8 roadster and spent the next few years on a sybaritic binge through the southwest. In 1919, suddenly bored with the life of a playboy, he rejoined his father, just in time to exploit a new oil rush in southern California. This boom made father and son multimillionaires.

There would be no taking time off this time. Getty bought leases and drilled for oil up and down the California coast. When the stock market collapsed, the acquisitive Getty expanded his holdings by buying up distressed oil company stocks. In 1930, Getty's father died and Jean Paul became president. The bulk of the senior Getty's ten-million dollar fortune went to his wife, then aged seventy-eight and in poor health.

Getty immediately began a battle with his ailing mother for control of the company. Legend has it that Getty was so ruthless in his business dealings that when he discovered a well he was drilling was bottoming out on someone else's property, he tried to sell it to his mother. When informed of the shenanigans, Mrs. Getty is supposed to have replied, "What you are trying to tell me is that Paul is a crook. But he's awfully smart, isn't he?"

Weary of the fight, Mrs. Getty finally relinquished her claim to the bulk of the Getty assets, and Paul quickly set out to build a global international oil company. He set his sights on the giant Tide Water Associated Oil, quietly buying up blocks of stock. It took Getty two decades of tussling with the John D. Rockefeller cartel to wrest control of the company and its twelve hundred service stations. It was the major triumph of his career and gave him the nucleus for a worldwide conglomerate of some two hundred companies.

While the financial wrangling was going on, Getty did not stray from his wildcatting instincts. In 1949, he paid $12.5 million for the rights to prospect for oil in the Neutral Zone, a barren tract of scrub desert between Kuwait and Saudi Arabia. It was one of the few remaining areas in the Middle East unexploited by oilmen. After nearly four years of dry holes, Getty struck oil with a last do-or-die drilling. By 1955 Getty had fifty-five producing wells in the

Neutral Zone; his wealth doubled.

With his unveiling as America's richest man, the public clamored for details on Getty's life. There was plenty to titillate the curious. Getty had divorced five wives, tiring of each almost before the ceremony was over. "My wives married me; I didn't marry them," he said.

There were stories of his miserly habits. In 1961 when he appeared on British television for the first time, he admitted that, yes, he really had waited five minutes to get into a dog show at a cheaper price. He personally washed his underwear every night— not, he explained, to save money on laundry bills, but because he didn't like the detergent his local laundry used.

Tragedy dogged Getty for the final years of his life. A young son died of a brain tumor, his oldest son committed suicide, and his grandson was kidnapped. The boy was returned only after having his ear severed and mailed to an Italian newspaper to convince Getty the plot was real. The old man paid an $850,000 ransom.

In the 1950s, Getty moved to England to be centrally located to his global empire. Once there, however, he seldom visited his Middle East holdings, and never once set foot in America again. He changed his will twenty-one times, using it as a weapon to set one person against another. When he died in 1976 at the age of eighty-four, Getty had ensured discord in Getty Oil. His company was sold to Texaco for $9.9 billion, history's biggest corporate takeover.

Goodrich

Dr. Benjamin Franklin Goodrich was born in the tiny hamlet of Ripley, New York in 1841. He was orphaned at eight years of age and grew up with relatives. At seventeen, Goodrich began studying medicine with his cousin Dr. John Spencer. At the age of twenty, Goodrich graduated from Cleveland Medical College and signed on with the Union Army as an assistant surgeon.

Dr. Goodrich emerged from the Civil War more interested in business than medicine. He entered into a real estate partnership in New York City and soon prospered. In 1869 the partners traded ten thousand dollars worth of real estate for stock in a small factory in Hastings-on-Hudson, New York—the Hudson River Rubber Company.

As Goodrich dug into the books of the rubbermaker, it became clear to him how financially crippled the firm was. He traded more real estate for full ownership and became president. His first step back to fiscal health was to move the business downriver to Melrose, New York and save money on rent.

Progress was slow, and Goodrich decided to break clean with New York and establish the first rubber plant west of the Alleghenies, out where there was power, transportation, fresh labor, and a fast developing country. On the train west, Goodrich met a stranger who spoke so glowingly of a town in Ohio called Akron that he decided to pay a visit.

While in Akron, Goodrich met with business leaders and both sides were impressed. One of the Akron men visited the rubber factory in Melrose and offered Goodrich a loan of $13,600 to establish his business in the small canal town of ten thousand. Akron was on its way to its destiny as the Rubber Capital of the World.

On the penultimate day in 1870, Goodrich, Tew & Company bought four lots on the Ohio Canal. At the time there were few commercial uses for rubber. Dr. Goodrich had watched helplessly as a friend's house burned to the ground when a leather hose froze and burst, so his first product was a cotton-covered rubber fire hose.

The rubber company struggled financially in the beginning, but the business community of Akron helped it through some rough times until sales increased. In 1880, the business officially became the B. F. Goodrich Company as sales climbed to over $500,000 a year.

Dr. Goodrich died prematurely at age forty-seven in 1888, but his company had by this time established the reputation that anyone needing to solve a manufacturing problem involving rubber would go to B. F. Goodrich. In the decades to come, this innovative thinking would result in a new rubber bicycle tire, automobile cord tires, and even the first modern golf ball.

Goodyear

In 1898, Frank A. Seibering was nearly insolvent. His family had started and operated several Akron enterprises, including flour milling, oatmeal production, banking, real estate, the Akron Academy of Music, a rubber company, and manufacturing of strawboard, mowers, and reapers. All were lost in the years of financial distress in the wake of the Panic of 1893.

Seibering was in Chicago to liquidate much of his holdings when he happened upon an Ohio business acquaintance who was looking to dispose of a seven-acre strawboard plant whose main assets were a small power plant and two dilapidated buildings facing each other on opposite banks of Akron's Little Cuyahoga River. He had invested $140,000 in the property, he said, but was seeking only $50,000. The desperate buyer accepted Seibering's offer of $13,500.

Seibering returned to Akron wondering what he was going to do with the old plant and how he was going to pay for it. He borrowed the down payment from his brother-in-law, and other relatives loaned him money to start a rubber company. He had worked around his father's Akron India Rubber Company, so the industry was not totally unfamiliar to him. His brother Charles, who had worked three years for India Rubber, joined him in the enterprise.

The new business was incorporated on August 29, 1898 as the

Goodyear Tire and Rubber Company—in honor of Charles Goodyear who had accidentally discovered the vulcanization of rubber in 1839 when he dropped rubber and sulphur onto his kitchen stove. Goodyear died insolvent in 1860 at the age of sixty.

The company named for him would be the largest tire company in the world in only eighteen years, with sales exceeding $100,000,000. Every dollar invested in Goodyear in the beginning was then worth hundred dollars.

Harley-Davidson

William Harley and Arthur Davidson were Wisconsin boys looking for a way to make their rowboats get to the fishing holes faster. Harley began tinkering with drawings a friend had brought back from France of a small, one-cylinder gas engine.

Davidson had worked as a patternmaker for Ole Evinrude, who was to become famous for outboard motors. Harley was working as an apprentice bicycle fitter. They read all available literature on gas motors. Davidson and Harley decided to work on motorized bicycles instead.

By 1903 they had their first prototype ready for the streets of Milwaukee. Their new motorcycle was painted gloss black and reached a top speed of twenty-five miles per hour. Harley, twenty-three, and Davidson, twenty-two, had no intentions of making their hobby a business, but friends began asking for a similar machine.

Working weekends in a backyard shed, two more motorcycles were constructed the next year. They chose the name "Harley-

Davidson" in recognition of Harley's original design. Davidson's aunt created the distinctive logo for the gas tank.

Arthur's older brother Walter quit his job as a machinist in a railroad shop to come on board full-time in 1904, as Harley entered the University of Wisconsin to gain formal engineering training. He paid expenses by waiting on fraternity tables.

Five motorcycles were handmade in 1905, and by 1907 there were 150 motorcycles in production. Everyone surrendered their outside interests, and the Harley-Davidson Motor Company was officially incorporated. Walter Davidson was named president, William Harley chief engineer, Arthur Davidson sales manager, and William Davidson—the eldest of the Davidson brothers—joined the company as production member. Each founding partner remained in his original position until his death.

In 1907 the American motorcycle market was glutted with small manufacturers. One way to stand out was to win highly publicized races. Harley-Davidson joined motorcycle competition in 1908 when Walter Davidson entered a two-day endurance ride in New York. Eighty-four riders representing twenty-two manufacturers started the race, and fewer than half survived the gutted country roads. Davidson won that race and another several weeks later, getting an estimated 188 miles per gallon.

Behind the renowned Harley-Davidson racing team, known as "The Wrecking Crew," sales grew. But the controversies and fluctuations that have always dogged the motorcycle industry had already begun. In 1920 Harley-Davidson sales reached to the twenty-eight-thousand-bike mark. They would not reach that level again until 1942.

William Davidson was the first of the partners to die, in 1937 at the age of sixty-six. As production manager he enjoyed a close relationship with his workers, often carrying personal debts he would never collect from his men. Shortly before his death, seven workers organized a union affiliation with the CIO, creating a rift in the close-knit Harley-Davidson plants. Two days after William Davidson saw his beloved production team become a union shop he died.

Walter Davidson ruled, often ruthlessly, as president until his death in 1942 at the age of sixty-seven. His tight-fisted operational style was necessary to keep Harley-Davidson a viable concern, especially during the lean years. In times of prosperity, like the early 1920s, the public could more readily afford cars, but in bad times they couldn't afford any transportation. Output dropped to less than four thousand motorcycles during the Depression. But Walter Davidson kept his company profitable.

Although William Harley relinquished much of the day-to-day design work on new motorcycles he remained a giant in the industry as the creator of the original, reliable Harley-Davidson bike. An avid outdoorsman, Harley increasingly became an automobile enthusiast through the years. He remained chief engineer until his death in 1943 at the age of sixty-three.

Arthur Davidson was the most outgoing of the partners. His biggest contribution to the firm was the creation of an extensive dealer network when the only Harley-Davidson claim to fame was Walter Davidson's road-racing triumphs. By 1921 there were Harley-Davidson dealers in sixty-seven countries. Arthur Davidson died at the age of sixty-nine in 1950, ironically, in a car crash.

Hertz

John Hertz left his fingerprints on nearly every facet of the early transportation industry. He started car agencies and cab companies and bus factories, but the one thing he didn't create is the business that will carry his name into the next century—Hertz Rent-A-Car.

The pioneer of auto renting was Walter Jacobs, who in September of 1918, at the age of twenty-two, opened a car rental operation in Chicago. Starting with a dozen Model-T Fords, which he repaired and repainted himself, Jacobs expanded his operations to the point where, within five years, the business generated annual revenues of about one million dollars. At this point he sold out to John Hertz, who called the concern Hertz Drive-Ur-Self System.

Hertz had been in the business world since 1890, when he ran away from home at the age of eleven. He ran copy for the Chicago *Morning News* and peddled papers for extra cash. His take each week approached three dollars, more than enough to cover his room and board. After a year his father, who had brought the family to Chicago from Austria six years earlier, found John and forced him to come home. He lasted six more months and then left home for good. He was thirteen.

He worked long nights at the paper, but the strange hours caused his health to break at only fifteen. A doctor told Hertz to get out during the day and rebuild his constitution. He landed a job driving a delivery wagon and spent nights in a gym boxing, building up a respectable record against local opposition.

Hertz rejoined the journalistic world as a sportswriter for the *Chicago Record*, but when the paper merged all the writers were fired. Hertz drifted into boxing management and developed two potential champions: Benny Yanger and Jack O'Keefe. Hertz soon had ten thousand dollars from his boxing stable, a considerable accomplishment for the day. But his girlfriend didn't approve of the shady boxing business and, despite its lucrative charms, Hertz left the fight game.

Through an acquaintance Hertz became a salesman for the newest novelty in Chicago: the horseless carriage. Sales were slow the first year, and Hertz earned only nine hundred dollars. Then he sold service along with the car—John Hertz was available night and day to help you with any car you bought from him. His commissions jumped to twelve thousand dollars his second year.

He quit to buy a quarter-share of a French car agency for two thousand dollars. The horseless carriage was catching on quickly, and sales topped $500,000 the first year. In 1910 his old friends at the Chicago Athletic Association contacted Hertz to operate a private cab service for its members and guests. Hertz used two of his own fleet and eight borrowed cars to forge his infant taxi business.

Intrigued by the potential of taxis, Hertz went to Europe to study the French taxi system. What he saw opened his eyes. The

French utilized small, economical cars stripped of luxuries as cabs, unlike their American counterparts who typically pressed leftover touring cars into service. Cab companies linked their fortunes to local hotels; In America there were no such concessions.

But most importantly, in France people simply hailed passing cabs from the curb. In the United States, passengers needed to phone for a pickup because all taxis looked different. There were countless incidents of people piling into private cars. Hertz immediately realized he needed distinctive, standardized cabs, recognizable from a mile away. He painted his cabs yellow, which he thought was a color easily spotted day or night.

The Yellow Cab Company, thirty cabs strong, picked up its first passengers on August 2, 1915. Hertz built short, sturdy, highly maneuverable cars designed to go 300,000 miles or more. It wasn't long before cities across the country were ordering similar cabs from Hertz. He installed receipt meters, heaters, interior lights.

With his cab business booming, Hertz turned his attention to buses. He engineered a merger with the Chicago Motor Coach Company and built sleek new buses as the Yellow Coach Manufacturing Company. A year later he added the rental car business to his transportation dynasty, establishing the first coast-to-coast network by 1925.

In 1925 the Yellow Cab Manufacturing Company was merged with General Motors in a sixteen-million-dollar deal, by which Yellow Cab was tabbed to build the corporation's trucks. Hertz Drive-Ur-Self was included in the merger, to remain a part of General Motors until 1953. John Hertz became chairman of the board of the Yellow Truck and Coach Manufacturing Company.

Approaching fifty, Hertz loosened his ties to the transportation industry. He became a partner in Lehman Brothers in 1934, a position he would hold with the investment banking firm until his death some thirty years later. Away from the office, Hertz built one of America's most renowned racing stables featuring the fabled 1943 Triple Crown winner, Count Fleet.

When Hertz was finally felled by ailing health in 1961, after more than seventy years in business, the Hertz Corporation operated more than seventeen hundred drive-yourself stations in one thousand cities and forty-six foreign countries.

Hess

Leon Hess was born to Lithuanian parents in Asbury Park, New Jersey in 1914. In 1925, after twenty years of kosher butchering, his father Mores quit to deliver fuel to homes in the beachside town. The Depression killed what little business Mores had built up over the years. Leon's two older brothers and sister attended college, but there was no money left for him. Leon Hess got the struggling oil business.

In 1933 that business was a single room in an old building in Asbury Park and an overmortgaged and undersized truck. Hess drove across bumpy pine-draped roads selling oil and coal by day and delivering on his return trip at night. The coal would soon be dropped from his tiny product line—literally. "I was basically lazy. I didn't want to carry hundred-pound bags of coal," he said.

In the late 1930s, Hess began to focus his meager resources on residual fuel—the tarry, gunky ooze that remained after refining. The sludge was useful only in massive boilers maintained by public utilities. From his attempts at peddling coal, Hess knew oil was replacing coal at power plants, and residual oil would become more profitable.

Residual oil had to be transported hot to keep it flowing; if it cooled it became the consistency of a newly tarred street in summer. Hess built a successful fleet of specially designed tankers to deliver the residual oil. He began shipping to distant markets and came in low bid on several federal contracts, submitting the only handwritten bids.

In World War II, Hess left the business with his brother Henry and went to battle as petroleum supply officer under General George Patton. He earned a bronze star, the rank of major, and invaluable experience in running a large organization efficiently.

He applied his lessons to his oil business, which steadily expanded. Hess trucks were soon seen as far away as upstate New York. He began importing residual oil, and Hess oil generated the electricity in seventy-five percent of New Jersey by the late 1940s.

In 1958 Hess built his first refinery, and two years later he marketed gasoline under his own name.

Hess built his business on business no one else wanted; now he was in the business everyone wanted.

He competed on price. He refused to comply with an agreement signed by other New Jersey stations to keep gas priced above a minimum price. He built huge stations to pump gas only, leaving repair business to others. His refinery was close to his stations, so the pennies saved in distribution were slashed off his gas prices. Hess grew from twenty-eight stations in 1961 to five hundred across the Northeast in twenty years.

By the mid-1960s, Hess Oil was profitable but he had no crude production, leaving him in a precarious position if his supply disappeared. After prolonged financial maneuvering and at considerable risk, Hess took control of Amerada Petroleum in 1969.

At the same time, Hess undertook the building of the world's largest refinery in the Virgin Islands, a United States territory not fully answerable to American law. Hess used political connections made by his father-in-law, a former attorney general of New Jersey, to pull off the deal. The refinery cost $600,000,000 and eventually produced 700,000 barrels a day.

Hess Oil was now steeply leveraged, but the Arab oil embargo paid off Hess's gamble. His fortunes continued to vacillate with the fortunes of the oil market but Hess, the owner of the New York Jets and a tyrannical but trustworthy businessman, had built his company into the country's seventeenth largest oil producer.

Honda

In a land of conformity, Soichiro Honda was a rebel. The son of a blacksmith born on the southern coast of Honshu in 1906, Honda

dropped out of technical high school and in the 1930s began racing cars. He built a small piston-ring company, reveling in the
sounds and smells of engines.

Honda set out to build his piston-ring plant, but because Japan
was hoarding materials in preparation for World War, he was
unable to obtain cement. Undaunted, Honda built the plant by
learning to make his own cement. The factory survived repeated
bombings in World War II, but was then destroyed by an earthquake.

From his ruined machine shop, Honda went into the motorcycle business. He once remarked that he happened on the idea
for fitting an engine to a bicycle simply because he did not want to
ride the incredibly crowded trains and buses in Japan.

The early postwar years were so lean that Honda once carried
heavy motorcycle parts in his clothing on an airplane because he
could not afford the excess baggage charges. A financially talent-
ed partner kept the business afloat, which freed Honda to wield
his technical skills (Honda would hold 360 patents) and test his
unconventional management philosophies.

Before Honda, a motorcyle in America meant "Hell's Angel."
Honda's plan was to sell motorcycles to those who had never
thought about it before. Singlehandedly, he sold the motorcycle to
the middle class as a leisure-time sport in developed countries. In
poorer lands, his motorbikes brought transportation within reach
of impoverished millions.

He made the smallest, lightest motorcycles available. He added
features to make the bikes easier to handle for women. His motorcycles ruled Grand Prix competiton, winning every possible racing
prize.

In the early 1960s, a UCLA undergraduate submitted an advertising campaign as a class requirement, featuring the theme, "You
meet the nicest people on a Honda." His instructor sent the paper
to Grey Advertising, and Honda adopted it. By 1965, one of every
two motorcycles sold in the United States was a Honda. From
scratch, in ten years Honda dominated the world industry.

In 1963 Honda went into the car business. By the 1960s, there
weren't many entrees for newcomers into the competition with the
established automakers of the world. Soichiro Honda produced a
gas-sipping car that caused less pollution as his mark. He did so,

not with expensive added equipment but by designing a more efficient engine. Honda's super-efficient four-cylinder engine was an
industry landmark.

His Honda Civic reached America in 1972 and the Accord in
1976 ("By the time we got into the business all the good names like
'Cougar' and 'Wildcat' were taken"). The incredibly popular cars
rank as all-time best-sellers. At an age when many Japanese businessmen were just assuming the top job, Honda, who favored
longish hair and loud socks, abruptly retired after the introduction
of the Civic.

He became an ambassador for his business philosophies,
speaking to youth groups on self-reliance, hard work, respect for
parents, and safe driving. "I'm not concerned with making money
anymore," he said. "You see, a life is like an airplane journey. No
matter how good the takeoff, no matter how good the flight, if
you have a crash landing, then it was all for nothing. I am coming
in for the landing now. The important part of my life is just
beginning."

Mack

In the early 1900s, as Americans began their love affair with the
automobile, trucks were an afterthought. Trucks were largely
assembled with surplus or obsolete car parts. John (Jack) Mack was
to change all that.

Jack Mack was one of five brothers raised on his German parents' farm near Scranton, Pennsylvania. In 1878 Jack ran away
from home to work as a teamster. He was fourteen years old. Mack
learned how to work steam engines, a talent which took him to sea.

He worked for several years around the United States and in the Panama Canal region.

Mack and his brother Augustus purchased a small carriage and wagon building firm in Brooklyn in 1893. The country was gripped by the Panic of 1893, and the Macks filled few orders. They did establish a reputation as first class repairmen for wagons, however.

Jack and Augustus began experimenting with new self-propelled vehicles. Many of their early creations ended up in the East River as fish-breeding environments. In 1900, after eight years of work, the first hand-crafted Mack motor vehicle was ready.

Powered by a Mack four-cylinder engine, utilizing a cone-type clutch and three-speed transmission the first vehicle was actually a bus designed to carry twenty sightseers through Brooklyn's Prospect Park. It was the first successful bus in the United States. The Mack was so rugged it served for eight years in the park and then was converted into a truck and retired seventeen years later with one million miles under it.

The prototype "Old Number One" was so successful other orders followed. The Macks' three other brothers joined in the formation of the Mack Brothers Company in the State of New York, with thirty-five thousand dollars in working capital. By 1905 they had outgrown their Brooklyn facility and moved home to Allentown, Pennsylvania as the Mack Brothers Motor Car Company with Jack Mack as its driving force.

But Jack Mack had no intention of building motor cars. He pioneered the design and manufacture of custom-built trucks using durable Mack-built components, not discarded car parts. Very early on he devised the seat-over-engine trucks which were the forerunners of modern cabs. The trucks could haul a capacity of seven and a half tons. Mack also turned out fire engines, railroad cars, and buses.

By 1911 Mack was the premier manufacturer of heavy duty trucks, making six hundred units a year. He needed more money to expand, and J. P. Morgan merged the Mack Company with the Saurer Motor Company to form the International Motor Company.

The company would eventually drop its other lines and revert back to Mack Trucks, but Jack Mack would be gone by then. Unhappy with the changes in top management of the new company, he and three of his brothers disassociated themselves from the new combine. Mack's name would live on, for it was his leadership and ingenuity that had been instrumental in establishing Mack's legendary toughness. Jack Mack was the first to "build 'em like a Mack truck."

Mercedes-Benz

Carl Benz received a patent for the world's first gas-powered velocipede in 1886. In 1888 he won a gold medal for his automobile at the Munich Engine Exposition, but generated no sales. Experts opined that the use of petroleum held no more promise for road travel than did steam. Benz did attract one prospect, however, but the man was literally carted off to a lunatic asylum before any money could change hands. The world's first new car buyer was certifiably insane.

Carl Benz's road to his first automobile was no less rocky than his drive for his first sale. Benz was born in Germany in 1844, and completed an education at Karlsruhe Polytechnikum before launching an immodest early career. In rapid succession he worked on locomotives, designed scales, and built bridges. In 1871 he set up a machine shop in a shed with a partner who turned out not to like anything about the business beyond setting it up. Benz floundered, and his business was kept from the auctioneer's gavel only by the value of its property.

Gottlieb Daimler had just built a four-stroke internal combustion stationary engine which convinced Benz he could develop a two-stroke engine he could mount on a movable vehicle. On New Year's Eve 1879, a nearly destitute Benz hit upon a workable model

with enough promise to land local financing. At first Benz built stationary engines, but in 1883 he set out to build a road vehicle.

But what was he going to build? No one had ever built anything that resembled a car. How would it ignite? How would it
steer? How many wheels should it have? Late in 1885 the first Benz
car rolled around the courtyard in his hometown of Mannheim. It
stopped when an ignition wire snapped. Then a chain drive broke.
After weeks of repair, Benz tried again. This time he drove his five-
hundred-fifty-pound vehicle into a brick wall—the first automobile
accident.

By early 1886, Benz was back on the streets with a three-wheeled
contraption. He test drove at night to avoid any embarrassment,
and his son ran down the road with him to refuel the car. Fearing
an explosion, Benz was careful to only put one and a half liters into
the tank at a time. But his tests were successful. Meanwhile,
Daimler had taken his faster engine and situated it in between the
two wheels of a bicycle to make the world's first motorcycle. Soon
he had driven a horseless carriage of his design eighteen kilome-
ters an hour.

Germans ignored these new cars, but the French were wildly
enthusiastic about motor transportation. Benz contracted with a
Parisien agent to sell his cars as more and more inventors introduced their own strange and wonderful contraptions. What better
way to determine the merit of these new cars than to stage a race?
On July 22, 1894 in Paris, twenty-one vehicles—eight steam-driven
and thirteen gasoline powered—rolled to the starting line in the
first-ever automobile race. It was more horseless carriages gathered together in one place than ever before.

Carl Benz was not enthusiastic about this sort of competition.
He knew others were working with more powerful engines and
thought a car should be judged on its reliability, not its ability to
reach a high speed for a short time. Indeed, the Benz car reached
the finish line in the seventy-eight-mile race well behind the
Daimler-powered engines in the field. But Benz instead pointed
with pride to another motoring achievement—a thousand mile,
three country tour undertaken by a Benz Viktoria car.

By the end of the nineteenth century, Benz had sold two thousand cars, making him the leading automobile maker in the world.
Benz thought thirty miles per hour was as fast as a car ever needed

to go, and he became increasingly disenchanted with his company's growing infatuation with racing. On April 21, 1903 he resigned his position as board member and advisor.

Gottlieb Daimler died in 1900 at the age of sixty-six, never having met Carl Benz, even though the two lived only sixty miles apart. The following year his company was commissioned by Emile Jellinik, a wealthy Austrian banker, to build a car. He wanted the engine in front, an unusual placement at the time, because "that was where the horse used to be." The car was named for Jellinik's eleven-year-old daughter, Mercedes Adrienne Manuela Ramona Jellinik. Emile Jellinik would die in prison in World War I, accused of being an Austrian spy.

World War I decimated the German automobile industry. Eighty-six car makers vied for sales in the war-ravaged country in the 1920s, causing Benz et Cie. and Daimler-Motoren-Gesselschaft to enter into a loose association where the firms shared technology and market information. In 1926 the merger became official, with the melding of the three-pointed Daimler star and the Benz laurel branches onto the new Mercedes-Benz. Carl Benz died three years later, at eighty-five, a recognized pioneer of the automobile industry. Mercedes Jellinik also died in 1929, impoverished after two failed marriages to Austrian barons.

Michelin

In 1889 a French cyclist arrived in the workshop of the Michelin et Compagnie rubber works asking for a repair of his punctured Dunlop tire. Edouard Michelin labored for three hours to repair the curious new tire and still the repair didn't hold. But when he tested it, the air-inflated tire gave such a comfortable ride he decided to look for a way to make the troublesome tire practical.

The rubber company, founded by Edouard's grandfather in the 1830s, had never made tires. Belts and hoses comprised the product line of the struggling company, which was on the verge of disappearing when Andre Michelin took the helm in 1886. Then thirty-three, Andre continued to tend his picture frame and lock business and recruited his younger brother Edouard from fine arts school to help him with the rubber shop. By 1889, a rubber brake pad for horse-drawn vehicles was Michelin's best seller.

Edouard set to work, and by 1891 he had designed a detachable pneumatic tire that was repairable in only fifteen minutes, not hours. The next year it required only two minutes to fix a punctured Michelin tire. In a twelve-hundred-kilometer race, a Michelin rider endured five punctures and still won by eight hours. The Michelin brothers organized another race and surreptitiously scattered nails across the route. The unwary riders suffered 244 punctures but proved how easily repairs were made with Michelin tires. In 1893, ten thousand Michelins were sold.

In 1894 the Michelin tire was adapted for horse-drawn Parisien cabs. The improved ride on the five test cabs produced so much extra business other drivers sabotaged the tires. Soon six hundred Paris cabs were outfitted with Michelins.

1895 saw Michelin introduce the first pneumatic automobile tire. The Michelin brothers themselves drove *Eclair*, meaning "forked lightning," in a June race that year. Only nine of the 19 competitors finished the 1,209 kilometer race in the allotted one hundred hours. *Eclair* was one, the first of many Michelin racing triumphs.

Approaching a new century, the tire business was intense; France alone sported 150 manufacturers. A strong brand image was crucial and Michelin came up with one of the best of all time. The Michelin Man, a rotund figure composed of tires, bounded onto the advertising scene in 1898.

Another Michelin institution was born in 1900 with the publishing of the first Michelin travel guide, the *Guide Rouge*. Distributed free, the journey planning advice and hotel listings were liberally spiced with tire information. By the end of the decade, guides were available for Europe, North Africa, and Egypt.

In 1910 the company published the first road maps of France designed for motorists.

The Michelin brothers were constantly on the lookout for new markets and applications for their tires. The English market opened in 1905, the Italian in 1906—years later when Michelin became the world's leading tire manufacturer France would account for less than one sale in six.

The Michelins sponsored an early aviation contest, designing a difficult course culminating with a dangerous landing on a mountain peak in quest of a hefty cash prize. Cynics accused the brothers of setting an impossible task for the sake of publicity, but the prize was won in 1911, on the third anniversary of its creation.

The Michelin commitment to aeronautics continued in World War I. One hundred bombers for the French air force were supplied free, and another eighteen hundred were built at cost. The postwar years brought a surge in motorized traffic and Michelin grew along with that surge. Michelin was in the forefront of road numbering and signposting throughout France.

Andre and Edouard Michelin guided the company, now focused entirely on tires, until they died—Andre in 1931 at the age of seventy-eight and Edouard in 1940 at eighty-one. The family was torn apart by the German occupation of France in World War II, but emerged with Michelin under family control, as it remains today.

Oldsmobile

Ransom Eli Olds was unique among the automotive pioneers whose names have flourished for nearly a century. Like David

Buick and Louis Chevrolet, history treated Olds shabbily. For a time his name was stripped from Lansing, Michigan's tallest building and leading hotel, both of which Olds built. His historic mansion, despite occasional preservation murmuring, was leveled as part of a highway project to enable cars bearing his name to speed over his former living room. But Olds did not struggle financially like Buick and Chevrolet; his worth was estimated at up to $60,000,000 and he died a millionaire.

On the other hand, Olds was in the best position of any car builder to establish an empire like Henry Ford or Walter Chrysler. But he lacked the competitive drive to build that sort of mega-business. What Ransom Olds really lacked was an ego.

Olds began building horseless carriages when he was twenty-one in 1885 in his father's steam-engine business. The next year he produced a three-wheeled steam-propelled horseless carriage that roared through the streets of Lansing in a predawn test run. Olds took his invention to the road in the middle of the night to avoid the jeers of spectators, but its crude noises caused people to leap from their beds and rush to the window anyway.

He improved his steam carriage over the years. The first of thirty-four patents Olds would claim over the years was granted in 1891 for an engine governor. In 1893 Olds sold his horseless carriage, now sporting four wheels, to an English company for use in India. It was America's first automobile sale.

By this time Olds was deeply involved in gasoline engines. In 1896, he organized the Olds Motor Vehicle Company in Detroit with a group of investors. Over the next few years, only four cars were sold as Olds vacillated over what type of horseless carriage to produce. For a while he made an electric "town car" in addition to a gas-powered roadster for the country.

In 1901 Olds settled on a tiny one-cylinder carriage with only a dash that curved upwards like a toboggan in front of the occupants. While he was on a trip to California that year, Olds's Detroit factory burned down. Only one curved-dash roadster was salvaged.

With a crippled capacity, Olds had to turn to outside suppliers for car parts. This stimulated the growth of the auto-support industry, which made Detroit the auto capital of the world. The plant fire is often romantically credited with creating the Motor City, but Olds had years earlier realized the need for outside suppliers to manufacture horseless carriages in quantity.

In 1902 the Oldsmobile trade name was registered, the oldest surviving American automotive marquis. Olds promoted his little runabout vigorously. It rapidly became the most widely advertised, best-selling car in America. He wrote dealers' instruction booklets, magazine ads, and fancy postcards. Oldsmobile billboards were commonplace in American cities.

Olds formed the Oldsmobile Club of America, announcing that all that was required of a member was "a good character and an Oldsmobile." "The former," the company suggested, "we can not always furnish, the latter is delivered on payment of the initiation fee, $650."

Olds also favored publicity stunts like driving up steps to demonstrate the little carriage's ruggedness and piling up to seventeen people on the sturdy runabout. Olds was one of the few automobile makers to use advertisements to attack the industry's primary competition—the often skittish horse.

After accepting outside capital in 1896, Ransom Olds's power in the business eroded rapidly. He argued that breakdowns and defects were inevitable given the limited technology available and the company could sell post-purchase service. "We have to sell parts, too," he maintained.

Company officials, stung by occasional criticism of the Oldsmobile's reliability, felt the best possible endorsement was a well-made quality car before it left the shop. Ransom Olds resigned his presidency in 1904. Oldsmobile enjoyed soaring sales for two more years, but was selling only a thousand cars annually in 1908 when William Durant bought the company for General Motors, claiming he was spending a million dollars for little more than billboards.

Meanwhile Olds diversified his business interests: real estate, a peat fuel company, a gold mine, and banking. Before 1904 was out, Olds was back in the car business. He formed the R. E. Olds Company, but was threatened with litigation from his former company. He changed the name to REO Motor Car Company, an acronym of his initials.

The first REO, clearly an automobile and not a horseless carriage, was ready in 1905. Its $1,250 price tag, while reasonable for a touring car, put the car out of the mass market being claimed by

Ford. REO became established as an industry leader, but Olds failed to keep up with changing designs and mechanical advancements. The 1911 model was still the 1905 REO.

In a brash new 1912 advertising campaign Olds announced "My Farewell Car." "Embodied here," read the copy, "are the final results of my twenty-five years of experience. I do not believe that a car materially better will ever be built." The REO climbed back to seventh place in car sales.

The copy was written for him, but it was frightfully prophetic. Olds had no plans to retire, but had not been actively involved in the business since 1907. He traveled extensively, vacationed much of the winter, and spent a great deal of time at auto shows. Always a better pioneer than manager, Olds relinquished the title of general manager in 1915. He gave up the presidency of REO in 1923 but kept the honorary position of chairman as his last tie to the industry.

Olds was not entirely content with the life of leisure. He continued to tinker and obtain patents. He created one of the first gas-powered lawnmowers in 1915 and headed the Ideal Power Lawn Mower Company. He developed a planned community in Florida which, although failing in his lifetime, eventually took hold. In 1929 he built the twenty-six-story Olds Tower in Lansing, next to the venerable Hotel Olds.

The Depression killed REO. The last car was made in 1936, although truck manufacturing would continue another four decades. For the first time in forty years, Ransom Olds was not involved in carmaking. He cut all ties to the auto industry.

Olds lived until 1950, when he died from complications of old age. Most of his fortune was split among his family. He eschewed national charities, convinced that most of the money went to pay staff salaries. Instead he showered benefactions on local libraries, Michigan State University, and the church.

In an interview a year before his death, the eighty-five-year-old Olds decried the high price of cars, advocating a stripped-down car that would sell for a thousand dollars. "Prices are much too high," declared Olds. "More people should have the benefit of this fine equipment. The public wants transportation, not gadgets."

Porsche

The first vehicle to carry Dr. Ferdinand Porsche's insignia was a tank. He designed tractors and the first Volkswagens, or "people's car." His automotive designs earned him two honorary doctorates. At his funeral in 1952, the West German minister of transport delivered this eulogy: "We are not only standing at the bier of a great designer, but we are burying with him the heroic epoch of the motor car." Still, Dr. Porsche never built an automobile that carried his name.

This legend of automotive design was self-taught in his home-town of Maffersdorf, Bohemia, a region of Austria-Hungary, when Porsche was born in 1875. As a teenager, Porsche chose not to fol-low his father into the tinsmithing trade, and instead pursued a fascination with electric motors. The Porsches became the first family in Maffersdorf to be wired for electric lights when Ferdinand rigged a generator into the house.

His design career began in 1898. Porsche joined the firm of Jacob Lohner & Co. to create carriages for the royal Austrian House of Habsburg. In 1905 he began an association with Austro-Daimler, the largest automobile maker in Austria, that would span nearly twenty years. One of Porsche's rare failed designs at Austro-Daimler was the Maja, a passenger car named for the daughter of a wealthy Austrian, Emil Jellinek. Another car designed for Jellinek's other daughter, Mercedes, did become a commercial success.

During World War I, Porsche's designs for the Austrian mili-tary—including a motorized gun carriage for light artillery—earned him the Austrian Officer's Cross and an honorary doctorate from the technical college in Vienna where he had studied briefly twenty years earlier but never bothered to enroll. In 1924, after leaving Austro-Daimler for Daimler in Germany, he won a second doctorate from the technical college in Stuttgart for his design of a Mercedes SSK racer.

Mergers in the German automobile industry compromised Porsche's autonomy and, in his fifties, he returned to Austria to head the engineering department for Steyr Motor Works. Here Porsche could work on the small, affordable cars he favored over the luxury vehicles Austro-Daimler had preferred. However, Steyr and Austro-Daimler merged in 1930, and Porsche left once again for Stuttgart, Germany and his own design firm, buoyed by nine Austrian engineers he took with him.

Porsche once again set out to become the Henry Ford of Europe. He designed three prototypes for the Volksauto, a car for the masses, but the cars were never produced. The car would be resurrected decades later as the car Americans know as the Beetle. Adolph Hitler, also seeking a car for the German masses, appointed Porsche as a director of the government's new car company and awarded him the title of professor. During World War II he designed tanks for the Third Reich, the first vehicles to carry the Porsche name.

After the war, Porsche was interned for several months at an American interrogation center while being questioned about his military activities. After he was released in November 1945, Porsche was invited to France to discuss the possibility of establishing an automotive factory there. Once again, Porsche was arrested and accused of war crimes. The seventy-year-old Dr. Porsche was forced to help design a Renault car before raising one million francs to secure his freedom. He had spent eighteen months in prison.

Ferdinand Porsche was broken upon his release in 1947. Porsche's son Ferdinand II, "Ferry," assumed management of the business. It was under his direction that the first Porsche automobile, crafted from spare Volkswagen parts, reached the market in 1948. The Porsche name would be carried on to future generations rightly as a high-performance sports car and not a utilitarian tank.

Rand McNally

William Rand learned his printing in the eastern United States; Andrew McNally learned his printing in Ireland. They teamed up in frontier Chicago in 1858, announcing "every description of printing on the most advantageous terms."

That first decade, the two men decided to concentrate their printing and publishing efforts in the field of transportation. The first sales division of the fledgling firm was railroad printing. Railroads went into places before cities, and people needed tickets to get to those places, so the young printers found plenty of customers. They published literary works on railroad timetables to give riders something to read on the train.

In 1868, the year the firm officially became Rand McNally & Company, Chicago was rapidly becoming the unofficial printing and engraving capital of the nation. Rand McNally published its first book in 1870, *The Business Directory of Chicago for 1870–1871*, and the following year brought out the first edition of the "Western Railway Guide." The "Guide" was a monthly periodical listing the latest timetables of various railway and steamboat lines.

The Great Chicago Fire of 1871 devastated the city. As flames licked the doors of their offices, Rand and McNally ran a relay race to safety with two ticket printing machines. Rand hauled them to McNally's stable three miles away and McNally carted the machines to the shore of Lake Michigan where he dumped them in the sand.

Three days later they were back in business in rented space.

In 1872 Rand McNally took out a small advertisement announcing its entry into the map engraving field. The huge growth of railroads had created a tremendous demand for maps. There were many other map manufacturers at the time, but Rand McNally innovated modern methods of engraving in wax to accelerate correction work. This single technique was responsible for their emergence in the map field. Rand McNally was able to draft and correct maps at a fraction of previous costs.

Railroad maps were given away by the thousands to promote train travel, many railroads distorting their own routes to display their superiority over rival lines. Rand McNally printed many maps in Swedish and Norwegian, which no doubt contributed to the Scandanavian settling of the west.

In 1876 Rand McNally published its first *Business Atlas,* which became the backbone of the firm's dominant map business. Rand retired from the business in 1899 and McNally died in 1904, just as the country's demand for road maps would indelibly stamp their names on American travel.

olls Royce

One was educated at Eton, the other studied at night school. One was a devil-may care racer, the other a no-nonsense engineer. One died spectacularly as the first Englishman ever killed in an airplane crash, the other died of overwork. Together they are responsible for the most luxurious car in the world.

Frederick Henry Royce was the son of a miller who was forced to sell newspapers on the streets of London when his father's business failed. By his twenty first birthday in 1884, he had already been in and out of the telegraph business, the railroad business, and the new electric light business. That year he borrowed seventy pounds and began manufacturing lamps and other electrical devices. With a fanaticism for detail and a normal workday that spanned sixteen hours, he was able to become prosperous.

In 1902 Royce treated himself by purchasing a new French auto. Royce was not happy with his new car; it was unreliable and worse, noisy. A self-styled engineer, Royce decided to build his own two-cylinder car. In fact he made three: one for himself, one for his partner A. R. Claremont, and a third for Henry Edwards, a new director in the firm of F. H. Royce, Ltd.

Edwards drove his car over to see a friend, Charles Stuart Rolls, who knew cars. Rolls, the son of an English baron, graduated with an MA in mechanical engineering and became a champion high bicycle rider. In December 1895 he imported a Peugeot from France, then the most powerful car made. It was only the fourth car in England. At the time, traffic laws forbade any self-propelled vehicle from moving more than four miles per hour—about the speed of a brisk walk—and a man carrying a red flag had to pre-cede the car on the highway. It took Rolls more than twelve hours to travel from London to Cambridge, a distance of less than fifty miles.

The experienced racer became convinced upon seeing Royce's little car that the superior engineering should be applied to a more powerful automobile. The two became partners in 1904, with Royce building in a shop in Manchester and Rolls, awash with influential contacts, selling in London. They quickly decided to concentrate on a single model, and with Rolls adding flare and style to Royce's meticulous engineering the first Rolls Royce auto-mobile reached the market in 1906.

It was called the Silver Ghost and was a landmark in automo-tive history. It was "quiet as a ghost," so solid that a penny would not be dislodged from the side of a radiator cap while the six-cylin-der engine idled. The car set speed records immediately and, with its distinctive grille, established standards for luxury and quality forevermore.

But already Charles Rolls was becoming bored with the auto business. An enthusiastic aviator he made 170 balloon ascents after discovering the sport in 1901, and founded the Aero Club in England in 1903. He became one of the first to fly with Wilbur Wright when Wright demonstrated his new airplane in France, and as a pilot he became the first to fly across the English Channel and back without setting down. Rolls died tragically on July 12, 1910 when a Wright biplane he was piloting at a flying tournament in Bournemouth crashed from a height of only twenty-three feet. England's first airplane casualty was only 33 years old. As a symbol of mourning the "R & R" was changed from red to black.

In 1911, Henry Royce suffered a breakdown from overwork. For the rest of his life he would not visit the automobile works in Derby—contributing designs and making approvals from his home. If Rolls had lived the company would inevitably have been involved in airplane manufacturing sooner, but by World War I Rolls Royce became the leading supplier of planes to the Royal Air Force. Half of Britain's air force of Eagles, Falcons, Hawks, and Condors carried Rolls Royce engines.

Production was stopped on the legendary Silver Ghost in 1925, after some six thousand had been built. In 1930, three years before his death, Royce was awarded a baronetcy of his own. Sir Frederick Henry Royce's death was a rare one for a member of the peerage: the lingering affects of overwork.

chwinn

Ignaz Schwinn was born in 1860 in the little town of Hardheim in the province of Baden, Germany. His father, the owner of a thriving piano factory, died when Ignaz was eleven, curtailing the boy's formal schooling. He apprenticed to a machinist where he turned out to be a gifted mechanic.

Like most young men of the time Schwinn was fascinated with the "wonder of the age," the high wheel bicycle. Seeking work he moved from town to town working on bicycles and bicycle parts whenever he could find the opportunity. In northern Germany he studied the new "Safety" bicycles imported from England.

Technology was advancing rapidly with the new bicycles, and many people—conservative villagers—were slow to respond to the "Safety" bicycles. Schwinn was enthusiastic, however, and purchased a drawing board where he could work out his own bicycle designs at night after his regular job. He showed his designs to Heinrich Kleyer, a bicycle maker and customer of Schwinn's machine shop. Kleyer was impressed and hired Schwinn to design and manufacture bicycles. These were some of the very first "Safety" bicycles produced in Germany.

Desiring to participate in the fast-moving technological advances occurring in America, Schwinn scraped together the funds to come to Chicago and the great World's Fair in the early 1890s. He worked around town designing bicycles and planning bicycle factories. In 1895 he teamed with Adolf Arnold to form Arnold, Schwinn & Company.

Schwinn designed the product and the tools to make it, selected machinery and equipment, engaged the personnel, and set up the factory. Annual production estimates at the time were set at approximately twenty-five thousand units. Schwinn's bicycles proved exceedingly popular, and Arnold's superior business ability gave the business a solid foundation.

In 1908, after several expansions, Schwinn bought the interests of his partner and became sole owner. Schwinn consistently brought design innovations to the bicycle industry. He sponsored bicycle racing, which accelerated the development of high performance parts that provided increasing value to consumer bikes.

During World War II Schwinn, then in his eighties, devoted all his time, energy, and resources to the production of war materials, as he had in 1917. For his efforts, Schwinn & Company was awarded the Army and Navy "E" for excellence of its war production performance. Devoted, as always, to the production of his bicycles, Schwinn visited the plant every day until his death in 1948.

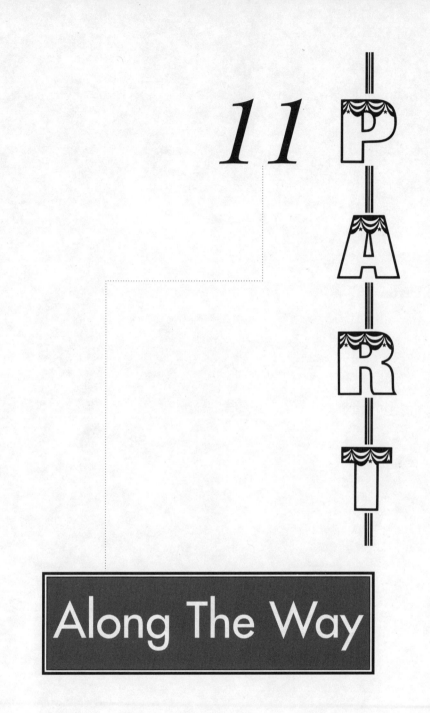

11 PART

Along The Way

Baskin-Robbins

Irvine Robbins grew up on his father's dairy farm outside Tacoma, Washington. He helped process and sell the milk, ice cream, and other products. When it came time to count up the profits each month, Irvine saw that the real profits were not coming in selling to groceries and drugstores, but from sales made from the family's little store in a Tacoma alley known as "Court C."

With the end of World War II, Robbins remembered his lessons from the farm and set up his own ice cream shop. Robbins, then twenty-seven, opened the Snowbird ice cream store in Glendale, California. Down the road in Pasadena, his brother-in-law Burton Baskin started another store in 1946. The goal was to make seventy-five dollars a week and have some fun.

The early years forged the business philosophy that would weld into Baskin-Robbins when the two became partners shortly thereafter: sell nothing but ice cream and offer a vast array of fun-to-choose flavors. Baskin-Robbins sold nothing but ice cream and sold it only in their shops. And they sold it even in the winter.

Soon there were eight stores and sales were booming, but the partners had no money. They decided to sell the stores to the managers; the company would supply the ice cream and merchandising ideas. The formula worked. Baskin and Robbins collected the payments and concentrated on the ice cream.

Baskin and Robbins inaugurated a rotating stable of thirty-one flavors, one for each day of the month. They had hundreds of exotic flavors to choose from. The names were as appealing as the flavors. When the Dodgers arrived in Los Angeles from Brooklyn in 1958 they were welcomed by baseball-nut ice cream: raspberries (for "razzing" the umpires) and cashews (for peanuts in the bleachers) mixed into vanilla (the all-time winning flavor). Lunar cheesecake ice cream commemorated the first moon landing in 1969.

All flavors were subject to a test panel. Not all flavors survived the scrutiny. Goody Goody Gumdrop—a seemingly ideal Baskin-Robbins fun combination of gum drops and ice cream—was withdrawn because of its tiny tooth-threatening frozen gumdrops. Ketchup ice cream and lox and bagels were allowed to quietly melt in the lab.

In 1967 Baskin and Robbins sold their company for twenty million dollars. Burton Baskin died suddenly only six months later, but Robbins carried on with the business. When Baskin-Robbins's 31 Flavors celebrated its thirty-first birthday in 1976, the sixteen hundred stores had a flavorful roster of over five hundred flavors to choose from.

Colonel Sanders

For half of his working life Harland Sanders made his way as a street car conductor, railroad fireman, and insurance salesman, to name just a few of the jobs he tried. In 1930, at the age of forty, Sanders started cooking chicken in a small restaurant in the rear of a service station he operated in Corbin, Kentucky.

Here he perfected his secret blend of eleven herbs and spices, seasonings he claimed stood on everybody's shelf, to flavor his chicken. The ingredients are still used in Colonel Sanders Kentucky Fried Chicken today and are still a secret, even from franchisees. In 1935, Kentucky Governor Ruby Lafoon named

Sanders an honorary Colonel for his contribution to the state's cuisine.

For a quarter-century Sanders prospered. Then in the mid-1950s a new interstate highway was planned that would bypass Corbin and his restaurant. Sanders was now sixty-six years old, an age when many business owner would retire and watch cars speed past his old restaurant.

But the Colonel auctioned off his operations and hit the road to display his patented pressure cooker and sell his fried chicken cooking process. He signed up only five restaurants in the first two years. Still he persevered. In two more years he had sold two hundred franchises. Over the next decade Colonel Sanders and Kentucky Fried Chicken would become famous the world over.

In Japan the Colonel, with his white hair, white goatee, black string tie, and double-breasted suit, is the most recognizable of all Americans. A life-size statue stands outside of every one of the Colonel's restaurants in Japan. The Colonel traveled more than 250,000 miles a year promoting his chicken.

In 1964 Sanders sold his interest in Kentucky Fried Chicken for two million dollars, but remained active promoting his chicken and starring in folksy commercials until his death in 1980 at the age of ninety. In honor of his achievements, his body lay in state in the rotunda of the State Capitol in Frankfort, Kentucky. His chicken was being sold in more than eight thousand outlets in sixty countries.

Famous Amos

According to Wallace Amos he was sitting in his friend Marvin Gaye's office talking to Gaye's secretary while they munched on some of his homemade chocolate chip cookies. At the same time, Amos was chewing on his future in the entertainment business. "Why don't we go into business together selling your chocolate chip cookies?" she suggested. And the first celebrity cookies were born.

Wallace Amos was born to illiterate parents in a black ghetto of Tallahassee in 1936. In 1948 his parents divorced, and Wallace and his mother went to Orlando, where he stayed only a short time before going to live with his aunt in New York City.

Amos worked part-time through school while dodging street gangs. When a school recruiter told him that "cooks make a lot of money" Amos enrolled in Food Trades Vocational High School. He was assigned to the pantry at the Essex House, but became discouraged at only making desserts and dropped out of school.

For the first time, Amos drifted. He gambled away his aunt's utility payments and lived on the streets. When he finally returned home, the seventeen-year-old Amos convinced his aunt to sign papers allowing him to join the Air Corps, where he learned to repair radar and radio equipment.

After his tour of duty, Amos came back to New York and worked as a stock clerk at Saks while attending the Collegiate Secretarial Institute. Working hard, he was promoted to an executive position at Saks and was sent to New York University to take retailing courses. Amos found math so troublesome he quit rather than try to be a buyer. He was twenty-five years old.

Amos next landed a job at the William Morris Talent Agency working in the mailroom and filling in as a substitute secretary. Again he worked hard and was promoted to become the first black agent at William Morris. Amos found success booking musical acts including the Supremes, the Temptations, and Simon and Garfunkel.

By 1967 Amos felt burned out and out of touch with the coming of acid rock in the music business. But more importantly, he felt he had gone as far as he could go as a black man at William Morris. He left to manage trumpeter Hugh Masakela, but the relationship ended quickly. Amos had bounced from one entertainment job to another when he went to see his friend Gaye.

Amos thought it was a terrific idea to sell cookies, but he didn't have any money. He turned to his friends in the entertainment industry. Helen Reddy pledged ten thousand dollars if he found other investors. Herb Alpert chipped in five thousand dollars and Marvin Gaye clinched the venture with another ten thousand dollars. The pivotal secretary suggested the name "Famous Amos" and he called his product the "superstar of cookies."

Amos set up shop at the corner of Sunset Boulevard and Formosa Avenue, a most unsavory location. Next door was the Exotica School of Massage, emblazoned with the sign screaming "Sindy's Nude, Nude, Nude Girls, Girls, Girls." Across the street was the American School of Hypnosis.

Wallace Amos was a natural showman. He donned a white Panama hat and set out to make his store opening a true Hollywood happening. He sent out twenty-five hundred invitations. Over fifteen hundred showed up, including many celebrities who sipped champagne and enjoyed a strolling Dixieland band.

He promoted cookies like rock stars. When celebrities enjoyed his cookies, he made certain the Los Angeles papers wrote about it. A friend took some cookies to Bloomingdale's in New York and they agreed to carry the "jet-set cookies." So did Nieman-Marcus. Amos set up a factory in New Jersey to help meet demand.

In 1977 he left Bloomingdale's for the basement at Macy's, with the proviso he could appear in the Macy's Thanksgiving Parade. For four years, Amos marched in front of twenty million viewers, becoming a media star himself. By 1979 his factories were baking over three tons of homemade cookies every day. His first store was featured on the Grayline Sightseeing Bus Tour of Hollywood.

As the company grew, Amos became less involved in the mundane everyday operations. He moved to Hawaii, further removing himself from the demands of the business. He neglected to franchise the stores, and owned only eight. Other competitors bit into the gourmet cookie market, and by 1985 Amos had to sell all but eight percent of the company to private investors.

Amos was not troubled by his shift in fortunes. "I started the cookie business just to make a living and that's still all I'm concerned with," he said. Although not running the business, he was still a popular spokesman for Famous Amos and an important campaigner for the Literacy Volunteers of America. When the Smithsonian Institute displayed a Business Americana Collection they asked for Amos's trademark embroidered shirt and Panama hat. His was the first food company in the exhibition, and he was the first black businessman to be represented.

Hilton

The first Hilton hotel was set up by Conrad Hilton in his family's adobe home in San Antonio, New Mexico in 1907. Business reversals in his father's general store necessitated the conversion of six of the rooms in the house into quarters for transient lodgers. Hilton, then nineteen, worked all day in the store and went to the train station at 1:00 A.M.. and 3:00 A.M. to meet the train and solicit guests. Room and board was $2.50 a day.

Slowly the Hilton family's financial health was restored. By 1912, Hilton became interested in politics, winning a position in the state legislature just when the New Mexico Territory was accepted into statehood. He introduced nine bills which became New Mexico law, but on balance found politics confining and frustrating. He came back home after two years.

Hilton decided San Antonio needed a bank. He organized a syndicate to establish the town's first bank, but the shareholders rewarded him by electing an aged former banker from Illinois as president and made Conrad Hilton a cashier. He began maneuvering for control of the bank. It wasn't much of a bank, but he had started it.

Hilton wrested control of the bank from the board of directors but there wasn't much time to savor the victory. He wore out hot, dusty Texas roads tracking down new depositors, and then World War I shattered his plans for a garland of New Mexico banks.

Hilton was off to France to serve in the Army.

In 1919, following the death of his father in an automobile accident, Hilton returned from the army. He left for Cisco, Texas, looking to buy an interest in a bank. When the slow pace of negotiations forced him to stay overnight, he found all the hotels in town overbooked. Instead of a bank, Hilton wound up making a deal for a hotel, the forty-room Mobley Hotel.

It didn't take Hilton long to become a hotel man. He surveyed every inch of the Mobley to eliminate non-revenue-generating space. He sawed the front desk in half and added a shop; he ripped out the dining room and spaced it off into bedrooms; he rented his own bed and slept on a leather chair in his office.

A few months later he purchased the Melba in Fort Worth, and in 1920 he added the 140-room Waldorf in Dallas. In 1925, Hilton committed himself to building a million-dollar hotel in Dallas, the first hotel to carry his name. When the Depression hit, Hilton controlled eight hotels. It was too much.

In 1931 Hilton defaulted on a $300,000 loan. His creditors hired him to manage his lost hotels, but it was a turbulent business marriage. Nine months later the business arrangement disintegrated into legal matters. Hilton eventually emerged from the Depression with five of his eight hotels; by 1937 he was free of debt.

Hilton began to take advantage of depressed hotel properties. In the next few years he took control of the Sir Francis Drake in San Francisco, the Town House in Los Angeles, the Roosevelt and Plaza in New York, and the Stevens and Palmer House in Chicago. In 1946 the Hilton Hotels Corporation was formed, the first hotel company to have its stock listed on the New York Stock Exchange.

Hilton cherished tradition. With each of these great houses he recognized an obligation to retain the atmosphere and individuality which gave it its prestige. In 1949 he realized a lifelong dream with the purchase of the Waldorf-Astoria in New York, America's greatest hotel. In 1954 Hilton executed the largest hotel merger in history, purchasing the Statler hotel chain for $111,000,000. Hilton clinched the deal by pleading with the widow Statler to keep the great hotels in "the hands of hotel people."

Hilton turned the presidency of Hilton Hotels over to his son, Barron, in 1966. The next year Barron Hilton persuaded his father to swap his Hilton International stock for TWA stock. The stock plummeted by half in the next eighteen months, and the eighty-year old Hilton lost the rights to his name overseas.

Conrad Hilton became the world's premier hotelier by acquiring America's most prestigious hotels. Only a handful ever carried his name. He assiduously avoided resort hotels and eschewed gambling houses. But under his son the Hilton name was franchised, and the Las Vegas Hilton and Flamingo Hilton were purchased. When Conrad Hilton died in 1979 at the age of ninety-one, the hotel-casinos were responsible for nearly forty percent of Hilton profits. The business he had built proudly on the grandest hotel rooms in the world was being supported by roulette wheels and blackjack tables.

Howard Johnson's

"I've spent my life developing scores of flavors," Howard Johnson once lamented, "and yet most people still say, 'I'll take vanilla.'"

Howard Dearing Johnson was born in 1897, the son of a tobacco merchant. He entered the retail business shortly after returning from France and World War I. His father died, and he inherited the cigar-store business, then heavily in debt. Johnson continued to sell cigars until 1924, when he liquidated the business and bought a run-down drugstore near the railroad station in his hometown of Wollaston, Massachusetts. He went from owing ten thousand dollars to owing nearly thirty thousand dollars.

The small patent medicine store featured a soda fountain, a candy and tobacco counter, and a newspaper stand. Johnson resurrected the business with the newspapers, organizing a staff of seventy-five boys delivering the news. Within a few years his newspapers had made his business prosperous. But it was ice cream that was his first love. He had only three flavors—vanilla, chocolate, and strawberry—and he thought a wider variety of flavors and a better quality ice cream were the keys to success.

Johnson bought an ice cream recipe from an elderly German pushcart vendor whose wares appealed to him. He paid three hundred dollars for the peddler's secrets: doubling the butterfat content of his ice cream and to use only natural flavorings. To expand his product line, Johnson used an old-fashioned freezer in the basement, hand-cranking the ice cream.

He was right. The customers began lining up for his twenty-eight flavors of ice cream. By 1928, Johnson was pulling in nearly a quarter million dollars a year from ice cream sold in his shop and at several nearby beach stands. He added frankfurters and other easily prepared foods and gravitated towards restaurants in 1929. Within seven years, Johnson had peppered twenty-five restaurants along Massachusetts highways.

He then persuaded a yacht captain on Cape Cod to build a restaurant, call it Howard Johnson's, paint it blue with a bright orange roof, and sell products Johnson would supply. Johnson also trained the new owner. The venture made money from the start. Howard Johnson had pioneered the art of restaurant franchising.

Johnson next developed the concept of convenience food. He maintained control over the food served in his franchises by preparing the food and processing it in centrally located company-operated plants where it was shipped to restaurants for final preparation and cooking. Johnson insisted that the food be plain, simple, wholesome American fare.

To make sure that the ice cream and food sold in the restaurants that bore his name remained at high quality, Johnson spent two days a week on inspection tours. He arrived unannounced and unrecognized, on the lookout for everything from dirty restrooms to sassy waitresses.

The ubiquitous orange-roofed restaurants begat motor lodges designed for the vacationing post-World War II family. The first Howard Johnson's motel franchise opened in Savannah, Georgia in 1954, five years before Johnson turned the company over to his son. Even in retirement, Johnson continued to scout for new restaurant and motel sites.

The entire time Johnson was building a $200,000,000-a-year

business he never lost his taste for the ice cream that made him famous. It was his favorite dish. He kept at least ten flavors in the freezers of his Manhattan penthouse. Every day of his life Howard Johnson enjoyed at least one ice cream cone.

Marriott

The Marriott name is known for its hotels and resorts, but it began as—and still primarily is—a food business. John Willard Marriott, known as Bill, was born in 1900. He grew up on the Utah range raising beets, herding sheep, and serving the Mormon church. He gained a measure of renown around Ogden when, at the age of fourteen, he shot two brown bears in one day.

Marriott worked his way through the University of Utah selling woolen sweaters and long underwear in logging camps in the Northwest. When he graduated in 1927 he was ready for his own business. He became intrigued with a root beer he enjoyed during hot summer Utah days. Marriott would drive up to the curb and a waitress would bring out ice-cold mugs of five-cent root beer to the car.

He learned that a man named Allen and a man named Wright had started A & W Root Beer a few years earlier in Sacramento, selling only ice-cold root beer at their drive-ins. In the summer, a good stand averaged five thousand mugs a day. So Bill Marriott decided to stake his future to root beer.

He had become enamored with Washington, DC during a Mormon mission back east, and that was where Marriott headed for his franchise. He leased eight feet of frontage from a baker and opened a nine-seat root beer stand on May 20, 1927—the same day

Lindbergh took off for Europe. Marriott placed a small radio on the countertop and prospective root beer buyers gathered round to hear the progress of America's greatest aviator.

Inevitably, Washington's torrid summers give way to chilly winters. Obviously demand for ice-cold root beer, would fall off. A & W franchises were required to sell only root beer but Marriott flew to Sacramento to obtain a special dispensation to include food on his menu. He didn't want standard burgers and franks but opted for Mexican food, a specialty from home not often enjoyed in the nation's capital.

When the heavily spiced chili and tamales and barbecued beef debuted, Marriott called his new restaurant "Hot Shoppe"—hot food with a touch of English affectation. The new restaurant was a hit, and Marriott barely waited for the cash register to fill before opening a second Hot Shoppe. Soon there was a chain of medium-priced family restaurants in the Washington, DC area. Marriott waited for the Depression to slow his business but it never did.

Marriott worked nonstop, but he was never more diligent than in selecting new sites for his restaurants. He opened a Hot Shoppe out by the Hoover Airport and noticed a trade had developed in passengers and crew taking out food for their flights. In 1937, Marriott started boxing lunches of ham or chicken sandwiches, a small carton of slaw, a frosted cupcake, and an apple for Eastern airlines. "Sky girls" served the first airline food along with hot coffee in thermos jugs.

Marriott's catering business soon picked up government cafeterias, and entered the hospital food service market as well. Bill Marriott had been in the food service business for thirty years when he opened his first hotel in Arlington, Virginia in 1957. Over the next few years, Marriott continued to open hotels as well as Hot Shoppes restaurants.

By 1964, Marriott was ready to slow down. Physically he had survived Hodgkins Disease, battled chronic nervous exhaustion, and weathered several heart attacks. While maintaining nominal control of the business he turned daily operations over to his son Bill Jr.

It was hard to let go, but Marriott could reflect back on the time his father had entrusted him with a herd of sheep to take to San Francisco on his own at the tender age of fourteen. His son was no less successful. By the time he succeeded his father as chief executive officer in 1972, Bill Jr. had quadrupled the size of the company. Marriott Corporation now owned the Big-Boy restaurant chain and started the Roy Rogers fast food chain.

The elder Marriott invested his time in the Republican party, entertaining political luminaries on his ranch in northern Virginia. He died at age eighty-four at his New Hampshire summer home. The business he started by selling root beer for a nickel was grossing four billion dollars a year.

McDonald's

By 1954 Ray Kroc was fifty-two years old. He had finally erased years of debt and struggle by selling Multimixers for milk shakes. He had even achieved a modest prosperity, buying a home in Arlington Heights, Illinois, one of Chicago's poshest suburbs.

One day Kroc received an order for eight Multimixers from a hamburger stand in San Bernadino, California. What was this? Each Multimixer had a capacity for six milkshakes. Kroc wanted to see for himself an operation that needed to make forty-eight milk-shakes at one time.

The McDonald's hamburger stand was run by Maurice "Mac" McDonald and his brother Richard. They had come to California from New Hampshire in 1928 to work in movies, a calling particu-larly ill-suited to their dour personalities. The McDonalds wound up managing a movie theater in Glendora instead.

They sold the theater in 1940 to open a hamburger stand in Pasadena. For eight years the McDonalds worked out their ideas for a self-service food operation, mostly to eliminate the groups of teenagers that hung around the restaurant. On December 12, 1948 they were ready to test their ideas at a new location in San Bernadino.

San Bernadino, fifty-five miles east of Los Angeles, was the terminus for famed Route 66. The town was in the center of postwar prosperity and the exploding automobile mentality. C-rations from World War II had also inoculated less discerning American diners with a homogenized diet.

The McDonald brothers devised an ideal food service operation for the new times. They sliced the menu to only four items: a hamburger with condiments already added that they sold for fifteen cents, crisp french fries warmed with innovative infrared heat lamps, soft drinks, and a twelve-ounce milkshake.

Everything the McDonalds did emphasized value, efficiency, and speed. There were no plates, no dishes, no condiments. The brothers were frugal and obsessed with cleanliness. Every part of their restaurant sparkled. When Ray Kroc arrived with his Multimixers he was astounded: "They had people standing in line clamoring for hamburgers. I figured that if every McDonald hamburger place had eight Multimixers, I would get rich."

Kroc was not the first to be impressed by the McDonalds' operation. The brothers had cautiously sold six franchises in California, but had no interest in growing larger. "More stores, more problems," they told Kroc. They pointed to a nearby hill where Mac, a bachelor, and Dick lived. Their houses and three Cadillacs—including one for Dick's wife—were all the McDonalds needed.

The brothers were conservative and suspicious of quick money. Only months before Kroc arrived in 1954, they had turned down another big chain offer. Neither was interested in Kroc's talk of nationwide franchises. Kroc persisted. Finally he left San Bernadino with a ninety-nine-year contract to represent McDonalds exclusively.

The arrangement would not last nearly that long. The taciturn brothers increasingly imposed restrictions on the franchises that Kroc found totally unacceptable. In 1960 he offered $500,000 for everything—trademarks, the Golden Arches, the name. Dick and Mac countered with $2,700,000—a figure they had arrived at that would yield each of them a million dollars after taxes.

Kroc was flabbergasted. The only financing he could obtain

would eventually cost him $14,000,000 to buy out the McDonalds
—which, of course, was still a bargain. The brothers had one more
surprise as the final papers were signed—they intended to keep
their cherished San Bernadino store.

Kroc did not want to lose the money-churning flagship store,
but he wasn't about to blow the deal over it. Instead he built a
gleaming new restaurant directly across the street. It was an exact
replica of the brothers' restaurant, which they had to rename "Big
M." Soon Mac and Dick McDonald were out of business.

The brothers traveled and returned to Bedford, New
Hampshire where they lived out their lives in obscurity as their
name became the most famous cultural icon in America.

Nathan's

In 1916 a small rebellion was stirring at Coney Island, New York's
fashionable seaside playground. It seems a couple of singing wait-
ers by the name of Durante and Cantor did not like the idea of
paying the inflated price of ten cents for their frankfurters. They
urged the young roll-slicer behind the counter to open his own
stand and sell hot dogs for a nickel.

Nathan Handwerker was a Polish immigrant who had arrived
penniless in New York only four years earlier when Jimmy Durante
and Eddie Cantor implored him to start his own hot dog business.
He was working part-time as a delivery boy for the Max's Busy Bee
eatery, making $4.50 a week. On Sunday afternoons he moon-
lighted at Coney Island dishing out Charles Feltman's famed ten-
cent franks. He decided to take the advice of his show-business
friends.

Handwerker took his life savings of three hundred dollars and with his new bride, Ida, opened a small open-front stand on the corner of Surf and Stillwell Avenues. He laced his hot dogs with Ida's secret spice recipe. The nickel franks caught on immediately with the thousands of resort visitors.

Handwerker displayed a natural flair for merchandising. In 1917, competitors spread rumors that Nathan couldn't be selling quality all-beef hot dogs for only a nickel. He fought the accusations by hiring a group of college students to stand around his counter wearing white professional jackets with stethoscopes dangling from their pockets. Word spread that doctors from Coney Island Hospital were taking their meals at Nathan's hot dog stand. The crisis passed.

Customers could always find pretty girls behind Nathan's counters. Clara Bowtinelli, a gregarious redheaded teenager, served up franks for a short time until one of her customers whisked her away to Hollywood. She would resurface as Clara Bow, one of the most glamorous of all the silent film stars.

In 1921, Handwerker finally christened his nameless stand "Nathan's Hot Dogs" after hearing Sophie Tucker perform the hit song *"Nathan, Nathan, Why You Waitin'?"* Handwerker built Nathan's into the largest hot dog stand in the world, acquiring surrounding property as it grew and expanded.

In 1923 the New York subway reached out to Coney Island, and thousands of people streamed off trains from the massive Stillwell terminal and headed for Nathan's across the street. Nathan's became a New York institution. President Rockefeller entertained at Hyde Park with Nathan's "red hots." Nelson Rockefeller told Handwerker during a campaign stop that, "No one can hope to be elected to public office in New York without having his picture taken eating a hot dog at Nathan's."

Nathan's had three restaurants when the company went public in 1968. The chain of fast food restaurants was quickly expanding when Handwerker semi-retired in 1972. He died two years later at the age of eighty-three as history's most famous purveyor of hot dogs.

tuckey's

Like so many others, William Stuckey was desperately searching for a way to make a living during the Depression. In 1931, the twenty-one-year old Stuckey borrowed thirty-five dollars from his grandmother—her life savings—to peddle pecans.

Stuckey walked from house to house in his native Georgia buying nuts. If he used up his thirty-five dollars too early in the day, he waited until the banks closed and wrote checks he knew he couldn't cover. On those days he stayed out selling pecans until he could be at the bank the following morning to cover checks.

Diligently he built his pecan business this way. In 1936 he sold $150,000 worth of pecans. He opened his first candy store in Eastman, a small town in central Georgia, in 1938. Wife Ethel was the candy cook.

When World War II ended, Stuckey was one of the first to recognize that Americans would become increasingly mobile. He began building distinctive pecan shops—with blue roofs and red and yellow signs—along the country's new highways. In addition to enjoying a pecan roll, weary motorists could fill up at Stuckey's pumps as well.

In eight years Stuckey had twenty-nine pecan shops, building his business on extensive billboard advertising. He awarded franchises to friends and employees. "A lot of people in town own interests in the stores," he boasted at one point. "They all profited by it. There are more Cadillacs in Eastman, Georgia than in any town this size in the South, I reckon."

Stuckey sold his business, now with 160 stores, to Pet, Inc. in 1964. He stayed with Pet as a vice-president and continued operating the highway stops until 1970, when he retired. Stuckey's chain had grown to nearly three hundred stores by then. Stuckey, a former Georgia state legislator, continued enjoying pecans until his death in 1977.

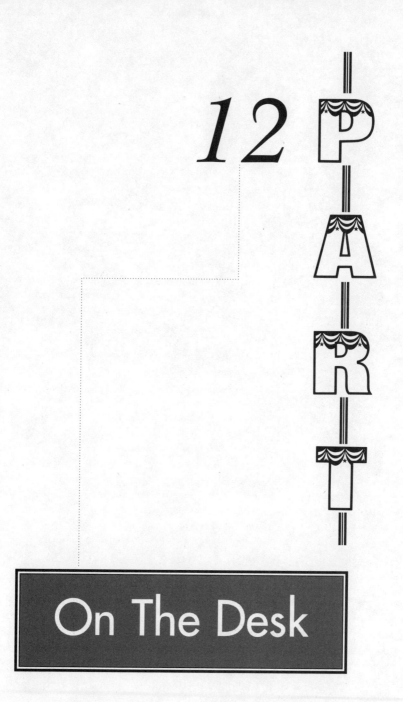

12 PART

On The Desk

ich

In 1945, Milton Reynolds introduced the first ballpoint pen in America. It sold for a pricey $12.50 but created a sensation when it hit the market. In 1949, Marcel Bich introduced another ballpoint pen. It was non-refillable, encased in a simple plastic stick, and sold for as little as nineteen cents. It created a revolution when it hit the market.

Marcel Bich was born in Turin, Italy to French parents in 1914. By age eighteen he was working the Paris streets peddling flashlights door to door. After a stint with the French Air Force, Bich landed a job with a French ink manufacturer. His career was interrupted by World War II. In postwar France he raised one thousand dollars to buy a leaky shed in the Paris suburb of Clichy, where he set out to make parts for fountain pens. In his spare time he worked on a disposable pen which could be used reliably and thrown away when the ink ran out.

The world had plenty of inexpensive ballpoints when the Bic, with the "h" dropped for simplicity, was introduced. They were also disposable—mostly because they leaked, smeared or clogged. The Bic disposable, however, worked with the fluidity of high-priced, prestigious ballpoint pens. By 1955 Bich was selling two million pens each week in France, and millions more across Europe.

Marcel Bich then looked across the Atlantic, where Americans were embracing the new "throwaway culture" like nowhere else. In 1958, Bich purchased the Waterman Pen Company, a Connecticut-based firm that had pioneered the fountain pen seventy-five years earlier but never saw the ballpoint pen coming. Bich gobbled up sixty percent of Waterman's stock and unleashed his Bic pen on America.

Americans had no trouble resisting the charms of the twenty-nine-cent point ballpoint. The market had been flooded by shoddy pens by this time. To convince the skeptical consumer that his pens were different, Bic launched an aggressive advertising campaign behind the theme, "writes first time, every time." Americans watched live television commercials featuring clear plastic Bic Crystal pens drilled through walls, fired from guns, and strapped to the feet of ice skaters—and come up writing.

Bich moved his pens from traditional stationery stores and sold them in grocery stores and at checkout counters. Within ten years it was hard to find an American student going to school without a Bic. Bich was selling five hundred million pens a year in the United States by 1967—more than two for every American.

Bich next took his reputation for inexpensive yet reliable products to disposable cigarette lighters. Gillette got to the market two years ahead of Bich—with its Cricket in 1970—when the assault began. Americans were enticed to "Flick My Bic" and they did—by 1984 Gillette pulled the Cricket from the market. Bich chased Gillette again in disposable razors in 1977, but this time the Good News disposable razor held onto its market share.

It was not the only American invasion where Marcel Bich came up short. Like another European magnate before him, Thomas Lipton, Bich set his sights on yachting's America's Cup. In 1970 he built and raced the "France" for three million dollars but lost in Newport, Rhode Island when the yacht got lost in the fog. It was a rare time when Marcel Bich's vision was obscured.

 inney & Smith

In 1864 Joseph Binney, an Englishman, launched a modest chemical company in Peekskill, New York to grind, package, and distribute hardwood charcoal called lampblack. The carbon extract was used for shoe polish, stove blacking, and ink, as well as the red oxide that has traditionally colored America's barns.

In 1885, Binney retired and his son and nephew formed a new partnership named Binney & Smith to continue the company. The cousins expanded the product line, and in 1900 the company bought a water-powered stone mill along Bushkill Creek near Easton, Pennsylvania, close to a slate quarry where pencils could be manufactured.

The pencils were successful. One salesman reported from the schools he sold pencils to that the chalk of the day was hard, scratchy, dusty and left really permanent marks on blackboards. Binney & Smith developed a dustless chalk that won a gold medal for excellence at the 1902 St. Louis Exposition.

But it was their next gold medal that was to bring Binney & Smith lasting fame. In 1903 the firm made their first box of Crayola crayons. The box cost a nickel and held eight colors: red, orange, yellow, green, blue, violet, brown, and black. Alice Binney, Edwin's wife, coined the word Crayola by joining "craie," from the French word meaning chalk, with "ola," from oleaginous, meaning oily. After taking the Gold Medal in 1904, the crayons were marketed as the "Gold Medal Line" and packaged in familiar yellow and green boxes.

Crayons had existed as far back as seventeenth century England. Thomas Jefferson wrote about them. But Crayola's colored wax sticks caught the public's fancy, virtually snuffing out the competition. Today Binney & Smith makes two billion Crayola crayons a year, and you'll have to go elsewhere for your lampblack.

Eberhard Faber

"If only I could sell one pencil to every American I could be rich." Well, that may not be exactly what Eberhard Faber was thinking when he arrived in New York City in the 1850s, but he did come to America to establish an import business, including pencils.

His great grandfather Casper Faber had perfected the process of binding powdered graphite and encasing it in wood in 1765. Faber used the fine Bavarian clay in the ground around his home in the village of Stein, near the ancient German city of Nuremberg. They were the world's first commercially marketed pencils.

In 1861, Eberhard Faber opened the first United States pencil factory on the site of the present United Nations building. Fire destroyed the plant in 1872, and Faber relocated his plant to Brooklyn—where it stayed for eighty-five years.

Until the Civil War, the goose quill pen was the writing instrument of choice in America. But soldiers on the march needed something convenient to write letters home, and demand for Faber's pencils literally exploded. By the time Faber died in 1879, the Eberhard Faber pencil was so well known that his twenty-year old son John legally changed his name to "Eberhard" when he took control of the family business.

Eberhard Faber II ran the company for the next sixty-six years. In 1893 he introduced the Mongol, named after Siberian graphite which was considered the world's finest. Each pencil received eight coats of paint—yellow paint. Yellow pencils became the rage and outsold everything else.

Loyalty to yellow pencils was so strong that as an experiment a thousand pencils were once made exactly the same—only five hundred were painted green and five hundred painted yellow. The green pencils were returned with complaints that they broke and were not as durable as the yellow ones. Today, seventy-five percent of Eberhard Faber's two billion pencils, still manufactured by Casper Faber's direct descendants, are yellow.

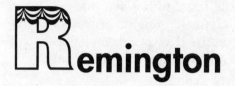emington

Like most young farm boys in 1816, Eliphalet Remington wanted a rifle. His father did not have enough money to buy his son a rifle, but Eliphalet did not sulk. Instead he set about gathering scraps of steel from his father's forge and welded a gun barrel. He then walked fourteen miles to Utica, New York to have it rifled. The result was such a phenomenal gun that his neighbors began commissioning him to make rifles.

Slowly Remington's Mohawk Valley forge grew into a great gun factory. Eliphalet Remington died in 1861 just as his company, E. Remington & Sons, was about to have a major impact on American history as a major supplier of arms to the Union Army.

The sons began diversifying the manufacturing concern after the Civil War, adding agricultural implements and sewing machines. About this time Christopher Latham Sholes began working on a writing machine in his home in Milwaukee, Wisconsin. In 1873, after six years of tinkering, what he called a "typewriter" was ready for a demonstration. The Remingtons were a well-known manufacturer he would try to impress.

Sholes was a shy man more comfortable around machines then men. A Pennsylvania oilman named James Densmore had been an enthusiastic proponent of the typewriter project, and Sholes invited him to Ilion, New York to make the demonstration for him. Philo Remington was not completely sold by the clunky machine, but was intrigued enough with its potential to purchase complete ownership on March 1, 1873. Sholes was destined to receive little or no money from the sale, but he seems to have been content just to have his invention reach the market.

It did in September of the same year. Remington was having success selling sewing machines at the time, so he mounted the typewriter on a sewing machine stand and decorated it with flowery designs. The first commercial typewriter was ready.

There was much to overcome.

No one knew how to use it. Why would anyone pay $125 for a

typewriter when they could write faster with a pen that cost but a penny? The popular story around the Remington offices was about a Kentucky mountaineer who returned a typewritten letter he had received with a marginal notation, "You don't need to print no letters for me. I kin read writin'."

Mark Twain called the typewriter a "curiosity-breeding little joker", but became one of the first to type his manuscripts in 1874. Still, when the Remington Model 1 typewriter was featured at the 1876 Philadelphia Centennial, practically the only revenue it generated was from selling samples of typewriting for twenty-five cents a piece.

In 1878 Remington introduced a shift key to enable the typewriter to print both upper and lower case letters and gradually it became more important in business. In 1903 Remington broke with the Union Typewriting Company and became the Remington Typewriter Company.

Smith-Corona

As hard as it is to believe now, there was a passionate debate over the merits of a new typewriter innovation in 1895—the typist could now see his work. At the Union Typewriter Company, management officials hotly contested the merits of the new typing methods.

The four Smith brothers were convinced that the future growth of writing machines depended on seeing the lines. Their partners with whom they had merged in 1893, Remington, Caligraph & Densmore, wanted to make typewriters the way they had since introducing the first commercial typewriter in 1873.

The Smiths left and formed the L. C. Smith Brothers

Typewriting Company in 1903. Back in 1887, Lyman Cornelius Smith led his brothers Wilbert, Monroe, and Hurlbut into the typewriting business to finance the development of a typewriter able to use both upper and lower case letters without shifting. The Smith-Premier typewriter from Syracuse, New York spread the Smith name to offices around the world.

Now the Smiths introduced Model 1, Serial 1 with 76 characters. That first machine was sold to the *New York Herald* where it operated in the newsroom twenty-four hours a day for eight years before it was traded for a newer model. It resurfaced in 1934 still going strong. With that track record for their very first machine, the brothers had no difficulty establishing a reputation for quality.

In 1925 L. C. Smith merged with the Corona Typewriting Company, and a year later Hurlbut Smith, the youngest of the brothers, retired at the age of sixty. He was always active in the community, supporting libraries, roads, and education. A religious man, Smith was legally adopted as a member of the Seneca Indian tribe in 1908.

But the company was hit hard by the Depression. Sales fell so sharply that Hurlbut Smith was recalled from retirement and elected president at the age of sixty-eight. Friends advised against returning to the floundering company, risking his health and reputation. But it was his family business.

Smith reversed the ebb of sales and restored Smith-Corona's vitality. He instilled pride and a sense of repsonsibility with the workers. He worked alongside the employees, ate in the cafeteria, and bowled in company leagues. And, most importantly, he did not reduce the work force of more than five thousand in hard times.

As the company recovered, Smith-Corona developed "quiet machines" in 1935. In World War II the factories hummed in support of the war effort, first turning out Springfield rifles and then cranking out typewriters. Smith ran the company well into the 1950s postwar prosperity. He had returned to his company at an age when most executives were winding down their careers and guided it to even greater heights.

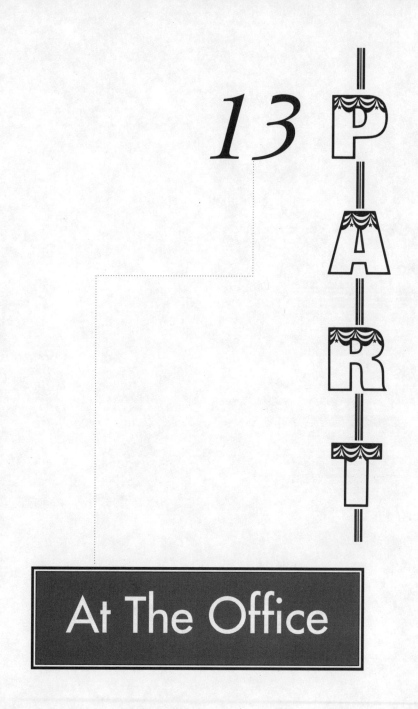

13 PART

At The Office

Dow Jones

Charles H. Dow and Edward D. Jones were reporters digging up stories in Providence, Rhode Island for the *Evening Press*, while looking for a way to advance their careers to New York City. Dow left first, landing as a job reporting on mining stocks in 1880. Dow worked in the Stock Exchange, scribbling shorthand notes on the cuffs of his shirt.

Financial news in those days went largely unreported, save for sporadic reports from the office of the John J. Kiernan News Agency. The financial bulletins, known as "flimsies" because of the thin paper on which they were printed, were delivered by messenger boys. Dow soon went to work for Kiernan and summoned his friend Jones to join him in the business.

By the fall of 1882 as their contacts increased, the two men developed their own ideas of how financial news should be reported and left to form Dow Jones & Co. in a basement at 15 Wall Street, next door to the Exchange. Dow and another former Kiernan man, Charles M. Bergstresser, were reporters who brought the day's news back to Jones at the desk. Jones wrote the stories on agateware stencils, and the copies were dispatched to clients by messenger. They called their paper the "Customers Afternoon Letter."

By 1887, handwriting bulletins was too slow to keep up with the increasing demand for timely financial news. A hand-cranked revolving cylinder began churning out the letter on five-by-nine inch pieces of paper. On July 8, 1889 the letter became *The Wall*

Street Journal, a four-page afternoon daily replacing the letter, although printed bulletins remained part of the business until 1948.

An out-of-town correspondent, Clarence W. Barron, joined the paper to contribute news from the Boston financial district. A ponderous "ticker" was developed in 1897 to provide instantaneous news. Dow Jones leased the machines—which had to be hand-wound every half-hour but still ushered in the information age.

A morning edition of the paper was added in 1898, and Jones retired the following year at the age of forty-three. In 1902 Dow sold the remainder of the business to C. W. Barron. Dow and Jones passed from the public eye, but not before they stamped their names permanently on the financial community.

Dun & Bradstreet

The Duns emigrated from Scotland and settled in Ohio in the early decades of the 1800s. All prospered greatly save for Robert Dun. He died in 1835, and his nine-year old son Robert Graham grew up as a poor relation in one of the wealthiest families in Ohio.

At sixteen, Dun began his business career as a store clerk. In 1851 he eagerly jumped at the opportunity to join the Mercantile Agency, founded in 1841 as America's first credit reporting firm. Credit and its management were the engines driving young America's commercial expansion. The agency provided information to manufacturers and retailers on far-flung country stores. The Mercantile Agency promoted and protected trade in the Untied States.

The industrious Dun was promoted to partner in 1854, and in 1859 he acquired the entire interest in the Agency, now a nation-wide credit-reporting agency with sixteen offices in the United States, two in Canada, and one in London. Three months earlier the Mercantile Agency's first *Reference Book*—complete with lock—had been published.

The book featured credit information on 20,268 firms, arranged alphabetically by town and state. The key, copied from a London firm, provided four ratings for each name and a summary. The name of the company issued to was embossed on a dark brown sheepskin cover. The *Reference Book* sold for two hundred dollars.

The *Reference Book* was published in part as a response to competition from John Bradstreet, to whose name Dun's would be linked long after his death. Bradstreet came to New York from Cincinnati to expand his business. He issued weekly reports, and in August 1857 produced his first bound volume of credit reports: *Bradstreet's Book of Commercial Reports*. The book featured a system of ratings composed of somewhat vague numbers, perhaps influenced by the threat of libel suits. It was the first serious competition to the Mercantile Agency.

Bradstreet died in 1863 in the midst of the Civil War, which crippled much of the credit reporting business. The Mercantile Agency not only lost its Southern clients during the war, but also the need to report on Southern markets. Dun himself believed the North would go bankrupt and the South would prevail, emerging as the "garden spot of the Continent."

Dun's success and Bradstreet's early profitability spawned so many rival companies after the war ended that even Dun's nearly ten thousand reporters couldn't keep track of them all. Dun worked diligently to keep his agency out of the inevitable scandals and accusations.

Prior to 1866, much of the credit-reporting in America tended to be highly subjective opinions based on a man's character. Dun's extensive reporting network used capital worth and statistical ratings. He took advantage of every new advance in technology to increase efficiency. In 1867 the Mercantile Agency became the first business to use typewriters, doing away with tedious copying of records by hand.

Dun's genius lay in his ability to secure and retain the services of men of the highest quality. Although he was sole owner of the business, the profits were shared with his associates. Under Dun's leadership the Mercantile Agency emerged from the bewildering array of credit reporting firms as the unqualified leader in the industry.

When Robert Graham Dun, art collector, wine connoisseur, avid bass fisherman and bird-hunter, died in 1900 at the age of seventy-four from cirrhosis, the Mercantile Agency consisted of 140 offices compiling information on business firms of all descriptions across the globe. Upon his death one editorial wrote, "R. G. Dun is known all over the world, and he has established an institution that will probably live as long as commerce lives."

E. F. Hutton

For someone who would be included among America's greatest capitalists, Edward Francis Hutton's business career got off to an inauspicious beginning. At seventeen he secured a position in the mailroom of a prestigious New York mortgage company. Hutton's climb from the ground floor didn't get far. He took an unauthorized vacation and was summarily fired.

Hutton next surfaced as a check writer in the Manhattan Trust Company. The president criticized his sloppy penmanship one day and suggested a stint in night school. Hutton quit in a huff. But he did enroll in Packer's Business School. Hutton became convinced that capitalism was the key to success. With a friend Hutton purchased a seat on the Consolidated Stock Exchange, forming the brokerage of Harris, Hutton & Company.

Strikingly handsome, Hutton hobnobbed in New York's high

society, where he fell in love with the daughter of one of the leading members of the New York Stock Exchange. When he asked for her hand in marriage Hutton was dismissed as a worthy suitor because the Consolidated Stock Exchange was viewed by the Big Board as a street bazaar for hucksters and third-rate brokers. Hutton didn't hesitate—he dissolved the partnership and married the girl in 1902.

On their honeymoon to the West Coast, Hutton realized that San Francisco and Los Angeles possessed no direct link to Wall Street. Financial information arrived slowly via a patchwork of telegraph feeds with stock quotes. Hutton became determined to establish a quality national brokerage to serve the West Coast.

He began his married life by accepting a partnership with his cousin in a Cincinnati bond house. Hutton found himself trapped in a sleepy, unaggressive house with no interest in his plans to set up a coast-to-coast financial network. He went back to New York and purchased a seat on the New York Stock Exchange with his friend George Ellis. E. F. Hutton & Company began trading on October 12, 1903.

Hutton proved to be a financial salesman extraordinaire. He beat the streets uncovering new accounts until he was ready to pursue his dream of a West Coast brokerage. His plan called for a private wire from New York to San Francisco providing investors with critical time for securities decisions. It wasn't going to be easy.

Western Union went only as far as Salt Lake City and was in no hurry to stretch from the Atlantic to the Pacific. Hutton proposed to shoulder half the price of construction and maintenance of a line from Utah to San Francisco, up to $50,000. When it was completed Hutton had the only private transcontinental wire in the country.

When the E. F. Hutton office opened in December of 1904 his San Francisco brokers could execute orders in minutes, as opposed to hours and more for other houses. The biggest players in San Francisco were soon E. F. Hutton clients. For years, many investors on the West Coast thought E. F. Hutton *was* the Stock Exchange.

Much less known in New York, the brokerage continued to be aggressive. Rather than wait for clients, Hutton established hotel branches for the convenience of wealthy travelers. Ellis proved to be the ideal partner for the mercurial Hutton; he was methodical, cautious and reserved.

Tragically, both his wife and son died before Hutton was forty-five. He married the daughter of C. W. Post, who founded the Postum Cereal Company. It was a curious pairing of opposite personalities, but his staid, proper wife convinced the impulsive Hutton to take the chairmanship of Postum Cereal. In 1923 he stepped away from his senior partnership in E. F. Hutton & Company.

With Postum, Hutton directed the merger of fifteen nationally known grocery manufacturing companies into the General Foods Corporation in 1929. Hutton served as chairman of the new conglomerate until 1935. Coincidentally, he divorced his second wife that same year.

In later years Hutton founded the Freedoms Foundation at Valley Forge, Pennsylvania, to give awards to individuals and organizations that promoted patriotic ideals. He penned a newspaper column titled "Think it Through" which appeared in more than sixty papers across America before he passed away at the age of eighty-six.

H & R Block

Henry Bloch does his own tax return. And he urges every American to do the same, "People should really fill out their own returns when they can because it'll teach them a lot about economics. There's nothing like getting into your own tax return to teach you where your money's going." Fortunately for his business, many Americans ignore his advice.

Henry and his older brother Leon borrowed five thousand dollars from a great-aunt to start the United Business Company in Kansas City in 1946 to provide advertising, accounting, and legal services for small businesses. The first year was so bad that Leon bailed out and went to law school.

Twenty-five year old Henry Bloch carried on during the lean year of 1947. He lived on fifty dollars a month from the GI Bill and fifteen dollars he received for keeping the books at a hamburger stand. Then his entrepreneurial brother Richard joined him from the University of Pennsylvania. Richard built the business and Henry managed the accounts.

As a courtesy, Henry and Richard Bloch did tax returns for their clients. In 1954 they made eighteen hundred dollars for three hundred returns. It was not worth the effort, and they planned to abandon the service. But many clients appreciated the little extra, and one persuaded the Blochs to take out a small ad in the local paper. If it failed the Blochs could leave the tax return business in good conscience.

But they made twenty-five thousand dollars in the short tax season; instead of dropping their tax business they dropped everything else. The Blochs changed the last letter of their corporate name from "h" to "k" to avoid any pronunciation problems in H & R Block. The Blochs were so successful in Kansas City they decided to open a New York office in 1956.

Neither brother wanted to leave Kansas City, so they alternated in New York for two weeks at a time. They grossed fifty thousand dollars but only broke even with the expenses. Clearly, one brother would have to relocate to New York. Still, neither one would leave.

So the Blochs took an ad in *The New York Times* to sell the business. The only respondents were two CPAs who offered ten thousand dollars, which was all they could afford. The Blochs weren't going to sell at twenty cents on the dollar, so they charged the new owners five to ten percent above gross revenues. As Henry later pointed out, "They became, in effect, our first franchise, though at the time we didn't know what a franchise was."

The new tax preparation service encountered vocal opposition from lawyers and accountants who considered tax returns their business. But the Blochs did the finest work possible at a fair price, and they stood behind their work.

Two things were in the Blochs' favor. Americans were realizing a rapid increase in income and the tax laws became increasingly complicated. All H & R Block tax preparers were trained thoroughly in an eighty-one-hour program their first year and annual refresher courses thereafter.

The Blochs worked to make a visit to the taxman as painless as possible. They offered free coffee (eight million cups were served by the early 1960s) and playthings for the kids (over 100,000 crayons were distributed during the same time). H & R Block preparers were friendly but serious. A typical session took forty-five minutes and cost around forty dollars.

H & R Block was carried for years by word-of-mouth advertising, but widescale ads began appearing in 1970 with Henry Bloch as his own spokesman. Bloch became so popular he began appearing in other companies' commercials as well.

But it wasn't an ideal time for expansion. The Tax Reform Act of 1971 lopped three million taxpayers off the rolls, exactly the people H & R Block served. The company would have to become less dependent on seasonal tax preparation. The early acquisitions, including a door-to-door handbill delivery service, were unsuccessful.

But Personnel Pool of America (employment agency), Compuserve (data transmission) and Hyatt Legal Services all did well. Through the expansion, H & R Block remained a family business. Richard retired in 1978 after being diagnosed with terminal lung center, which he has successfully battled.

Henry, who retained forty-five percent of the stock when the company went public in 1962, and his son Thomas have managed the more than nine thousand H & R Block offices since 1978.

Hewlett-Packard

David Packard came to Stanford University as a track star from Pueblo, Colorado. William Hewlett was an underachieving student who came to Stanford University from Ann Arbor, Michigan because his father was an alumnus. Together they were star students in electrical engineering.

They graduated in 1934, Packard taking a job with General Electric in Schnectady, New York and Hewlett going on for his master's degree at MIT. After three years Packard surrendered his secure job (in the middle of the Depression) to return to Stanford and join his friend Hewlett, who was engaged in making an oscillator.

The two men put together $538 and went to work in Packard's garage. In a short time they had invented a weight-reducing machine, an electronic harmonica tuner, and a bowling alley foul light indicator. But Hewlett's oscillator was their star product. The first sale was to Walt Disney, who bought eight oscillators at $71.50 each to use on his sound track for *Fantasia*.

First year sales totalled $5,369 worth of electronics, and Hewlett and Packard moved to Stanford's eight-thousand acre industrial park as one the pioneers in Silicon Valley. Company sales reached $100,000 when Hewlett was called into active duty in World War II. Packard ran the company during America's first high-tech war. Orders for sonar, radar, and other electronics flooded the assembly plant in Santa Clara Valley. Hewlett returned to discover two hundred employees building two million dollars worth of electronics.

But the government orders disappeared after the war. Hewlett and Packard were forced to pare the work force by half. The move traumatized the partners. They vowed never to be so dependent on the vagaries of government orders again, orders that were the lifeblood of high-tech firms. They would finance growth and research only through earnings.

The cutback spawned an intense devotion to Hewlett-Packard

employees. They promised never to lay off employees again—and they never did. Recessions forced cuts in hours and wages, but never jobs. A liberal profit-sharing plan was instituted. The partners were routinely known as "Bill" and "Dave" to employees. Their style of informal management became known as "management by walking around."

By the late 1950s, Hewlett-Packard made more than three hundred products. Ten years later there were 2,163. Hewlett-Packard's 13,340 employees tested the informal structure of operation. Packard left for Washington in 1969 to serve as deputy secretary of defense for three years. Now it was Hewlett's turn to run the company.

Sales rose but profits dipped as Hewlett-Packard's technological prowess didn't always translate to markets. They introduced the minicomputer in 1967, but were quickly superseded by rivals and switched to the time-sharing market rather than compete in the mass market.

Prior to the 1970s, Hewlett-Packard never made consumer products. Then in 1972 they announced the HP-35, a revolutionary hand-held scientific calculator. Market research experts called it a toy, company executives said it didn't adhere to Hewlett-Packard's philosophy, but Bill Hewlett persisted. Overnight the calculator replaced the venerable slide rule in the pockets of engineers. Suddenly Hewlett-Packard was thrust into an enormous mass market.

Texas Instruments immediately seized the low end of the calculator market and challenged Hewlett-Packard with cheap knockoffs of the scientific calculator. Flustered, Hewlett-Packard fought back not with price cuts but with technological advances. But their new wrist-calculator, selling for $795, hardly sold at all.

It was a rare misstep for the partners. In 1978 Hewlett and Packard departed to buy a cattle ranch in Idaho. Packard donated his 450,000 shares of Hewlett-Packard to the David & Lucille Packard Foundation they had set up in 1964 to support scientific and health research. The shares were worth more than two billion dollars.

Kelly Girl

William Russell Kelly ran a business where companies dropped off work at Kelly's office for typing, calculating, duplicating, and mailing. One day a swamped customer called Kelly to send over a typist and the temporary help industry was born.

Kelly may have stumbled onto a new industry, but it wasn't total happenstance. He was born in British Columbia in 1906. His oil pioneer father took the family across the world before dying in 1928, leaving no estate. Kelly worked through the Depression as a car salesman and accountant for the Great Atlantic & Pacific Tea Company.

He volunteered during World War II and helped establish a system to move crucial food supplies to the troops. After the war he saw the United States poised for a tremendous expansion which would no doubt be accompanied by a crush of paperwork. Kelly planned to apply the organizational skills he learned in the military to help ease this burden.

Kelly chose Detroit as the site for his new business, since it was the center of the automobile industry. He used ten thousand dollars in savings to rent an office and hire two clerical workers. After three months, he had billed only $847.72. Kelly had guessed correctly about the volume of work, but didn't foresee that companies would try to do it all themselves. When he sent out his first temp as a courtesy, Kelly realized that what was needed was not office equipment but skilled operators.

When clients called they asked to have one of "those Kelly girls" sent over. Kelly adopted the Kelly Girl name. When temporary workers arrived on their assignment they introduced themselves by saying, "Hello, I'm your Kelly Girl."

Kelly had not only tapped into a valuable market niche—he also uncovered an enthusiastic pool of employees. Women had filled in admirably as wartime workers, and many still harbored a desire to work as they dutifully returned home to start families. Temporary clerical work was an ideal way to have both worlds—

they could always refuse an untimely assignment.

In the twenty-five years after the war, the number of American clerical workers doubled from seven million to fourteen million, and ninety-five percent of the increase was women. Kelly opened his first branch in Louisville in 1952, and by 1955 Kelly Girl was in twenty-nine cities. By the end of the decade there were eighty-four thousand Kelly Girls.

Kelly conducted careful market research in the 1960s and introduced Kelly Marketing, Kelly Labor, and Kelly Technical. Many of the new recruits for part-time work were men, forcing a name change to Kelly Services in 1966.

Thousands of temporary help agencies entered the market in the 1970s but Kelly Services, with William Kelly still serving as chairman into his eighties, was billing over $1.6 billion on their fortieth anniversary in 1986.

Merrill Lynch

Charles Merrill believed there were thousands of potential investors who weren't being served by traditional brokerage houses. He would service the small investor and collect their paltry ten-dollar commission checks while the big brokers would stay with the social and economic elite.

Merrill had come to New York from Amherst College and the University of Michigan in 1907 to work in the financial office of a textile group. In 1909, he started on Wall Street at George H. Burr & Company, a commercial paper house looking to expand into bonds. Merrill became that bond department.

At the 23rd Street YMCA, Merrill met Edmund Calvert Lynch,

a Johns Hopkins graduate who was making his way selling soda fountain equipment. The two forged a lifelong friendship and Merrill found a place at Burr & Company for his new pal.

In January 1914, Merrill left to test his ideas about selling securities to the proletariat. He began in sublet space, and in May moved to his own tiny place at 7 Wall Street. He persuaded Lynch to join him, and in 1916 Merrill Lynch & Company was formed. Both men were twenty-nine.

The firm began as a distributor of new securities, especially in the emerging chain store business. Merrill Lynch brought out stock issues for S.S. Kresge, J.C. Penney, Western Auto, and Safeway. From the beginning, Merrill believed in educating the public about markets and showing them how to become investors. They set standards that a broker must consider the customer's particular circumstances when suggesting investments. This was especially important when dealing with small investors.

By the late 1920s, Merrill became worried by the speculative excesses of the stock boom. In 1928 he wrote his customers: "Now is the time to get out of debt. Sell enough securities to lighten your obligations or pay them off entirely." The advice was so diametrically opposite of other financial advisers at the time that Merrill was racked with self-doubt and consulted a psychiatrist. After a few visits his therapist handed his portfolio to Merrill to sell, saying, "If you're crazy, then so am I."

He had a tougher sell with his own partner. Merrill drafted a stern letter to Lynch early in 1929 stating that the firm must liquidate its debts. Lynch replied from Paris, "I don't agree with your thinking, but I will not disagree with your actions. If you wish, please sell all my holdings."

Merrill Lynch weathered the Stock Market Crash in 1929, but Merrill decided to sell his retail commission business and concentrate on investment banking, which he did for several years. Lynch died in 1938 at the age of fifty-three, as the brokerage business was slumping. Merrill searched for a new direction for the firm.

He was one of a very few Wall Streeters to notice a 1939 Roper public opinion survey which showed almost total distrust, disinterest, and misunderstanding of financial markets. Stockbrokers were routinely considered legalized bandits. Worse yet, one out of every eleven people thought the Stock Exchange was the place their butcher went to order pork chops.

Merrill ordered his own study to find out what people wanted in a securities firm. He came up with a blueprint for a new company that would be a "department store of finance bringing Wall Street to Main Street." Merrill advertised not only to build trust in his new firm, but in Wall Street as well. By the end of 1940 he had twelve thousand new accounts out of an entire investor pool of fifty thousand. He was on his way to two million accounts.

But the average transaction brought in ten dollars and cost fourteen dollars. Merrill Lynch, completely unprecedented in the brokerage business, published an annual report listing a loss of $309,000 in 1940. Increased efficiency in effecting transactions stemmed the losses. Profits would reach five million dollars by 1943.

Merrill then suffered a severe heart attack. Afterwards, he was only able to return to the office on few occasions, but kept a steady stream of memos and phone calls flowing from his house. He remained very much the directing partner until his death in 1956.

tis

One day in 1852, Josiah Maise decided he needed a hoist in his bedstead factory in Yonkers. He summoned his master mechanic Elisha Otis and explained his requirements. Otis studied the problem and constructed the hoist, adding a ratchet safety device to hold the platform should the hoist break.

It was the first elevator ever equipped with an automatic device to keep it from falling.

Otis was not particularly impressed with his invention. To him it was just another device he had rigged to keep the factory operating smoothly. He busied himself with plans to join the Gold Rush in California. But just as he was about to leave he received an unsolicited order for two "safety elevators." Otis was in the elevator business.

Otis had been tinkering practically since he was born in Halifax, Vermont in 1811, already the sixth generation of the Otis family in America. He was anxious to leave the family farm, and traveled to Troy, New York to work in the building trade as soon as his father released him to do so.

He returned to Vermont and built a grist mill, which proved unprofitable. Otis spent seven years crafting fine carriages, but when the carriage business slowed he started building a sawmill. The project proved financially daunting, and Otis built a water-turbine factory to make machinery. He did well for two years and seemed to have finally found prosperity. But the city of Albany, New York appropriated his stream and he was back in debt.

He was applying his inventive mind primarily to the bedstead factory when the elevator opportunity presented itself. At the same time Otis began building elevators, the United States' first World's Fair, the Crystal Palace Exposition, was under way in New York. Otis demonstrated his elevator with a flair that suggested his showmanship talents were being wasted in the manufacturing trade.

The New York Tribune wrote, "We may commence by referring to an elevator exhibited by E. S. Otis of Yonkers—which attracts attention both by its prominent position and by the apparent daring of the inventor, who as he rides up and down the platform occasionally cuts the rope by which it is supported." As word spread about a safe freight elevator, orders arrived from across the country. By 1855 twenty-seven Otis elevators were in service.

In 1857 Otis installed the first passenger elevator in the five-story store of E. V. Houghwout & Company, dealers in glassware and china. The elevator was belt-driven, and ushered in the age of the skyscraper. The safe elevator made the erection of multi-story buildings practical.

Otis succumbed to a diphtheria epidemic in 1861, leaving a small company worth five thousand dollars to his two sons. In the generations to come, every major development in elevator technology could be attributed to the Otis family business.

Pitney Bowes

There are better ways to make your fortune than dealing with the United States government. Arthur Pitney received a patent for his postage meter in 1902, but it was not until 1920, four administrations and half a dozen postmaster generals later, that the United States Postal Service accepted metered mail rather than stamps.

Pitney was born in Quincy, Illinois in 1871. As an infant he was stricken by polio and left with a shortened left leg. In 1890 he came to Chicago as a clerk in a wallpaper store. When Chicago staged the Columbian World's Fair in 1893 Pitney spent days looking at the marvelous mechanical inventions on display.

He soon became involved in mailing operations at work. Bulk mailing in the 1800s was not only slow and tedious but costly. At times it seemed as many stamps disappeared as made it onto envelopes. Stamp robberies were common. Pitney thought there had to be a better way.

He began to experiment with a machine to imprint envelopes with postage, which would be prepurchased at the post office. Others in England, Germany, Norway, and even New Zealand had tried to develop similar machines, but it is probable that Pitney had never heard of any of them. The idea of a postage meter drove him.

He found a partner and formed the Pitney Postal Machine Company even before receiving his patent in 1902. The gamble seemed to pay off when he was invited to demonstrate his machine for the postmaster general in 1903. The machine worked flawlessly, but the United States Postal Service didn't see the need for such a device.

Pitney went back to work at the wallpaper store, continuing to try and win approval for his machine. Years passed. Money became scarce while Pitney waited for approval from the Postal Service. Tension from the situation cost Pitney his marriage in 1910.

Meanwhile, testimonials from companies who had seen demonstrations of the machine piled up in Pitney's files. To help increase recognition of his machine, Pitney changed the name to the American Postage Meter Company, with a former Chicago postmaster as titular president. Pitney quit his job to work as the company's only full-time employee.

In 1912, nine years after Pitney's first demonstration, another test was ordered. As the machine performed splendidly for amazed onlookers, Pitney stood in a corner, struck by the realization that he could make the machine more practical by designing the printing and registering mechanism to be detachable for easy transport to the post office. He stopped the demonstration and the Postal Service agreed to a new test with the improved machine when it was ready.

Pitney quickly redesigned his postage meter. But months went by without any government action. Dejected, Pitney resolved to forget the machine and left for Chicago for an advertising job in Joliet, Illinois. He was there only a short time when he learned the Postal Service was interested in a full-scale test.

Pitney placed six machines in offices for use for three months. The first experimental machine was in use on January 28, 1914 and headlines screamed the next day across the country: MAY TAKE THE PLACE OF STAMPS AND MACHINE TO STOP STAMP LOSSES.

There were raves from the companies involved. The Chicago postal committee officially endorsed the postage meter. Pitney was ecstatic. But when war broke out in Europe, the necessary enabling legislation was shelved. Pitney then received a letter from the Postal Service, ". . . we see no need for such a machine as an adjunct to the Postal Service."

A despondent Pitney took a job selling insurance.

Walter Bowes was a natural-born salesman. As a young employee of the Addressograph Company, he smashed all sales records. After barely a year of working, at the height of his earning power, Bowes quit and went sailing on his twenty-three-foot sloop.

In 1908, the twenty-six-year-old Bowes was back selling check endorsing machines. In 1909 he bought the Universal Stamping Machine Company. Two years later he began selling a letter-canceling machine to the Postal Service. To Bowes, however, stamps were stupid in an age of mechanization. He set out to make his own letter-canceling machine obsolete.

Bowes had an idea to print stamp facsimiles on letters and use a counter to verify usage. He used his post office contacts to promote the idea. But the concept would allow anyone to enter the stamp-making business without complete safeguards. Why don't you talk with this fellow Pitney, who is working on a similar idea, he was told.

Bowes invited Arthur Pitney to visit him in Stamford, Connecticut in 1919. The plodding, singleminded inventor travelled east to meet the flamboyant, mercurial super-salesman. They formed the Pitney-Bowes Postage Meter Company. Pitney would work on improving the meter and Bowes would promote the idea in Washington.

Bowes won another test in 1920, and the postage meter was finally accepted for use in the United States postal system. They were now licensed to distribute postage meters, but had to put together a factory, find capital, and hire personnel. Their easiest task was in the marketplace. The postage meter was not a hard sell.

By 1922 there were branch offices in a dozen major cities and 404 postage meters were in use. Each meter printed only a single denomination—two cents, for instance—and sold for $1,350, with a ten dollars monthly leasing fee. The company was blossoming, but neither Pitney or Bowes was enjoying the success.

The two men were constantly at odds. During a board meeting in 1924, an obscure matter detonated Pitney's pent-up frustrations. He scribbled a resignation notice, handed it to Bowes, and limped out of the room. Pitney sold his entire stock for two hundred thousand dollars.

For Bowes, selling the meter to the Postal Service was the climax of his life. He had no interest in the details of running a business. An accomplished sportsmen, he devoted much of his time to racing yachts and horses.

The government continued to hassle the young industry. Several federal hearings were held in Washington. At one investigation, Arthur Pitney sadly denounced his life's work, claiming permit machines, which he was now manufacturing, were the best way to mail letters. Others championed the cause of the postage meter.

Pitney suffered a stroke in 1927 and died in 1933. Only his dogged persistence led to the adoption of the postage meter as standard office equipment. His efforts brought him little joy.

Walter Bowes was shifted from president to chairman of Pitney-Bowes in 1938. But even that honorary position took too much time from steeplechases and point-to-point races. He retired with a ten-year consulting contract in 1940. Bowes continued to enjoy the good life until his death in 1957 at the age of seventy-five.

14 PART

The Conglomerates

Dow

"Crazy Dow" they called him. The twenty-four year-old newcomer to Midland in 1890 was trying to tap into the vast prehistoric salt-water sea lurking beneath Michigan. But it wasn't salt he was after like everyone else. Herbert Henry Dow was determined to distill bromides—used in photography and medicine—from the brine.

Even if some townsfolk could appreciate the value of chemicals they were used to evaporating to get salt, no one could comprehend Dow's methods. He planned to separate bromides from the brine with electric current—at a time when electricity was so foreign that President Harrison refused to touch the newly installed light switched in the White House for fear of electrocution.

Dow, a chemistry teacher at Case Institute, interested three Cleveland businessmen in his venture to extract bromide from brine. Dow first tried in Ohio, but was unable to get by his inherent pumping problems. As the Canton Chemical Company was going under, Dow was already laying plans to start again in Midland, where the bromine-rich brine lay near the surface.

Using his patents as a lure, Dow attracted new investors to form the Midland Chemical Company in 1892. Dow was put in charge of setting up the plant, but the money men quickly tried to ease him out. Relieved of his responsibility at the plant he had built, Dow worked on removing chlorine from the waste leftover after the bromine was successfully removed from the brine.

Dow's new process produced bleach, but he couldn't interest

Midland Chemical in its mass production. Back to Cleveland he went for backing—this time to the academic community. The Dow Chemical Company was created on May 18, 1897. Dow perfected his process in Navarre, Ohio and again prepared to return to Midland. He leased the land next to Midland Chemical and bought their waste brine.

Dow envisioned the time when he could produce nine tons of bleach a day. But he was constantly thwarted by small explosions in the laboratory. Dow and his men worked around the clock in shifts looking for a solution until the problem was solved, and production indeed jumped to nine tons daily. Dow then finished his plans to buy out his former partners in Midland Chemical and merge the company with Dow Chemical in 1900.

Herbert Dow had forged the new American chemical industry. He set out to export his products and break the German and British stranglehold on the world market. The foreign suppliers immediately slashed their bleach prices in half, driving all American bleach makers out of business—except Dow. Dow continued producing bleach at a loss, plunging deeper into debt as he fought for market share.

By 1909 the tide was turning, and the Europeans began to withdraw from American markets. After the bromide war, a real war finished the German chemical industry in the United States. The German naval blockade forced American industry to rely on American chemical producers. After the war, Congress protected the chemical industry with high tariffs so the country need never rely on foreign manufacturers again.

By 1920 Dow Chemical sales soared over four million dollars a year. The stock price climbed to five hundred dollars a share before the market crashed. "Crazy Dow" was now "Doctor Dow" around Midland. From the strange experiments he conducted in a shed on the edge of town he now employed sixteen hundred people in town. Dow hired landscape architects to spruce up the town. When he died in 1930 at the age of sixty-four, the company he started by extracting bromide from brine now had a roster of five hundred products.

DuPont

On a wet, blustery day in the winter of 1801, a French immigrant was invited on a hunting trip in the wooded, rolling hills south of Philadelphia. Time and again Eleuthere Irenee du Pont leveled his shotgun, only to have the gun misfire. The dampness of the air was ruining his gunpowder.

Eleuthere Irenee du Pont took little game that day, but returned home with something more important: a business idea. The du Pont family, headed by his father and brother, had arrived in New Jersey a year earlier with intentions of being land speculators. Eleuthere Irenee, then thirty-one years old, listed his occupation on his passport as "botanist" and planned to work the land and do seed exchanges with other naturalists back in Europe.

But since their arrival the du Ponts had not prospered. Now Eleuthere Irenee saw an opportunity in gunpowder. He had studied with Antoinne Lavoisier, the French government's chemist in charge of manufacturing gunpowder. Du Pont returned to France to bring back the technology necessary to launch his own black powder enterprise.

Du Pont rode up and down the east coast searching for a suitable location for his new mills. Eventually he returned to the site of his hunting trip several months earlier. The Brandywine River in northern Delaware was in a region central to the existing states. The Brandywine flowed swiftly, generating abundant water power. The surrounding hills were blanketed with virgin timber which du Pont would use to make charcoal, one of the three ingredients needed to make black powder. And du Pont, who always struggled with the English language, drew comfort from a large French population in Wilmington at the time.

From the beginning, a constant lack of operating capital precipitated one crisis after another for E. I. du Pont de Nemours and Company. President Thomas Jefferson, a family friend from his diplomatic days in France, supplied du Pont with encouragement and an occasional government order.

Du Pont's black powder immediately gained acceptance as a superior gunpowder and blasting powder for clearing stumps, digging canals, and building roads. During the War of 1812 the United States Government became a regular customer, and for a time the company grew into the young nation's largest industrial firm. But after the war there was excess capacity and idle mills.

Du Pont was a dour, responsible man who shouldered the burden of the family debts. Twice a week he dutifully made the thirty mile trip to Philadelphia to meet the obligations of his bank notes. Finally in 1834 du Pont paid off the last of his notes. He left the bank, walked around the corner, and fell dead in the street.

Du Pont's sons built on the debt-free company their father had left them. The last DuPont black powder was sold in 1972, decades after anyone even remembered the company made the stuff.

Procter & Gamble

1834 was a particularly joyful year for the Norris family of Cincinnati. Young Elizabeth Ann married a young soapmaker named James Gamble, who was just ending an eight-year apprenticeship and opening his own shop. Sister Olivia also wed that year to a widowed, thirty-one-year-old Englishman, a candlemaker by trade. His name was William Procter.

Both Procter and Gamble had settled in Cincinnati under distressed circumstances. Gamble was the son of an Irish minister who came to America in 1819 to join countrymen in Illinois. On the boat trip down the Ohio River, sixteen-year-old James became violently ill, sending the family to shore in Cincinnati. The Gambles found a prosperous community making beer, building ships, and above all else, trafficking in hogs. They decided to stay and make their way in "Porkopolis."

Several years later, a woolen goods shop opened in London. The new business attracted attention not just from customers. When William Procter returned to his store the next morning, his entire inventory of merchandise had been stolen. Stunned and not knowing how he was going to repay his eight-thousand dollar debt, Procter headed to America with his wife to start over.

His destination was a town he had heard about on the "Falls of Ohio." As their flatboat approached Cincinnati, Martha Procter was stricken with cholera. Procter hurried to shore, but his wife was dead within days. Totally dispirited, Procter traveled no further. He saw little hope of ever repaying his debts and opened a small candle shop, a skill he had learned in his youth.

In 1837 the new brothers-in-law were in parallel businesses; both were buying animal fats from the great hog butchering centers of Cincinnati. Inevitably, the two men joined forces to form the Procter & Gamble Manufactory. It was a natural partnership— Procter managed the office and sales and Gamble directed operations in the factory. In busier times they wouldn't see each other until Saturday night when business notes could be compared.

At the time, eighteen other local firms in Cincinnati were making soap and candles. Procter & Gamble gained a reputation for fair dealing—"Suppliers of fats and oils could take a signed order from Procter & Gamble and pass it along in lieu of cash," reported one newsman—and by the Civil War, the business was the largest in town.

Shrewdly, the partners planned for hostilities by buying rosin by the boatload at a dollar a barrel. When war broke out and rosin prices leapt to fifteen dollars a barrel, Washington authorities visited the Procter & Gamble plant. Impressed with the operation, the partners were rewarded with an order to supply all Union encampments with soap and candles.

A thousand cases of supplies a day rolled out of the factory. Each was stamped with a distinctive half moon and a cluster of stars stamped on the top to identify its contents for the many illiterate dockworkers and quartermasters. Procter & Gamble crates served as chairs and tables in Army camps, and when troops scattered across the country after the war they knew the name and symbol of the Cincinnati soapmaker.

As sales spread across the nation, the founders left more and more business decisions to their sons. Both William Proctor and James Gamble remained involved into their eighties. In 1879 a worker accidentally left a stirring machine on too long and the soap bars became laced with air bubbles. The airy soap that floated on top of the murky bath water became so popular all Procter & Gamble soap formulas were changed. Ivory soap became the linchpin the next generation of Procters and Gambles would build upon.

Tandy

During World War II, Charles Tandy was stationed in Hawaii. He noticed that huge amounts of leathercraft were being used in base hospital and recreation centers. He wrote a letter home to his father—who was in the leather business selling sole leather and other shoe repair supplies—suggesting this might be a good market for leather.

Charles Tandy returned home in 1950 and opened two retail stores devoted exclusively to leathercraft, one in El Paso and the other in San Antonio. He realized a hundred percent return on his investment with the help of mail order sales—an eight page catalog to inquiries from a two inch ad in *Popular Science*.

Dave Tandy and his pal Norton Hinckley had formed the Hinckley-Tandy Leather Company in the 1920s to supply shoe dealers in Fort Worth, Texas. Now, Hinckley was not impressed with this leathercraft. The men worked out an agreement where they would split the partnership and Hinckley would retain the shoe business and leave the leather purse and moccasin kits to the Tandys.

The Tandys targeted the school, hospital, and armed forces markets. Leathercraft was the principal recreation during the nuclear submarine US's *Triton*'s round-the-world underwater sea voyage. Supported by direct mail, the company expanded to 150 stores through the 1950s.

In 1960, Charles Tandy became president of the Tandy Corporation. They expanded into other do-it-yourself hobbies, opening the Tandy Mart in Fort Worth in 1961. The Tandy Mart features twenty-eight hobby-related shops.

The organization acquired similar businesses: a tannery, a saddlemaking firm, and then Cost Plus (now Pier I imports). In 1963, Tandy took over a chain of nine failing Boston electronics stores specializing in selling equipment to ham radio hobbyists. They applied principles of selling leathercraft to electronics, and when Dave Tandy died in 1966 at the age of sixty-seven, Radio Shack was the fastest growing chain in America.

Westinghouse

In the first seventy years of railroading, there were 955 patents for brakes. Train length and engine speed were both dependent on reliable brakes. The patent that finally produced the ideal train brake belonged to a twenty-three-year-old inventor named George Westinghouse.

Westinghouse patented a rotary steam engine at the age of nineteen, and spent three years developing a compressed air brake that vastly improved the safety of train travel. Faster trains pulling larger loads translated into bigger profits for the railroad barons. The Westinghouse Air Brake Company began generating enormous revenue.

Between the years 1880 and 1890, Westinghouse received 134 patents, almost one every twenty days. He took out twenty additional patents to improve his railroad brake. He turned his attention to railroad yards and formed the Union Switch & Signal Company to supply the first electrically controlled railroad signals.

Next Westinghouse pioneered the delivery of electricity over great distances. Thomas Edison had harnessed electricity, but he was able to transmit his direct current only two miles. In 1885, the Westinghouse Electric Company introduced alternating current which sent electricity over long distances through intermittent transformers.

Edison and Westinghouse locked in the "Battle of the Currents." Westinghouse had by far the superior product; Edison's only advantage was safety, since he operated at lower voltages. Victory for Westinghouse was sealed when he won the bid to provide electricity for the Columbian Exposition in 1893. Ultimately, ninety-five percent of all electricity customers would use alternating current.

But it was a hollow victory. Edison, operating with J. P. Morgan, gained the ability to produce both currents, and Westinghouse needed to pay steep litigation fees. The two men agreed on co-patents and Westinghouse Electric fell behind and never recovered in its battle with Edison's General Electric. Westinghouse would never be closer than a distant second to GE in electrical consumer appliances. Westinghouse Electric went into bankruptcy for a brief period and Westinghouse retired in 1911.

But Westinghouse's other companies, including the air brake, were still pumping out profits. Westinghouse was one of the largest employers in the world with 50,000 people on his payrolls. He was a leader in worker relations and originated half-Saturday holidays back in 1871.

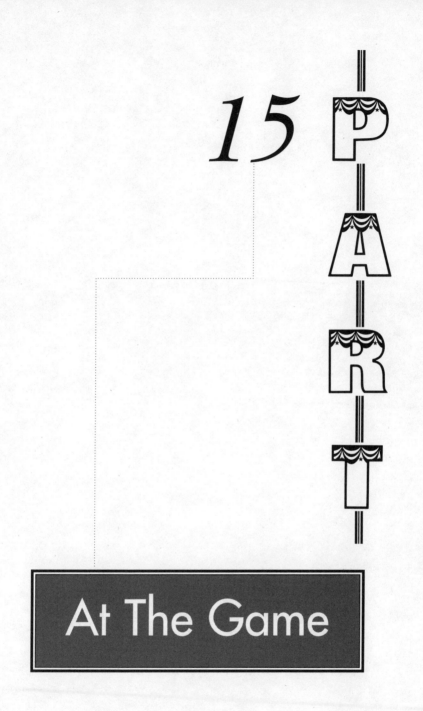

15 PART

At The Game

Duncan

The yo-yo has been known for at least twenty-five hundred years:
an ancient Greek bowl dating to 450 BC depicts a boy playing with
a disk on the end of a string. The toy was a popular entertainment
in the imperial courts of Europe, and it is said that Napoleon's soldiers passed the time between battles practicing with yo-yos. But
the American yo-yo was born, not in tony parlors of Europe, but
the jungles of the Philippines.

Although it is most likely the yo-yo reached the Philippines by
way of China, some legends maintain that Filipino hunters developed the yo-yo as a hunting weapon, throwing a stone and retriev-
ing it with an attached throng. However it arrived in the
Philippines, by the nineteenth century the yo-yo was ingrained in
the lives of Filipino children—with a twist. Literally. Instead of a
single-string European design which returned immediately, the
Philippine yo-yo's string was looped around the axle with the two
branches of the loop twisted tightly together. Thus the Philippine
yo-yo hesitated a few seconds before returning, enabling skilled
handlers to develop a repetoire of tricks.

It was this yo-yo—the name derives from the Philippine
Tagalog language to describe the action and sound of the toy—
that Donald F. Duncan saw in the late 1920s. As Filipinos made
their way to the United States in the early 20th century the toy
began appearing in Philippine neighborhoods. Pedro Flores, a
Filipino hotel worker, registered his "Flores Yo-Yo" with the U.S.

Patent Office about the time Duncan learned of the toy.

Envisioning a big-selling toy, Duncan manufactured his first yo-yo in 1929, but his patent application was turned down as an infringement on the Flores Yo-Yo. Undeterred, Duncan bought Flores's rights and marketed the first Genuine Duncan Yo-Yo in 1932. Duncan singlehandedly made the yo-yo a national craze. He hired groups of Filipino men to demonstrate the yo-yo, and sent them on tours of the United States to promote the Duncan Yo-Yo. The arrival of a Duncan troupe and their routines of gravity-defying tricks became an annual rite of spring in America.

When the novelty of the yo-yo faded by World War II, Duncan was able to re-vitalize the toy by taking his demonstrations to television. The maple and ash yo-yos gave way to the all-time best-selling plastic Duncan Imperial in the late 1950s, and the yo-yo boom was bigger than ever. But Duncan's greatest ploy was in securing the rights to the term "yo-yo" itself. It was not until 1965 that the courts ruled that the toy was a yo-yo, not a Duncan yo-yo. But by that time Duncan was selling about nine of every ten yo-yos in America, a figure it still approaches today.

Fisher-Price

For millions of Americans during the Depression, toys were the most frivolous of luxuries. But Herman Guy Fisher, Irving Lanouette Price, and Helen Schelle were determined to market their line of sturdy toys crafted from New York Ponderosa pine. They sold enough toys to stay in business until 1938, when Fisher-Price introduced Snoopy Sniffer at the Toy Fair. Snoopy was a loose-jointed, floppy-eared pull toy who woofed when you pulled his wagging spring tail. Snoopy Sniffer was an instant hit that bred a toy empire in a small upstate New York town.

Irving Price had come to East Aurora, New York when he retired from his position as Eastern District Manager for Woolworth's at the age of thirty-six. Price became involved in community work, serving on the school board. In 1928 he assumed the responsibility of attracting new industries to town.

In his search he met Herman Fisher, a Penn State graduate who had worked his way through school peddling Fuller brushes. After graduation, Fisher had worked in sales, promotion and advertising for several toy and game companies, and was now ready to start his own toy company. A third partner was Helen Schelle, who operated a Penny Walker Toy Shop in Binghamton.

The three came together to establish the Fisher-Price Toy Company in 1930. They raised $71,600 from local businessmen and their own workers to convert an old frame and concrete house into a factory. Fisher had a clear idea of the toys he would make. He wanted to make children "toys that played with them." Fisher-Price toys would have intrinsic play values, strong construction, and action.

Fisher, Price, and Schelle called their first brochure "Sixteen Hopefuls." All the toys were constructed of Ponderosa pine blocks with color lithographs, and they all did something comical. Ducks quacked, tails wagged, and beaks moved.

In 1936 Fisher-Price brought out their first "educational" toys, a line of blocks. The company gained a reputation for "good toys"—toys that were fun, safe, and educational. With the success of Snoopy Sniffer, Fisher-Price became the leading toy manufacturer in America. They were the first to license Disney characters for their toys. By the late 1930s, Fisher-Price was producing over two million toys a year.

During World War II, the toys became ship fenders and medical chests, but Fisher-Price was ideally positioned for the postwar suburban baby boom. In 1949, plastic was substituted for pine blocks to keep up with demand. In the 1960s, Fisher-Price introduced play people as an integral part of the toy increasing the play value. They built a nursery school and watched kids play. Their observations led Fisher-Price to become the largest maker of preschool toys in America.

When Price retired in 1965 at the age of eighty-one, revenues that were $116,000 in 1932 had mushroomed to $26,000,000. Four years later Fisher sold the company to Quaker Oats for $50,000,000. He was seventy-one years old. In the next twenty years the toy market exploded with high-tech toys, monsters, video games, and war toys. But Fisher-Price stayed true to Fisher's philosophy of "good toys" for children. In 1990 Fisher-Price educational toys with built-in play values were producing nearly $400,000,000 in sales.

Hillerich & Bradsby

It seems that Pete Browning, "The Gladiator," was in a slump. The celebrated hard-hitting batsman for the Louisville Colonels went in search of a new bat. He stopped by the small woodworking shop of J. F. Hillerich, then noted for its wooden butter churns.

Hillerich's teenage son Bud turned a piece of white ash while Browning tested it every few turns until just right. Browning banged out three hits the next day and publicly gave credit to the bat. Baseball players are a superstitious lot, and after the game the rest of the Louisville team showed up at the Hillerich shop for bats.

It was 1884. Until that time, players bought bats already formed by woodturners, or tried to carve their own. Hillerich's first custom-made bats became all the rage. He called them "Louisville Sluggers" after the power-hitting Browning. Soon Hillerich was turning out only baseball bats, and the wooden churns that had been the shop specialty were forgotten.

As batters became more exacting, Hillerich began burning each player's name into his bat. Famous nineteenth century stars like Cap Anson and Honus Wagner used Sluggers. Hugh Duffy hit .438 in 1894 with a Slugger, the highest average of all time. The early greats were followed by Ty Cobb, Rogers Hornsby, Babe Ruth, Lou Gehrig, and Joe DiMaggio. More Sluggers were made for Babe Ruth than anyone else. The Bambino favored gargantuan pieces of lumber weighing up to fifty-four ounces, fifty percent heavier than most bats.

Hillerich sold bats directly to the players, recording their required specifications on cards still retained by the company. Behind the baseball scene, every player knew Bud Hillerich. In 1910, Frank Bradsby joined the company to expand sales outside major league baseball. Everyone wanted to use the same bats as the big league stars, and by the time Bradsby died in 1937, the company was turning out two million bats a year.

The tiny woodworking shop grew into a ten-acre timber yard. Trainloads of white ash rounds, the only wood used for major league bats, were stacked to allow air to season and dry the wood. Over five million sticks of forty-inch ash would always be on hand. Each piece was carefully graded before turning on lathes, with the very best ash reserved for the major leaguers.

When Hillerich died in 1946 at the age of eighty, the "Louisville Slugger" trademark had been burned on over one hundred million baseball bats and Pete Browning, the original Louisville slugger, was forgotten.

Lionel

Joshua Lionel Cohen was not much impressed with store displays as he window-shopped on the streets of New York City in 1901. What was needed, he thought, was some sort of eye-appealing

action display. He went home to fashion a toy train to pull the
merchandise around the store window.

Cohen created an unlikely looking gondola car with a small
fan motor under the car. He attached a dry cell battery directly to
the track, and there was no way to regulate the speed. He called
his new train car the "Electric Express" and sold it to a store owner
for four dollars.

The next day Cohen had to make another train car. It seems
people were buying the advertisement, not the goods. Soon Cohen
was spending long hours in a cramped third floor loft with his new
electric toy train business. He named his new company the Lionel
Manufacturing Company, after his middle name. "I had to name it
something," Cohen would shrug later.

The first toy electric train was adapted in 1835 by a struggling
New York blacksmith as a demonstration of how electricity could
be used for America's new railroads. He couldn't sell the concept
and the first electric trolley wouldn't operate for another fifty years.

Through the 1800s toy trains were pull toys, propelled by springs
or fueled by burning alcohol. By 1877, when Joshua Cohen was
born—the eighth of nine children to an immigrant capmaker—
steam engines were popular.

Cohen was not studious, but became fascinated with electricity
and the storage of power. He dropped out of the City College of
New York and Columbia University to take an apprentice position
assembling battery lamps. In 1899 Cohen received his first patent
for a device igniting a photographer's flash, called a "Flash Lamp."

The United States Navy was interested in Cohen's invention,
but not to take photographs. They gave Cohen an order for twenty-
four devices as detonators for mines. With the Navy order filled,
Cohen had a stake for his own business. He had a company but no
product.

Cohen experimented with a flashlight and an electric fan, but
settled on his electric trains. Carlisle & Finch in Cincinnati had
been selling electric trains since 1896, and Cohen quickly realized
he needed more excitement from his product than a gondola. He
introduced a trolley car called "City Hall Park."

The first Lionel train set, made entirely of metal, included thirty
feet of track. "Every feature is carried out to the minutest detail,"
boasted Cohen's ads. The set sold for seven dollars with a primitive

battery at a time when the average worker's salary was $9.42 a week and a Kodak camera sold for a dollar. The expensive electric train became a toy for special occasions like Christmas and birthdays.

From the beginning Cohen realized the importance of accessories, and his first sixteen-page catalog in 1902 emphasized suspension bridges and tunnels as well as trains. In 1903 the first Lionel locomotive was available. In 1906 Cohen completely revamped the Lionel line by adding a trademark third rail to carry the electric current—like real city railroads.

The toy train business grew increasingly competitive, especially with foreign manufacturers, and Cohen, who changed his name to "Cowen" in 1910, hammered away relentlessly at his competitors, boasting of Lionel quality in ads. Cowen's "wish book" catalogs fascinated children, and sales climbed over two million dollars by the 1920s. In the peak years of the 1950s, the Lionel catalog would be one of the most widely distributed catalogs in America, behind only general merchandise retailers Sears and Montgomery Ward.

Lionel trains were hard hit by the Depression. Cowen essentially had a one product company, and an expensive one at that. He introduced an electric range for girls but it was overdesigned and sold for $29.50—more than a teacher made in a week—and few were sold. Cowen became embroiled in a bank scandal involving his brother-in-law, damaging his ability to borrow money, and Cowen was forced to put Lionel Manufacturing into receivership in 1934.

The company was saved by new streamlined trains and by the introduction of a train whistle that faded away like the real thing in 1935. Lionel created a handcar with Mickey Mouse and Minnie Mouse which became their biggest seller. During World War II, Lionel Manufacturing converted over totally to military production, but in peacetime the company was ideally positioned to become an integral part of postwar culture.

In 1948, Lionel brought out the Santa Fe diesel. The sleek silver, red, and yellow engine became Lionel's all-time best seller, so popular that Cowen was able to get railroads to pay for using their name. In 1952, the company's fiftieth anniversary, Lionel was producing 622,209 engines and 2,460,760 cars. All real-life railroads combined had 43,000 engines and 1,800,000 cars.

The glory years lasted less than a decade. By 1958, airplanes were carrying more passengers than railroads for the first time. The romance of the train was ending, and little boys grew up wanting to be pilots, not engineers. In the toy business a new half-sized toy train, HO scale, was sweeping the market. Model race cars were taking the place of trains under Christmas trees.

Cowen, who was forced to take the company public in the bleak years of the Depression, was increasingly disenchanted with Lionel management. Electric cattle guards and stereo cameras were produced with disastrous results. An attempt to attract girls with a completely fake pink train set was even worse. In 1959 Cowen sold his shares in Lionel to his great-nephew Roy Cohn for $825,000, causing his son to lose control of the company.

Cowen enjoyed golf and tennis, but his passion was always trains. Each year he and his wife took a train trip to the west coast and sailed to Hawaii for eight to ten weeks before returning home by rail. But as he retired to Florida, both Cowen and his former company quickly disassociated themselves from each other. The first economy move of the new management group was to sell Cowen's prized collection of antique Lionel trains he kept in the company showroom.

When Cowen died in 1965, no mention of his passing was made at Lionel's next board meeting. For his part, Cowen's headstone read "Joshua L. Cohen", making no mention of the Lionel name which stirred dreams of boys the world over.

Milton Bradley

Life isn't like it used to be. The game that is. When Milton Bradley first introduced the "Checkered Game of Life" it had as its theme high ideals of morality and happy old age. The modern version of "Life," introduced on the hundredth anniversary of the game, stresses personal achievement and monetary success. Milton Bradley would not be pleased.

Bradley was born in Haverhill, Massachusetts and showed an early talent for math and science. In 1854, with savings of about $250, he enrolled in Lawrence Scientific School at Cambridge. Living at home and making the arduous commute was the only way he could afford to stay in school. His parents, however, moved to Hartford, Connecticut in 1856 and Bradley had to abandon his studies.

If that wasn't bad enough, he couldn't find satisfactory work in Hartford and had to travel up the river to Springfield, Massachusetts, where he caught on as a draftsman for the Wason Locomotive Car Works. Bradley became fascinated with lithography, but at the time the only press in the country was in Boston. Somehow that press became available in Providence, and Bradley went there and bought it.

He stayed in Providence long enough to learn how to operate the press, and on January 31, 1860 he brought it back to Springfield. His first commission was a book of designs for a local monument maker.

Returning Springfield men from the 1860 Republican national convention suggested that Bradley produce and sell photographs of the parties' impressive new candidate—a fellow by the name of Lincoln. He readily agreed, and hastily produced hundreds of thousands of copies of Abraham Lincoln.

Lincoln won the election, but Bradley would not cash in on the speculation. His photos had portrayed a clean-shaven Lincoln. When Lincoln grew a beard before going to Washington, Bradley's portraits were nearly unrecognizable. He destroyed his large inventory of lithographs.

The Civil War delivered a further blow to Bradley's young company. Business ground to a halt and the press stood idle as bankruptcy loomed. But an inventor appeared with a new game he called "The Checkered Game of Life." Bradley bought the game and printed 45,000 copies of "Life" in the first year. By 1868, Milton Bradley was the leading manufacturer of games in America.

In 1869 Bradley attended a lecture by Elizabeth Peabody,

founder of the kindergarten movement in the country. He became an enthusiastic proponent, printing teaching aids at a loss for many years before making a profit. But Bradley, who founded his company with the goal of providing America's children a gift of happiness and pleasant instruction, was more interested in education than money.

The good works started by Bradley formed the basis of Milton Bradley's lucrative educational game business in future years, just like the shifting priorities of the game of *Life* indicate.

Parker Brothers

What would a life devoted to playing games be like? Would a life of fun and games be, well, all fun and games? Such was the life of George S. Parker.

Parker was born in 1867 in Salem, Massachusetts, the third youngest son of a well-to-do merchant. George was a tall, gangly youth who dreamed of world travel as a foreign correspondent. George and his friends were great games enthusiasts who formed an informal club playing old favorites like chess, checkers and dominoes.

The boys also played America's first board game, The Mansion of Happiness, created by a minister's daughter. No one in the club liked "Mansion" much. As with all board games of the time, it was preachy and piously moral. America's Puritan heritage died hard; 250 years after the Pilgrims, playing cards and dice were forbidden as the tools of the devil. George believed that the purpose of a game was to provide fun, not to teach moral principles.

In 1883, sixteen-year-old George Parker invented the Game of

Banking. The object of the game, consisting of 160 cards and a "bank," was to see who could profit the most from speculation and borrowed money. At the end of the game the richest player was declared the winner.

The club enjoyed the game immensely, and Arthur Wellington, a member of the group, suggested to Parker that other people might like it too. He persuaded George to try and sell it to a company that produced games. Parker took Banking to two Boston book publishers. Both turned it down, but one suggested that George try and publish the game himself since he thought so much of it.

Parker borrowed fifty dollars to have five hundred sets of cards printed and packaged in boxes. With ten dollars left over, he took a leave of absence from school and embarked on a sales trip through southern New England. By Christmas he had sold all but two dozen copies of Banking and cleared almost one hundred dollars in profits.

Despite his success, George Parker was skeptical about becoming a games inventor and publisher on a permanent basis, but his brother urged him to pursue his love of games. He founded the George S. Parker Company, spending the majority of his time developing new games and playtesting them.

To insure that all the games he published remained fun to play time after time, he played every game with employees, friends, and anyone else he could persuade to sit down with him. He noted the points over which they seemed confused, and the time when the pace of the game seemed too slow. Even though George was a busy head of a fast-growing business, he personally wrote the rules of every new game.

By 1888, Parker's catalog described twenty-nine games, most of which he invented himself. With the games business booming, George persuaded his older brother Charles, an shrewd and practical oilman, to join the company full-time, and they renamed it Parker Brothers. Edward Parker, the oldest brother, came on board in 1898.

Ironically, profits from the moralistic games, the rights to which he bought, fueled money for Parker's fun games. But by the 1890s, known as the Gay Nineties, the public was eager for fun. Parker Brothers experienced a great period of growth with games reflecting the times.

Over the years Parker Brothers introduced games based on the Spanish-American War (*The Siege of Havana* and *Battle of Manila*), the Alaskan Gold Rush (*Klondike*), the automobile (*The Motor Carriage Game*) and individuals like Lindbergh, Byrd, and America's G-Man.

Since bridge was banned by millions of conservative American families, Parker saw the need for a substitute card game that would not be associated with gambling. *Pit* and *Flinch* became best-selling card games in the early 1900s, and in 1906 Parker Brothers brought out Rook. It was not an immediate success but by 1913 was the largest selling game in the country. Some fifty-five million decks have been sold.

Always searching for a pleasurable pastime, Parker Brothers decided to apply a puzzle technique to pictures. The first jigsaw puzzle used reproductions of paintings by the masters laminated onto wood. Demand for puzzles was so overwhelming, production of games had to be curtailed in the Salem plant until a special building could be outfitted.

The Depression ravaged many businesses, especially a games company. In 1934, at the height of hard times, Charles B. Darrow of Germantown, Pennsylvania arrived at Salem with a new game. After an initial play-test by company executives, the game was unanimously turned down. Not only that, Parker identified fifty-two fundamental playing errors, not the least of which was that a game of *Monopoly* couldn't be completed in forty-five minutes— Parker's idea of a family's attention span.

Darrow went home and started selling his game on his own. Reports of brisk sales led Parker Brothers to reconsider, and they purchased the rights in 1935. *Monopoly* was the biggest thing that had ever hit Parker Brothers. More than 20,000 sets a week were leaving the plant. At Christmastime so many orders poured in that they were stuffed in huge laundry baskets and stacked in hallways.

Still, George Parker considered *Monopoly* a fad. On December 19, 1936 he personally issued orders to cease production of the game in anticipation of a sales slump before inventories grew too large. But it was only the beginning of *Monopoly*'s popularity, not the end. The greatest board game of all was to eventually be printed in twenty-three languages.

In 1953 Parker died at the age of eighty-six. His company was poised to introduce three of their most successful board games: *Clue, Risk* and *Careers*. Chances are he still couldn't believe that he had been able to spend his whole life playing games.

Spalding

Albert Goodwill Spalding was the best known baseball man in the United States in the nineteenth century, having played a part in every major development in the early history of professional baseball. He shrewdly used his fame to build the greatest sporting goods empire in the world. Whenever Americans thought about going out to play, they thought Spalding.

Spalding was born outside Chicago in 1850 into a family of some means. His father died when he was eight, and his mother, who had an inheritance from the death of her first husband, moved the family to Rockford, Illinois.

Here Spalding showed natural baseball talent, excelling as a pitcher for the local Rockford nine. At the age of seventeen, Spalding was a strapping six foot one and 170 pounds. He began establishing a widespread reputation as a pitcher for the powerful Forest City Club. In 1871, Spalding signed a contract for fifteen hundred dollars with the Boston Red Stockings in baseball's first professional league.

Pitching virtually every game, Spalding became the premier pitcher in the game. The Red Stockings finished in second place in 1871 and then reeled off four consecutive league championships. Spalding, in succession, won 21, 36, 41, 52, and 56 games. He was baseball's first 200-game winner.

In 1876 Spalding had a hand in forming the new National

League. He went to Chicago to play for and manage the Chicago White Stockings franchise. In addition to his two-thousand dollar salary, Spalding received twenty-five percent of the gate receipts. Before the season started, Spalding took his team on a two-week Southern swing of exhibition games with amateur teams, each selected for their largest profit potential. It was baseball's first spring training.

Spalding's White Stockings won the first National League championship with a 52-14 record. Spalding personally won 46 of those games. But in 1877 an injury limited Spalding to only four starts and the team tumbled to fifth place. Spalding was heavily criticized for his managing and accused of "having too many irons in the fire." He retired from playing and managing after 1877 to become Secretary of the White Stockings.

One of Spalding's "irons" was a sporting goods house he opened in 1876 with his brother Walter. Other players had entered the bustling sporting goods trade, but Spalding soon overwhelmed them all. His national reputation as a pitcher helped, but his connection with the White Stockings, whose owner was also National League president, was his biggest asset.

A. G. Spalding & Brother occupied the same offices as the Chicago ballclub. Spalding received the contract to supply all National League baseballs in exchange for the designation as "Official Major League Baseball." In 1879 Spalding began to manufacture his own products when he bought a croquet-and-baseball bat company. The firm was renamed the Spalding Manufacturing Company.

Spalding gained exclusive rights to publish the first "Official League Book" in 1876. At the same time, he introduced "Spalding's Official Baseball Guide." It was not connected with the National League in any way but Al Spalding did little to dissuade that natural assumption. Spalding was soon selling fifty thousand Guides a year, which not only promoted Spalding's sporting goods and Spalding himself, but attracted advertising dollars as well. By 1892 Spalding's American Sports Publishing Company was a separate concern, eventually producing three hundred different publications on every conceivable sport or physical activity.

Lest anyone not know who the authoritative author of the Guide might be, Spalding printed a full-page, autographed picture of himself inside. Spalding was not the first to recognize the money-making possibilities of sport, but he was the best. As a promoter he was often mentioned in the same breath as the other great entertainment promoter of the times, P. T. Barnum.

Spalding promoted his team heavily through the newspapers. To him, controversy and criticism were as important as praise; like George Steinbrenner a century later, Spalding was often at the center of any ruckus. He tried to stage a game between his White Stockings and a team of "picked nine from other teams in the evening under electric lights." Baseball's first all-star game and first night game did not materialize, but Spalding used his lights to illuminate a toboggan slide in the park.

The White Stockings won the pennant in 1880 and 1881 and Spalding became president in 1882. The powerful club won again in 1882, 1885, and 1886. Spalding arranged the first postseason championship matches, again to make Spalding money. His Chicago team, at the instigation of players, drew baseball's color line by refusing to play against the few blacks in professional baseball in 1884. It would be another sixty-four years before blacks again played in the major leagues.

Spalding had first become involved in lucrative barnstorming baseball exhibition to other countries in 1875 when he arranged a baseball and cricket tour of England. In the 1888 off-season, Spalding organized the first round-the-world tour of major league baseball players. Publicity-generating events like these were important to Spalding to establish his reputation as "America's leading sportsman."

In the 1890s, Spalding sponsored and managed a bicycle team at the height of the bicycle craze. He was head of the American delegation to the second modern Olympic games in 1900 in Paris. Each venture, of course, sold Spalding's wide array of sporting goods. Spalding was not only the major supplier of the 1904 St. Louis Olympics but built the stadium as well.

Albert Spalding viewed baseball as a railroad baron or oil tycoon looked at their businesses. He crushed employee revolts, like the Players' League in 1890, and stifled competition from rival leagues and franchises whenever possible. In 1891, owner of the largest sporting goods firm in the world and weary of his baseball battles, Spalding retired. But his activities hardly slackened.

His formal retirement lasted ten years, when he returned to thwart an attempt to turn baseball into a monopolistic National

League Baseball Trust with all players, owners, and franchises owned by a single corporation that would "arrange" competitions. A contemporary sports magazine wrote: "So A. G. Spalding is coming back into baseball, eh? Pray, when did he ever leave it? You may not have observed him but he was there all the time."

In 1902, at the urging of his second wife, Spalding became a member of the Raja Yoga Theosophical Society and moved to San Diego, California. He ended his direct involvement in baseball and in business but worked on special projects. Spalding authorized a baseball history, *America's National Game*, in 1911. Much of it was factually questionable, including Spalding's fabrication of Abner Doubleday as the inventor of baseball, but the book was hugely influential in baseball lore.

In 1910 Spalding ran for the United States Senate from California. He always believed baseball prepared men for life, and regarded political service as the ultimate extension of this rise to respectability. Spalding had always sought to make the rough-hewn baseball of the nineteenth century a "respectable" game. To this end he banned liquor and Sunday games in Chicago.

Still, he accepted his nomination with reluctance. He attached conditions to his drafting: no special interests, no personal canvassing of the state, and he would only spend seventy-five hundred dollars—the same amount a United States Senator earned. Spalding assumed the nominating committee would reject his demands, but he was wrong.

Despite not entering the race until mid-July Spalding carried the majority of the Senatorial and Assembly Districts, but the California Legislature elected to send another candidate to Washington, ending his political career.

Albert Spalding died of a series of strokes at the age of sixty-five in 1915, the same year a Baltimore youngster by the name of George Herman Ruth hit his first major league home run. Spalding was elected to baseball's Hall of Fame in 1939. His plaque in Cooperstown reads:

ORGANIZATIONAL GENIUS OF BASEBALL'S PIONEER DAYS. STAR PITCHER OF FOREST CITY CLUB IN LATE 1860S, 4-YEAR CHAMPION BOSTONS 1871-1875 AND MANAGER-PITCHER OF CHAMPION CHICAGOS IN NATIONAL LEAGUE'S FIRST YEAR. CHICAGO PRESIDENT FOR 10 YEARS. ORGANIZER OF BASEBALL'S FIRST ROUND-THE-WORLD TOUR IN 1888.